VAT Gap in Poland: Policy Problem and Policy Response

Polish Studies in Economics

Edited by Ryszard Kokoszczyński

Volume 15

Dominik J. Gajewski (ed.)

VAT Gap in Poland: Policy Problem and Policy Response

PETER LANG

Berlin - Lausanne - Bruxelles - Chennai - New York - Oxford

Bibliographic Information published by the Deutsche Nationalbibliothek
The Deutsche Nationalbibliothek lists this publication in the Deutsche Nationalbibliografie; detailed bibliographic data is available in the internet at http://dnb.d-nb.de.

Library of Congress Cataloging-in-Publication Data
A CIP catalog record for this book has been applied for at the Library of Congress.

This monography is the result of scientific research carried out as part of the grant from the National Science Centre on "Vat Gap in Poland: Policy Problem and Policy Response" – OPUS 16 (No. 2018/31/B/HS5/00234).

ISSN 2191-8848
ISBN 978-3-631-90874-7 (Print)
E-ISBN 978-3-631-91640-7 (E-PDF)
E-ISBN 978-3-631-91641-4 (E-PUB)
DOI 10.3726/b21666

Published by Peter Lang GmbH, Berlin, Deutschland

info@peterlang.com - www.peterlang.com

This publication has been peer reviewed.

Table of contents

Dominik J. Gajewski (SGH Warsaw School of Economics)

Introduction

In the European Union (EU) – as well as in many other jurisdictions[1], Value Added Tax (VAT) constitutes the backbone of the tax system, raising substantial part of the tax revenues[2].

The key strength attributed to VAT is neutrality to the economic processes (contrary to, say income taxation). Levied on the value added at subsequent steps of production chain, it is collected fractionally, via a system of partial payments and deductions (or reclaims). In other words, businesses collect VAT from buyers of their products, and deduct VAT they paid themselves at earlier stages of the production chain, buying, for example, raw materials or business services.

Due to its design, it is hardly surprising that VAT was also the first tax harmonized within the EU (in subsequent so called 'VAT directives'[3]). '*It was evident that if there was ever going to be an efficient, single market in Europe, a neutral and transparent turnover tax system was required which ensured tax neutrality and allowed the exact amount of tax to be rebated at the point of export*'.[4] Moreover, Council Decision 70/243 of April 21 1970, established VAT-based system for financing the EU budget.

VAT harmonization had been an important step in establishing the EU-wide Single Market, design for value creation chains spanning from one Member State to another – as illustrated by successful airplane manufacturer Airbus. On the other hand, the tax collection remained in the hands of Member State administrative apparatus. Thereby the key problem surfaced – maintaining VAT neutrality at the points of import/export from one Member State to Another.

---

1 For map of worldwide VAT application see: https://www.imf.org/external/np/fad/tpaf/pages/vat.htm (Accessed Oct. 31, 2023)

2 This monography is the result of scientific research carried out as part of the grant from the National Science Centre on '*Vat Gap in Poland: Policy Problem and Policy Response*' – OPUS 16 (No. 2018/31/B/HS5/00234).

3 The key milestones involved: First Council Directive 67/227/EEC of 11 April 1967 on the harmonisation of legislation of Member States concerning turnover taxes; Sixth Council Directive 77/388/EEC of 17 May 1977 on the harmonization of the laws of the Member States relating to turnover taxes – Common system of value added tax: uniform basis of assessment; Council Directive 2006/112/EC of 28 November 2006.

4 Commission.europa.eu (Accessed Oct. 31, 2023)

The solution – rules for taxing Intra-Community delivery and Intra-Community acquisition – turned out a threat to the whole harmonized VAT system, as it created an opportunity for so called '*Missing Trader Intra Community fraud*' (MTIC fraud). Its most elaborated form, so called 'carousel fraud' – based on artificial movement of goods (or just invoices) in a circle involving repeated Intra-Community deliveries and acquisitions – provided organized crime with financial *perpetuum mobile*, powered by taxpayers money extorted as undue VAT reclaims.

Coupled with more traditional forms of tax evasion, known also in sales tax systems (like sells underreporting as well as total or partial operation in so called 'shadow economy'), MTIC frauds represented forms of VAT noncompliance – leading to the loss of state revenues.

Macroeconomic attempt to proxy these losses is the concept of so called 'VAT gap' (also referred to as a 'compliance gap'),broadly defined as the difference between the total amounts of theoretically collectable VAT (as based on the applicable tax law) and the total amounts of VAT actually collected in a given period (see Chapter 1).

The concept of 'tax gaps' – the rough indicators of tax revenue loss gained widespread attention among scholars and policymakers in the aftermath of the global financial crisis. The problems were essentially foresaw by the International Monetary Fund, who warned domestic authorities that '*with the economic downturn, tax agencies are encountering growing compliance risks*' as '*an economic downturn tends to worsen taxpayer compliance in important aspects*'[5]. Specifically, it warned that crisis could shift in economic activity from the formal (taxed) sector to the so called '*shadow economy*' (studies like e.g. Mai, Schneider[6] provided evidences confirming that prediction).

Although the Global Financial Crisis starting in 2008 – and the Eurozone Sovereign Debt Crisis erupting few years later – constitute important part of the VAT noncompliance story, the state capacity and the policy choices are another important factor.

That is particularly true as far as Polish VAT compliance crisis is concerned. Despite the fact that Poland have not experienced recession after Financial and

---

5 Brondolo J. (2009). Collecting Taxes During an Economic Crisis, IMF Staff Position Notes, 2009 (017), A001. Retrieved Oct 16, 2023, from https://doi.org/10.5089/9781462339440.004.

6 Mai H., & Schneider F. (2016). Size and Development of the Shadow Economies of 157 Worldwide Countries: Updated and New Measures from 1999 to 2013. Journal of Global Economics, 4(3), pp. 1–15.

Eurozone crises, the size of its 'VAT gap' almost reached the levels recorded by Greece – the hardest hit EU Member State (see Figure I.1.). Thereby, growth in its 'VAT gap' could not be simply dismissed as a consequence of cyclical downturns.

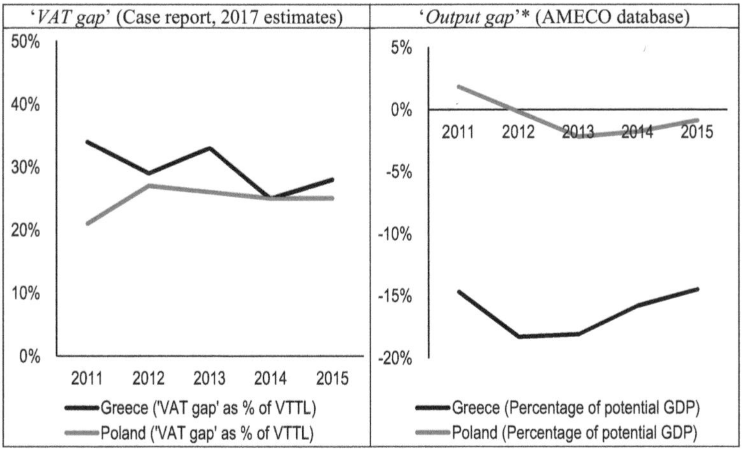

Figure I.1. Comparison of VAT noncompliance ('VAT gap', left panel) and business cycle ('Output gap', right panel) of Poland and Greece

*- Gap between actual GDP and potential GDP, percentage of potential GDP (AVGDGP)

Source: 'VAT gap' – European Commission, 2017; 'Output gap' – AMECO Online (Current Version 2023-05-15 11:00)

Given the popularity and importance of VAT in the EU and overseas, in depth examination of Polish noncompliance crisis is important for both the scholars and policymakers. The goal of this book is to examined it from the policy-making perspective. It depicts the state apparatus as facing red flags, indicating the problem, struggling to grasp its importance and underlying mechanics – and to develop and implement policies.

Noteworthy, the VAT noncompliance problem cut across traditional realms of legal scholarship (tax law, fiscal-criminal law, criminal law) and state apparatus organization (tax administration, crime control apparatus). Thereby, developing effective policy requires substantial coordination effort. The very same is true as far as scientific inquiry is concerned.

As a consequence, this book had been organized into two broad thematic blocks.

The first one deals with the overall description of 'VAT gap' crisis, and includes first three chapters. It illuminates the process of learning about the compliance crisis, with emphasize on various macro-level indicators available to the decision-makers, and the narratives formed to make sense of these evidence.

The second part deals with the activities undertook, in order to handle the crisis. They had been divided into three broad areas, covered in the subsequent chapters. The starting point is the response form broadly defined tax administration apparatus – the first line of the defence against VAT frauds and the migration of the economic activity to the 'shadow economy'. The reshuffling of tax administration apparatus, carried out in 2017 in order to improve its effectiveness in countering VAT fraud was described, together with two groups of control activities. The backward-looking controls aimed at spotting past noncompliance in an attempt to establish and recover VAT liability – as well as real-time activities like blocking fraudulent VAT reclaims, to prevent budget losses at the first place.

Then, the legislative response in the area of tax law is examined, with focus on key instruments implemented by the lawmakers in order to curb VAT noncompliance. The earliest instruments were discussed, together with later, wholesale, economy-wide interventions like so called Single Control File (Polish JPK).

Finally, the legislative response in the area of criminal law was examined, with focus on the severe sanctions introduced for issuing so called 'empty invoices' – the necessarily component of 'MTIC' fraud (as well as less sophisticated fraudulent activities).

While this book aims at the description of the policy response to the problem of Polish VAT noncompliance, as gauged by expanding 'VAT gap' over 2011–2016 period, it is not sort of authoritative inquiry into the causes of the crisis, its chronologies, nor a political exercise in blame-game. Also, there are reasons to believe, that fight against the VAT frauds is not finished yet, thereby it is still to early for an authoritative history of the crisis.

To this day voluminous materials had been assembled in order to allocate the blame for the crisis, trace its dynamics and – sometimes – outline lessons learned. Interested reader could consult:

(i) The report of the Parliamentary Investigative Committee (with separate opinion and numerous appendices);
(ii) The Supreme Audit Office (Polish: NIK) reports for VAT-related audits;
(iii) The Polish Economic Institute (Polish: PIE) report;
(iv) Series of English-language UN Global Compact reports on 'shadow economy' in Poland.

References

Brondolo J. (2009). Collecting Taxes During an Economic Crisis. *IMF Staff Position Notes*, 2009(017), A001. Retrieved Oct 16, 2023, from https://doi.org/10.5089/9781462339440.004.

Mai, H., & Schneider, F. (2016). Size and Development of the Shadow Economies of 157 Worldwide Countries: Updated and New Measures from 1999 to 2013. *Journal of Global Economics*, 4(3), 1–15.

Legislation

First Council Directive 67/227/EEC of 11 April 1967 on the harmonisation of legislation of Member States concerning turnover taxes.

Sixth Council Directive 77/388/EEC of 17 May 1977 on the harmonization of the laws of the Member States relating to turnover taxes – Common system of value added tax: Uniform basis of assessment; Council Directive 2006/112/EC of 28 November 2006.

Dominik J. Gajewski (SGH Warsaw School of Economics),
Kamil Joński (SGH Warsaw School of Economics)

Chapter 1 Gauging the depth of the crisis: The Polish 'VAT gap' evolution

Abstract: The chapter introduces the dynamics of Polish 'VAT gap' as estimated by various providers, including internal estimates of Polish Ministry of Finance and Fiscal Control apparatus. It emphasizes problems with the real-time availability of 'VAT gap' data to the policymakers, but also review alternative data indicating compliance problems.

Keywords: 'VAT Gap', VAT fraud, shadow economy, financial crisis

1.1. General comments

The dynamic of so called 'VAT gap' in Poland constitutes the natural departure point for the analysis of Polish VAT compliance crisis and policy responses formulated and implemented to counter it. However, as will be discussed, the real-time availability of 'VAT gap' estimates had been problematic, and assumptions taken during its estimation could result in skepticism of some policymakers.

Worse still, what we know as a 'VAT gap' is in fact an aggregate representing revenues missing due to honest errors, bankruptcies 'shadow economic' activity as well as several categories of frauds, including those run by organized crime groups. As the appropriate countermeasures depend on the mechanisms behind missing revenues, 'VAT gap' estimates fail to provide policymakers with the crucial piece of information required to craft effective policy response.

Thereby, this chapter also reviews alternative gauges available to the policymakers in the real time, and outlines a simple approach to the top-down 'VAT gap' estimation that would enable distinguishing between the two categories by building upon the minimal set of data available to the tax authorities[1].

Finally, the chapter briefly introduces three narratives on VAT compliance crisis, formulated in various policymaking or expert circles, as recovered from testimonies before the parliamentary investigation committee on VAT (hereafter

1 Gajewski D. J., & Joński K. (2022). 'VAT Gap' Estimation: Distinguishing Between Informality and Fraud. EC Tax Review, 31(3), pp. 124–130, https://doi.org/10.54648/ecta2022012.

'VAT investigative committee') and other open sources (in particular produced at the real time, to avoid so called 'hindsight bias').

1.2. Estimating the 'VAT gap'

The notion of 'VAT gap' originated over three decades ago in the United Kingdom, where *Her Majesty's Revenue and Customs* (HMRC) begun to compare VAT revenues with an estimate of the hypothetical VAT[2] revenue under perfect compliance[3]. Similar exercises had been carried out in other EU Member States: Germany, Denmark, Italy and Sweden[4].

In 2009, so called '*Reckon report*'[5] had been published, aimed at quantifying and analysing the VAT gap in each EU Member State over the period 2000–2006. This study provided the methodological foundation for future, ongoing project of the '*Study to quantify and analyse the VAT Gap in the EU-27 Member States*', carried out by CASE – Center for Social and Economic Research[6] on behalf of the European Commission (hereafter CASE reports). This project is now considered as an authoritative source of data about the 'VAT gap' defined as a '*difference between the theoretical tax liability according to the tax law and the actual revenue collected*' – the former referred to as an '*theoretical VAT tax liability according to the law (VTTL)*'[7].

2 Keen M., & Smith S. (2007). VAT Fraud and Evasion: What Do We Know, and What Can be Done?, IMF Working Paper, WP/07/31, pp. 15–16.

3 Estimates for 1992–2008 period see: Thackray M. (2012). The UK Tax Gap, slides available at: https://www.imf.org/external/np/seminars/eng/2012/asiatax/pdf/thackray.pdf (Accessed Oct. 31 2023).

4 European Commission, Directorate-General for Taxation and Customs Union. (2009). Study to quantify and analyse the VAT gap in the EU-25 Member States: report 2009, Publications Office of the European Union. https://data.europa.eu/doi/10.2778/018525, pp. 97.

5 European Commission, Directorate-General for Taxation and Customs Union. (2009). Study to quantify and analyse the VAT gap in the EU-25 Member States: report 2009, Publications Office of the European Union. https://data.europa.eu/doi/10.2778/018525, p. 97. Named after economic consultancy that prepared the report on behalf of the European Commission, see: https://www.reckon.co.uk/.

6 See: https://www.case-research.eu/en.

7 European Commission, Directorate-General for Taxation and Customs Union. (2013). Study to quantify and analyse the VAT gap in the EU-27 Member States: report 2013, Publications Office of the European Union. https://data.europa.eu/doi/10.2778/456646, pp. 21. On the definition of the 'VAT gap' and techniques of its calculation see also European Commission (2016) and IMF (2017).

From the methodological point of view, two approaches had been followed in order to estimate the extent of VAT noncompliance.

The '*bottom-up*' methodologies begin with micro-economic data, typically generated by tax administration itself (for example via tax audits). Such individual level data are then applied to estimate the components of the gap[8] – separately for different taxpayer groups and types of non-compliance[9]. Thereby, '*bottom-up*' approach provides more information about the structure of the estimated gap.

On the contrary The '*top-down*' approaches (including abovementioned CASE reports) begin with aggregated national accounts data (like GDP and consumption)[10], that are assumed reasonable proxies of VAT base. Thereby, they could be multiplied by appropriately estimated effective tax rate (representing differences in statutory rates and consumption structure) – producing theoretical amount of VAT due under perfect compliance. The 'gap' is a product of a comparison of this theoretically collectable amount and the actual amount of VAT revenues, collected by tax administration within specific time frame.

As 'VAT gap' is by definition estimated not observed and measured, obtained results could be sensitive to the assumptions made and input data quality. Figure 1.1. summarizes four available estimates of Polish 'VAT gap' covering the period of compliance crisis. Noteworthy, estimates provided in subsequent CASE reports were noticeably revised (thereby they were summarized as a range, for detail discussion see Section 1.3.), while Polish Ministry of Finance split their internal estimates depending on the statistical framework of input

8 In this context it is useful to distinguish 'bottom-up' approaches based on risk-based tax audits and random enquiry programmes. While risk-based tax audits are much more effective from tax administration point of view (targeting fraudsters), it would be tricky to generalize from the data obtained from such audits. That is not the case for random enquiry programmes, basically providing random sample of business activity in a country over audited period (see European Commission, 2022, pp. 141–144).

9 FISCALIS (2016) The Concept of Tax Gaps Report on VAT Gap Estimations by FISCALIS Tax Gap Project Group (FPG/041), available at: https://taxation-customs.ec.europa.eu/system/files/2016-08/tgpg_report_en.pdf (Accessed Oct. 31 2023), pp. 23–28; European Commission, Directorate-General for Taxation and Customs Union, Poniatowski G., Bonch-Osmolovskiy M., & Śmietanka A. (2022). VAT gap in the EU: report 2022, Publications Office of the European Union. https://data.europa.eu/doi/10.2778/109823, pp. 141–144.

10 In this context it is usefull to distinguish traditional, 'consumption-side' approach and 'production-side' approach, utilized in IMF's RAGAP. The latter estimates VAT liability separately for each sector of the economy (see Table no. 2.1), (see European Commission, 2022, pp. 141–144).

macroeconomic data collection (ESA1995 and ESA2010) to indicate their discontinuity.

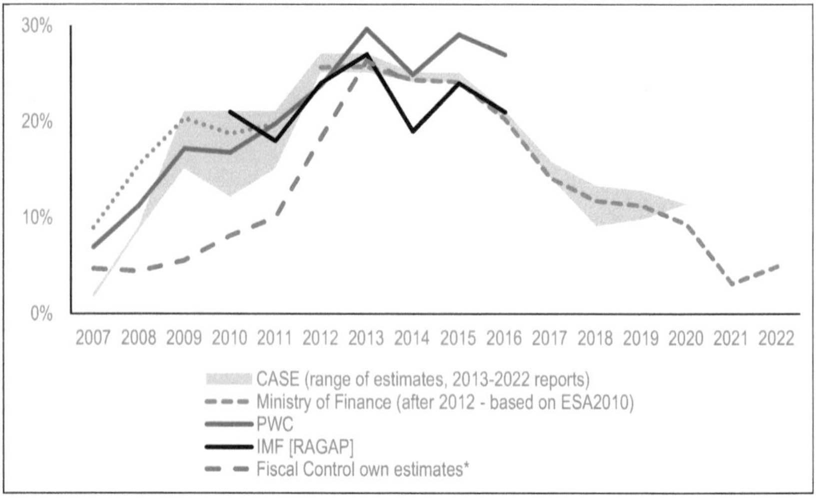

Figure 1.1. Estimates of Polish 'VAT gap' over 2007–2022

*- for more information about Fiscal Control apparatus see Chapter 4 Section 1a.

Source: CASE: (European Commission, 2013; 2014; 2015; 2016; 2017; 2018; 2019; 2020; 2021; 2022); Ministry of Finance: (The Republic of Poland, 2021; 2023); PWC: media release available at, *https://www.pwc.pl/pl/media/2016/2016-11-23-luka-vat-2016.html*

2016-11-23-luka-vat-2016.html (accessed Oct. 31 2023); IMF: Thackray and Ahmed (2018). Figure is a refined and updated version of Fig. 1 from (Gajewski & Joński, 2022); Fiscal Control own estimates adapted from Fig. 3 in (Ministry of Finance et al., 2015, p. 11).

With the benefit of hindsight (i.e. knowing all of the estimates and their subsequent updates), available metrics provides quite clear and consistent story of the 'VAT gap' build-up. There is little doubt, that the 'VAT gap' grew – albeit with different pace – since 2007 (Poland joined Schengen Area Dec. 31 2007), plateauing between 2012–2016 at around one-fourth of theoretically estimated VAT revenues.

In the subsequent years there are evidence of substantial narrowing of the gap, however there seems to be uncertainty over 'VAT gap' in the last two years – as 2022 *CASE report* provided estimates up to 2020[11]. Admittedly, the economic

11 European Commission, 2022.

developments (including double-digit inflation) involving the consequences of COVID pandemic and Russian invasion of Ukraine – as well as policy responses aimed at mitigating them (in particular the temporary changes in VAT rates for specific goods) – made estimating 'VAT gap' in 2021–2022 a daunting task.

1.3. The Fog of War: Evolution of 'VAT gap' estimates (CASE) for Poland - 2007–2020

Keeping in mind the uncertainty around 2021–2022 levels of 'VAT gap', it is important to remind the importance of so called '*hindsight bias*' (or knew-it-all-along phenomenon) in the analysis of the policy-making process. In particular, it is important to take into account the real-time availability of the 'VAT gap' estimates and the relevancy of data revisions – as these problems became particularly acute over 2010–2015 period. The uncertainty around 'VAT gap' estimates turned out particularly high during the 'gap' build-up in 2013–2015 (see bulging range of the CASE estimates for 2009–2011 period on Figure 1.1.).

It took almost four years since '*Reckon report*', to publish the first '*CASE report*'[12] presenting EU Member States 'VAT gap' estimates reaching beyond 2008 – the year when Global Financial Crisis erupted.

As presented on Figure 1.2, this study could led Polish policymakers to conclude that 'VAT gap' remains at manageable levels with medium-term downward tendency (as 2009–11 gap levels were lower than, say, 2000–2004).

The quantitative – and indeed, qualitative picture had hanged the very next year, as subsequent '*CASE report*' had been published[13]. First, it substantially revised upwards 2009–2011 estimates (by 4–6 percentage points – while leaving unchanged 2000 and 2005 estimates). Second, it reported jump in the 2012 'VAT gap' to 25% of theoretically collectable VAT revenues.

Such rapid change could indeed (i) surprise the policymakers and (ii) undermine the credibility of CASE-estimated 'VAT gap' as a gauge of taxpayers'

12 European Commission, Directorate-General for Taxation and Customs Union. (2013). Study to quantify and analyse the VAT gap in the EU-27 Member States: report 2013, Publications Office of the European Union. https://data.europa.eu/doi/10.2778/456646.

13 European Commission, Directorate-General for Taxation and Customs Union, (2014). 2012 update report to the study to quantify and analyse the VAT gap in the EU-27 Member States: report 2014, Publications Office of the European Union. https://data.europa.eu/doi/10.2778/571352.

compliance. Moreover, the reasons behind the revision were not discussed in greater detail[14].

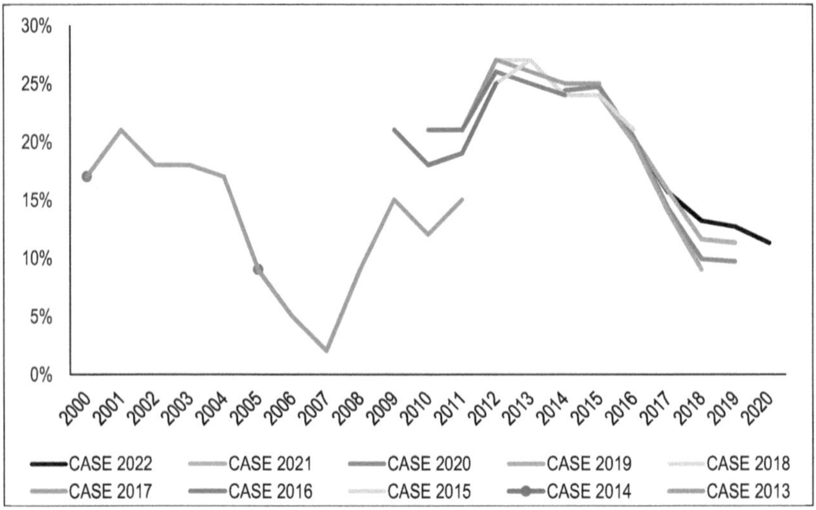

Figure 1.2. Polish 'VAT gap' as a percentage of VTTL: Subsequent CASE estimates for the European Commission

Source: European Commission, 2013, 2014, 2015, 2016, 2017, 2018, 2019, 2020, 2021, 2022

Indeed, in their testimonies before the *VAT investigative committee* both the Minister of Finance J. Rostowski and Chief Economist at the Ministry, L. Kotecki, stressed the magnitude of the 2013–2014 'VAT gap' revision. Admittedly, the scale of revisions in subsequent CASE reports were much lower (see Figure 1.2).

However, it is important to mention that Ministry of Finance policymakers had access to some internally calculated gauges of VAT compliance. For example the 2014 Convergence Programme update (Republic of Poland, 2014, p. 24) refers to the '*VAT tax gap*' described as the '*difference between VAT revenues*

14 As explained in (European Commission, 2014, p. 58): '*trends revealed for 2009–2011 in the 2013 VAT Gap report are similar for most countries, but in some the levels are different. At one extreme, the revised estimates for Slovenia are virtually identical, on average, to the previous ones. At the other extreme, the revised estimates for Malta have changed substantially due to a correction to the treatment of gambling exports … Other notable outliers are Poland (+5%), Italy (+4.6%), both countries on account of finer estimates of rates applicable to food and beverages*'.

and the indicator of the VAT tax base expressed as a percentage of VAT revenues (2005=100)'. The '*indicator of the VAT base*' included '*the private consumption, investments, net purchases by general government*'. The unusual property of 'gap' designed in this way was the fact, that MoF '*VAT tax gap*' could be either positive or negative[15] – quite unintuitive compared to the established definitions of 'VAT gap', like the one presented in '*Reckon report*' published in 2009.

Moreover, the report assembled by the Ministry of Finance, Ministry of Interior and the Prosecution General, prepared in July 2015 (Ministry of Finance et al., 2015, p. 11) plots the 'VAT gap' estimates assembled internally by the Fiscal Control (these estimates are compared with PWC's one). While these estimates were relatively optimistic prior to 2012, in the subsequent years they indicated rapid growth of VAT noncompliance, with magnitude similar to other available estimates of the 'VAT gap'(see Figure 1.1).

1.4. Crude indicators: VAT-to-GDP and nominal VAT revenues in Poland – 2007–2022

Admittedly, back in 2013–2014, CASE report 'VAT gap' performed quite poorly as a real-time indicator of the Polish VAT compliance crisis. However, the decision-makers had an access to much simpler gauges, that could be considered both intuitive and quite persuasive.

The simplest possible metrics, nevertheless clearly indicating VAT compliance problems, could be found in the budget planning and implementation data. Figure 1.3 summarizes the two key variables: VAT revenues forecasted (or assumed) during the budget planning process and the VAT revenues actually collected. Both are expressed in nominal terms (i.e. not corrected for inflation). Leaving aside three reasonable outliers (2009, 2020 and 2022)[16] it is visible that

15 See chart 4 in (The Republic of Poland, 2014) Convergence Programme 2014 update, available at: https://commission.europa.eu/publications/2014-european-semester-national-plans_en (Accessed Oct. 31 2023), p. 24. In a response to the request for public information dated Nov. 7th 2023 (No BMI1.0123.2850.2023), MoF confirmed that abovementioned 'gap' is not equivalent to 'VAT gap' understood as a difference between the actual and theoretically collectable VAT. Specifically it is not taking into account 'any data regarding VAT rates'. Noteworthy, since January 2011 the top VAT rate had been increased from 22% to 23% according to the Law of 16th December 2010 (Journal of Laws reference no. Dz.U.2010.257.1726). Thereby, the resulting revenues increase could be interpreted as a cyclical effect.

16 During the analyzed period, three years could be reasonably considered as outliers – thereby explaining the difference between planned and collected VAT. First, 2009,

in 2012 and 2013 MoF forecasters clearly overestimated the VAT revenues. Moreover, in 2013, the nominal amount of VAT declined. Perhaps as a consequence, in 2014 budget the value of VAT revenues had been planned quite conservatively (i.e. lower).

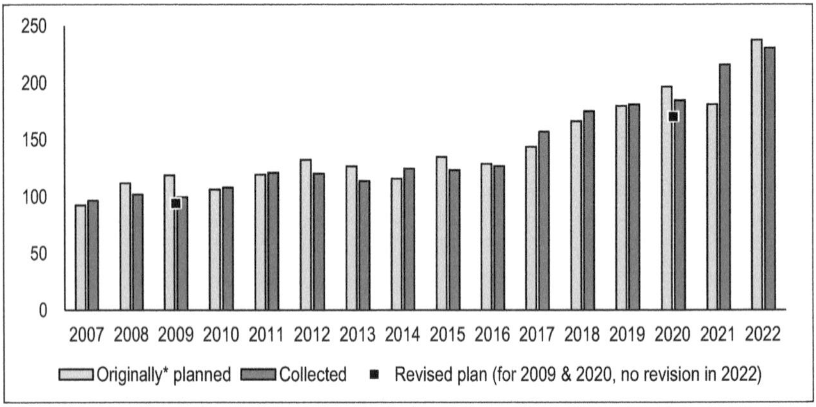

Figure 1.3. Polish nominal VAT revenues and VAT-to-GDP ratios: 2007–2022 [PLN billion]

Source: Subsequent budget laws (and selected amendments) and GUS Statistics Poland annual macroeconomic data available at: https://stat.gov.pl/wskazniki-makroekonomiczne/ (accessed Oct. 31 2023).

Noteworthy, comparing changes in VAT revenues in absolute terms neglects both economic growth and price dynamics. To this end, it is useful to employ some relative metric, linking VAT revenues to some macroeconomic aggregate like GDP (or, at more fine-grain approach, macroeconomic indicator of VAT tax base). Figure 1.4 plots nominal VAT revenues and GDP, rebased to 2007 – accompanied with VAT-to-GDP ratios[17]. This metric had been discussed in

marked the beginning of the acute phase of Global Financial Crisis. Thus budget law of Jan 9th 2009 (Dz.U.2009.10.58) had been amended by law of July 17th 2009 (Dz.U.2009.128.1057). Second, 2020 was the outbreak of COVID pandemics, marked with unprecedented policies like series of countrywide lockdowns. Thus budget law of Feb 14th 2020 (Dz.U.2020.571) had been amended by law of Oce 28th 2020 (Dz.U.2020.1919). Finally, 2022 marked Russian invasion of Ukraine, with massive refugees influx to Poland and global commodity process turbulence.

17 Noteworthy, the distance between the black (GDP) and red (VAT revenues) lines on Figure 1.4. somehow resembles the 'VAT gap'. Indeed, assuming that: (i) 2007 'VAT

policymaking circles during the compliance crisis – for example Supreme Audit Office (NIK) report on 2012 budget implementation[18] pointed out to the '*decline in the tax revenues to the GDP*'.

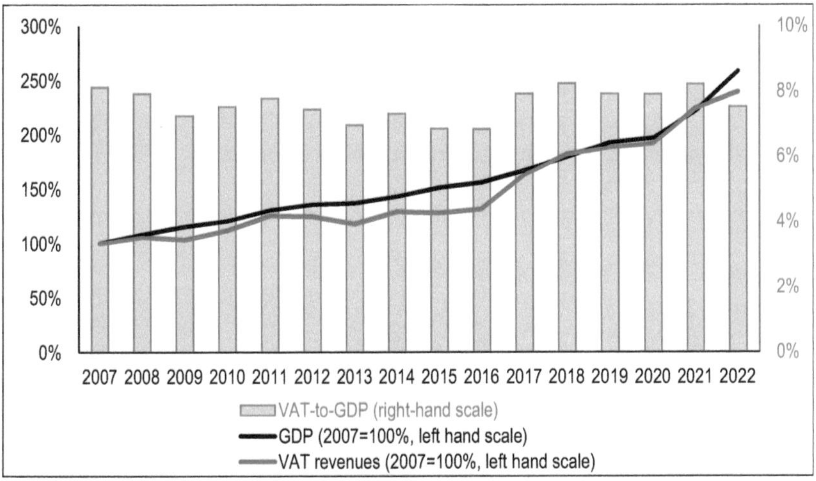

Figure 1.4. Polish VAT revenues and GDP (rebased, 2007=100 %) and VAT-to-GDP ratio: 2007–2022

Source: GUS Statistics Poland annual macroeconomic data available at: https://stat.gov.pl/wskazniki-makroekonomiczne/ (accessed Oct. 31 2023).

Last but not least, valuable insights into the severity of Polish VAT compliance crisis could be gained from specific markets. Although such sectoral perspective could not replace economy-wide view provided by indicators described earlier, it supplements it and could provide facts, able to pinpoint specific narratives.

---

gap' equated zero, (ii) relation of VAT tax base to GDP over 2007–2022 was constant, (iii) statutory VAT rates were constant and (iv) the structure of tax base with respect to applicable statutory VAT rate and respective exceptions were constant – it will be the equivalent of 'VAT gap' (and VAT-to-GDP ratio would convey precisely the same information as 'VAT gap' estimate). However, as abovementioned assumptions clearly not hold, the gap between both lines – as well as VAT-to-GDP ratio – are quite imperfect proxies of 'VAT gap' dynamics.

18 Supreme Audit Office. (2013). Analiza wykonania budżetu państwa i założeń polityki pieniężnej w 2012 r., available at: https://www.nik.gov.pl/analiza-budzetu-panstwa/archiwum/, (Accessed Oct. 31 2023), p. 76.

Perhaps the most striking fact of this kind was marked decline of (official) liquid fuel consumption in Poland during 2011—2014 (Figure 1.5). Bulk of the effect occurred in diesel market (the benefit of hindsight allows us to compare it to COVID 2020, marked by economy-wide lockdown affecting transportation) – and was hard to explain by anything short of massive fraud. Indeed, report commissioned by The Polish Organization of Petroleum Industry and Trade in Ernst & Young consultancy documented the extent of fraud on the market (study involved multiple methods, including 'detective' ones, as field observers counted tanks arriving through the state borders).[19]

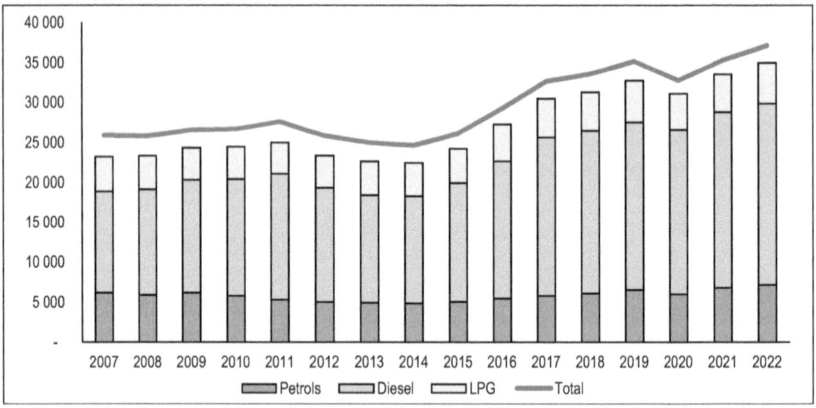

Figure 1.5. Estimated domestic liquid fuel consumption [m^3 thousands]: 2007–2022
Source: Annual reports of The Polish Organization of Petroleum Industry and Trade (Polska Organizacja Przemysłu i Handlu Naftowego, POPiHN), available at: https://popihn.pl/raporty-i-konferencje/, (accessed Oct. 31 2023).

Importantly, it pointed out to the role of missing traders – coupled with the sheer magnitude of the drop in the official fuel consumption, that would suggest involvement of organized crime.

Another important red flags came from the enforcement apparatus in both fiscal and crime-control realm. First, the value of 'fake invoices' identified during fiscal controls[20] grew steadily until 2016 (also the number of such invoices increased sharply in 2015, see Figure 1.6.). Noteworthy, 'fake invoices'

19 See testimony of P. Niemczyk before the VAT investigative committee.
20 For more information about Fiscal Control apparatus see Chapter 4, Section 1.1.

are – among others – the ones produced by the 'Missing Trader' in MTIC frauds schemes, runs by the organized crime groups.

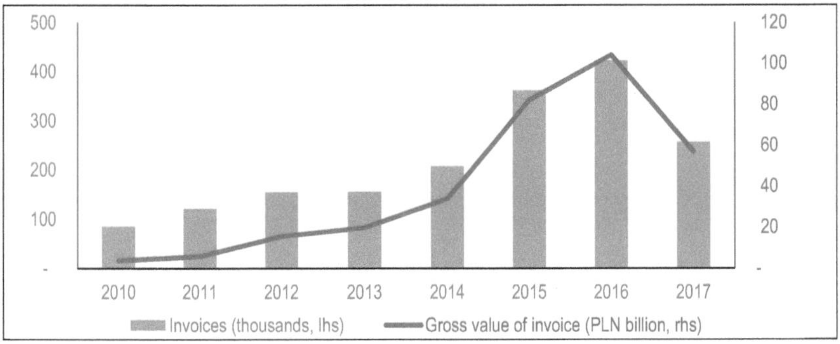

Figure 1.6. Number and gross value of 'fake invoices' identified during Fiscal Controls
Source: Annual reports of the Fiscal Control, (NIK, 2018, pp. 26)

And indeed, as the volume and value of 'faked invoices' grew, the law enforcement apparatus data on the structure of organized crime (see Table 1.1) revealed, that 'economic' groups outnumbered the second largest category – namely 'drug-related' groups.

Table 1.1. The structure of organized crime groups* investigated by selected services, 2014–2016

	Police's Central Investigative Bureau [CBŚP]				**Border Guard**				**The Internal Security Agency [ABW]**		
	'economic'	**'drug-related'**	**'criminal'**	**'multi-crime'**	**'economic'**	**'drug-related'**	**'criminal'**	**'multi-crime'**	**'economic'**	**'drug-related'**	**'multi-crime'**
2014	388	268	155	109	145	36	94	18	179	4	4
2015	320	237	190	65	156	29	118	42	134	2	5
2016	341	290	143	100	121	42	123	26	87	11	9

*- The number of groups should not be added, as single group could be investigated by more than one services.
Source: Ministry of Interior annual reports on the security developments (Polish: Raport o stanie bezpieczeństwa) available at: https://archiwumbip.mswia.gov.pl/bip/raport-o-stanie-bezpie/18405,Raport-o-stanie-bezpieczenstwa.html and https://isp.policja.pl/isp/aktualnosci/7789,Raport-o-stanie-bezpieczenstwa-w-Polsce-w-2014-r.html (Accessed Oct. 31 2023).

1.5. Cashing checks on the government: The dynamics of VAT Reclaims

Even before the creation of the Single Market, the false claims for VAT credit or refund had been well-known soft underbelly of VAT design. For example, Tait[21] reported that 44% of VAT frauds investigated in the Netherlands took the form of false claims for VAT. At that time, fraudsters typically produced invoices for non-existing purchases (or real, but exaggerated) which give grounds for VAT refund claims[22].

However it was the Single Market, with its (i) abolition of custom controls on internal borders, and (ii) VAT rules for Intra-Community transactions[23], that gave rise to what is called *Missing Trader Intra Community* fraud (*MTIC fraud*, see more detailed description in Chapter 2 Section 2). If VAT invoice can be dubbed '*a check written on the government*'[24], with MTIC the sole fraudsters and organized crime groups invented tool allowing them to produce – and indeed cash in – such checks in extraordinary quantities[25].

As presented in the Figure 1.7, the dynamics of collected VAT, VAT reclaims and the difference between these two – the VAT revenues (reported in cash) – behaved quite similar over 2008–2011 period. However, in subsequent years they visibly diverged, with VAT reclaims growing noticeably faster than VAT collected, thereby diminishing the total VAT revenues (in other words, the ratio of VAT reclaims to VAT collected increased from 35,9% in 2008 to 41,1% in 2013).

21 Tait A. (1988). Value Added Tax, International Practice and Problems, International Monetary Fund: https://doi.org/10.5089/9781557750129.071, p. 307.

22 European Commission, Directorate-General for Taxation and Customs Union. (2018). Study and reports on the VAT gap in the EU-28 Member States: report 2018, Publications Office of the European Union. https://data.europa.eu/doi/10.2778/013500, p. 8.

23 Specifically, '*The general VAT rules indicate that VAT-registered suppliers are entitled to apply a zero rate on their intra-Community sales (ICS) to VAT-registered buyers in other Member States under the condition that the goods are dispatched or transported from one EU Member State to a destination in another Member State*' (European Commission, 2018b, pp. 9)

24 Bird R. (1993). Review of 'Principles and Practice of Value Added Taxation: Lessons for Developing Countries, Canadian Tax Journal, 41(6), pp. 1222–1225.

25 Gajewski D. J., & Grzybowski T. (2018). *Abuse of law in value added tax added, Scientific journals of administrative justice*, 5, 9–31.

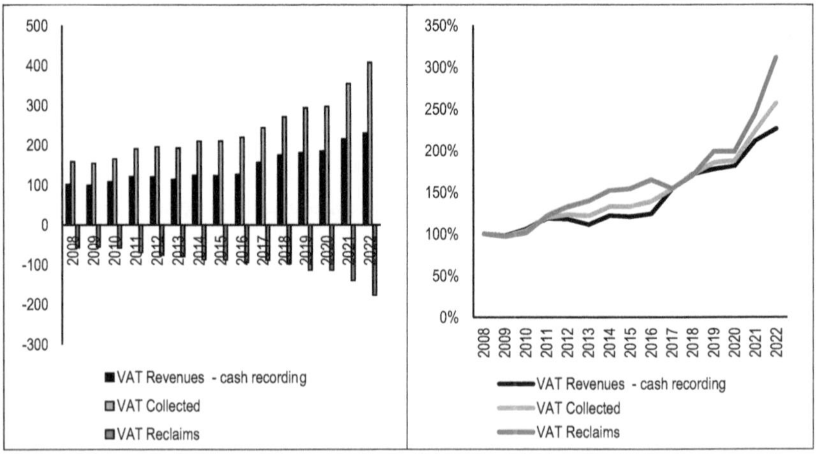

Figure 1.7. VAT collected, reclaimed and net VAT revenues: 2008–2022: nominal (PLN billions, left panel) and rebased (2008=100 %, right panel)

Sources and the raw data listed in the Appendix 1. Figure is a refined and updated version of Fig. 2 from (Gajewski &, Jończski, 2022).

Interestingly, in 2017 – as 'VAT gap' shrunk, the dynamics of the three variables aligned again (in 2017 the ratio of VAT reclaims to VAT collected was again 35,9). However, the growth rate of VAT reclaims accelerated again, and in 2022 the ratio of VAT reclaims to VAT collected reached 43,4% – the highest value in 2008–2022 sample. Unfortunately, extraordinary macroeconomic situation after COVID pandemic and Russian invasion of Ukraine – as well as temporary unavailability of well-established 'VAT gap' estimates – put serious limitation on the interpretation of these numbers (once again illustrating the pitfalls of real-time gauging the scale of VAT noncompliance).

Noteworthy, the comparison of dynamics of VAT collected and VAT reclaims demonstrates the importance of decomposing 'VAT gap' in general – and the importance of quantifying the effects of MTIC frauds in particular[26]. Unfortunately, CASE reports fail to provide such decomposition.

Some insights can be gained from IMF RAGAP project estimates, utilizing *top-down 'production-side'* approach. According to their estimates, substantial

26 For literature review (see: European Commission, 2018b, pp. 16–19).

fraction of 2012–2014 'VAT gap' can be attributed to the Trade and transport sector (Table 1.2).

Table 1.2. IMF's RA-GAP Compliance Gap – Four key contributing sectors

	2010	**2011**	**2012**	**2013**	**2014**	**2015**	**2016**
Professional services	0,4	0,4	0,4	0,4	0,4	0,5	0,4
Utilities	0,2	0,2	0,3	0,3	0,2	0,4	0,3
Construction	0	0,1	0,1	0,2	0	0,1	0,2
Trade & transport	0,6	0,3	0,9	1	0,5	0,4	0,2
Compliance Gap, % of GDP	**2**	**1,7**	**2,4**	**2,6**	**1,7**	**2,3**	**1,7**

Source: Thackray Ahmed (2018), Appendix Table 16. The Compliance Gap by Sector.

Another piece of evidence came from (monetary) shadow economy estimates prepared in 2020 by the EY consultancy.[27] It employed cross-country econometric model (so called currency demand approach, CDA, see Dybka et al., 2019) to estimate size of '*monetary shadow economy*' – expressed as percentage of the total monetary economy. That in turn had been used to calculated the VAT revenues lost as a consequence of the monetary shadow economy. Finally, EY team subtracted these lost VAT revenues from the overall top-down 'VAT gap' estimate provided by the MoF,[28] decomposing 'VAT gap' into the '*monetary shadow economy*' component and '*other factors, including organized VAT fraud*'.

Also Gajewski and Joński[29] proposed simplistic approach for decomposing the 'VAT gap' using data on VAT collected and VAT reclaims[30]. To this end, they isolated the component of '*unexplained VAT reclaims*' – i.e. amounts of VAT reclaims that grew faster than VAT collected (see 'gap' in the right panel of Figure 1.7).

27 On EY study see: https://www.ey.com/pl_pl/news/2020/02/analiza-ey-polska-szara-strefa-w-polsce-stanowila-10-8-pkb-w-2018-roku; results are summarized in the presentation available in Polish at: https://assets.ey.com/content/dam/ey-sites/ey-com/en_pl/topics/eat/pdf/03/ey-szara-strefa-w-polsce-final.pdf (Accessed Oct. 31, 2023).

28 As presented in the Wieloletni plan finansowy państwa na lata 2019–2022, available at: https://www.gov.pl/web/finanse/wieloletni-plan-finansowy-panstwa (Accessed Oct. 31, 2023).

29 Gajewski, & Joński, 2022.

30 On limitations of such exercise see: (Gajewski, & Joński, 2022, pp. 127–128).

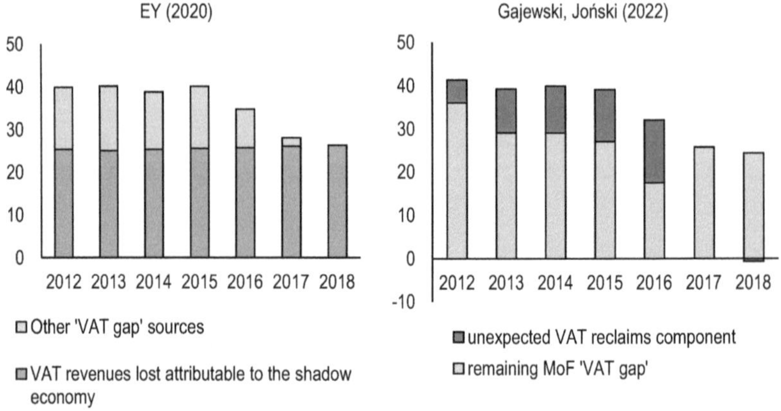

Figure 1.8. Decomposition of MoF 'VAT gap' estimates: EY CDA approach (left panel) and Gajewski and Joński (2022) 'unexpected VAT reclaims component' [PLN billion].
Source: Gajewski and Joński (2022) Fig. 4.

Figure 1.8. compares results of both empirical exercises. Given that they had been carried out using different input data and methodologies (CDA model of '*monetary shadow economy*' and discrepancies between growth rates of VAT collected and reclaimed), one can conclude that they provide reasonably similar pictures of '*shadow economy*' and '*reclaim extortion*' in the overall 'VAT gap'.[31]

1.6. The situational awareness: Interpreting the VAT compliance crisis in policy circles

After presenting the key data aimed at illustrating the development of Polish VAT compliance crisis (and discussing the issue of their real-time availability), it is useful to assess how they had been interpreted in the policy circles. Since people tend to think and argue using narratives – in other words, telling the

31 Jaras, T., Whittle, E., Patel, K. et al. (2015) Implementing the 'destination principle' to intra-EU B2B supplies of goods – Feasibility and economic evaluation study – Final report, Publications Office, 2015, https://data.europa.eu/doi/10.2778/216975 building upon the data provided by the Tax Authorities of Austria, Bulgarian, Czech Republic, Cyprus, Finland, France, Slovakia, Slovenia and United Kingdom reported that '*On average, according to the Tax Authorities 36 % of the VAT gap is due to VAT fraud*'.

stories ('*analytics+storytelling=influence*'[32]) – this section discusses three of them, emphasizing different meaning, that their authors ascribed to various pieces of the data.

For the sake of presentation, three vivid public figures, representing distinct views had been picked. All of them (i) belonged to what can be dubbed 'policy circles' (either as decisionmakers or advisors), (ii) presented their views in writing as the crisis unfold and (iii) testified before the VAT investigative committee, having opportunity to review their views with the benefit of hindsight. However, one have to keep in mind that what follows is not a systematic review of 'VAT gap' related discourse, nor detailed account of views and opinions of these three individuals. Instead, it is a nutshell summary of three distinct views – or interpretations – of unfolding VAT compliance crisis, that informed the policy formulation process.

1.6.1 The 'inherent flaw' view

The first of analyzed interpretations was vocally advocated by W. Modzelewski – Warsaw University professor, legal counselor and former deputy Minister of Finance, responsible for introduction of VAT in Poland back in 1993. It stated that harmonized EU VAT is inherently flawed by its very design, as far as intra-community trade is concerned[33]. Moreover, he vocally criticized so called '*reverse charge*' applied by various Member States on particularly fraud-prone markets. For Modzelewski, the key problem of VAT system management regarded rapidly growing VAT reclaims[34]. In his view, the key role in effective curbing TAX noncompliance should be played by Head of Tax Offices, deciding on VAT reclaims (as they transfer real taxpayer money, sometimes to the hands of fraudsters, thereby generating irreversible loses). He also claimed that so called penalty rate (30% of the documented underpayment of VAT) was an appropriate deterrent tool, and abandoning it in 2008 (as part of 'red-tape-cutting' and business-friendly agenda) was a serious policy mistake.

---

32 To borrow from preface in Knowles S. (2018). *Narrative by Numbers: How to Tell Powerful & Purposeful Stories with Data*. Routledge, Abingdon, Oxon.

33 See also, for example: Keen M., & Smith S. (2007). VAT Fraud and Evasion: What Do We Know, and What Can be Done?, IMF Working Paper, WP/07/31.

34 See: ISP. (2014). Raport podsumowujący najważniejsze doświadczenia 10-lecia podatku od towarów i usług oraz podatku akcyzowego w Polsce (lata 2004–2014), Biuletyn Instytutu Studiów Podatkowych, nr 7, p. 14.

1.6.2 The 'gangster' view

Another, although somehow related interpretation had been formulated in the circles of Polish crime-control apparatus. This view, presented for example by retired agent and parliamentary committee for secret services expert P. Niemczyk implied that Polish VAT fraud had been organized by relatively small number of criminals, who developed fraudulent schemes and apply them from one market to another (for example from steel rods to fuels). Thus, the appropriate response would require policing tools aimed at countering organized crime groups[35].

1.63. The 'automatic stabilizer' view

Perhaps the most outrageous interpretation of the data indicating the scale of VAT compliance crisis had been provided by L. Kotecki, deputy Minister of Finance (2008–2012) and, subsequently, Chief Economist in the Ministry of Finance (2012–2015).

In his testimony before the VAT investigative committee – Kotecki claimed that VAT noncompliance can be viewed as a form of… fiscal stimulus to the economic growth[36]. Noteworthy such view had been presented in the economic literature even before his interview. Brondolo[37] admits that '*a drop in taxpayer compliance may have some countercyclical effects on the economy, but complicates fiscal management, and tolerating noncompliance is not an appropriate response to the crisis*'. Also IMF[38], noted that '*increased noncompliance may have acted to some degree as an automatic stabilizer – but a very second-best one… Turning a*

35 See also Niemczyk P., Foryciarz K., & Kielan B. (2015). Nowe formy przestępczości zorganizowanej na przykładzie wybranych form przestępczości gospodarczej [in:] E. Pływaczewski, W. Filipkowski, Z. Rau, *Przestępczość w XXI wieku zapobieganie i zwalczanie. Problemy prawno-kryminologiczne*. Wolters Kluwer, Warsaw, pp. 736–754.

36 In his testimony he went as far as to draw parallel between declining VAT revenues and cut in social contributions, believed to provide fiscal stimulus for Polish economy during 2009 slowdown. Polish quote: '*lepszy przykład. Mianowicie w 2009 r. Polska była jedynym krajem, który nie poszedł pod wodę …To wynikało z tego, co się stało w 2007 r. … pani minister Zyta Gilowska, bo to ona była pomysłodawcą tych obniżek, spowodowała, że Polacy mieli netto więcej w tych swoich portfelach. To pomogło bardzo mocno np. przy konsumpcji … Gdybyśmy tym podatnikom odebrali te pieniądze, które są w tej luce, to tego wzrostu by na pewno nie było*'.

37 Brondolo, 2009, p. 7.

38 IMF. (2015). Current Challenges in Revenue Mobilization – Improving Tax Compliance, Policy Papers, 2015(005), A001. Retrieved Oct 16, 2023, from https://doi.org/10.5089/9781498344890.007, p. 13.

blind eye to noncompliance might have some beneficial effects on activity. But it risks damaging the credibility of enforcement'.

One can reasonably argue that each of these narratives convey some merits, although they fail to grasp the whole reality of the VAT noncompliance as a policy problem. It seems that improved handling of VAT reclaims and modifying the VAT rules for Intra-Community transactions (notably W. Modzelewski advocated collecting VAT from buyers '*graniczna płatność z tytułu WNT*' – instead of '*reverse charge*' – and such design was implemented in so called 2016 '*fuel package*') would not be sufficient to curb organized crime groups. On the other hand, countering these groups with police toolkit – without closing legal loopholes fixing tax apparatus – would be insufficient since new groups will proliferate as long as fraudulent activities would be profitable and relatively low-risky business.

However, it seems that the '*automatic stabilizer*' view was the most harmful. Leaving ethical considerations apart, interpreting VAT noncompliance in terms of automatic stabilizer of the economic growth could only make sense under the assumption that it is generated by otherwise honest businesses, extraordinarily cutting corners in difficult times. This assumption was hard to reconcile with growing evidence of criminal activities. Stimulating the economy by funneling taxpayer's money to the organized crime groups via VAT reclaims is hardly a sensible macroeconomic policy.

As Kotecki explained before the VAT investigative committee, there was no 'decision' to use VAT noncompliance as policy tool.[39] Also, he acknowledge that the literature estimates that VAT fraud accouns for '*20–35 percent*' of the overall 'VAT gap'.[40] Admittedly it would be hard to imagine EU Member State Minister of Finance deciding to tolerate tax frauds as part of growth-boosting policy mix.

However, one could hypothesize that such narrative would allow what D. Vaughan[41] dubbed '*normalization of deviance*'. Assumption, that there is nothing particularly bad in declining VAT revenues, would push compliance issues further down the agenda. It could also result in downplaying or explaining-away the contradictory evidence arriving from various sources (confirmation

39 Polish quote: '*W żadnej mojej wypowiedzi nie było słowa "decyzje". Tam, znaczy, to nie było tak, że ktoś podejmował decyzje, żeby opóźniać działania przeciwdziałające nadużyciom podatkowym*'.

40 Polish quote: '*to jest jakiś element, nawet nie potrafimy do końca powiedzieć. On jest szacowany w literaturze między 20 a 35 % całej luki*'.

41 Vaughan D. (2016). *The Challenger Launch Decision: Risky Technology, Culture, and Deviance at NASA*. Univ. of Chicago Press.

bias). Just like NASA bureaucrats reassured themselves, launch after launch, that repeating O-ring failures are not creating grave danger for the space shuttle, Ministry of Finance bureaucrats looking at 'VAT gap' through the lens of '*automatic stabilizer*' failed to grasp the policy problem that they faced.

Vivid examples of such cognitive limitation (assuming lack of bad faith) can be found in annual documents submitted by Poland to the European Commission as part of so called European Semester – review of public finance sustainability of the Member States.

The document submitted in 2013, observed '*a high growth was noted (significantly exceeding the growth rate of the tax base) in the VAT tax returns paid into taxpayers bank accounts by the tax office. This is due to the deterioration in the liquidity of enterprises which increased the preferences of taxpayers to obtain a return in the form of direct tax refunds (compared to a return settlement consisting of a reduction in future tax payments). In addition an excessive increase in the VAT tax arrears was noted in 2012. All those mechanisms constitute the elements that form automatic economic stabilizers, whose activity becomes visible in periods of economic slowdown*'[42].

In the following year, with alarm bells ringing all around (just to mention the fall in nominal VAT revenues or official liquid fuel consumption), the Convergence Programme update submitted by Poland put even greater effort to explain them away as a mere consequence of '*deterioration in the macroeconomic environment and the deepening of the output gap*'[43]. The Ministry of Finance pointed out at '*growth rate of the indicator of the VAT tax base (a sum of nominal values of private consumption, investments and net purchases of the general government)*' amounting to just 1%, and '*the pro-cyclical nature of taxes (the elasticity of taxes in relation to GDP, as well as in relation to the indicator of tax base, observed in Poland, is pro-cyclical), strengthening the activity of the automatic stabilisers*'. Moreover, the MoF-calculated '*VAT tax gap*' (see Section 1.3) had been used – but not to indicate the compliance crisis – but instead to reinforce the argument on '*the pro-cyclical nature of tax elasticity*'[44]. Noteworthy, the '*pro-cyclical tax*

42 The Republic of Poland. (2013). Convergence Programme 2013 update, available at: https://commission.europa.eu/publications/2013-european-semester-national-plans_en (Accessed Oct. 31 2023), p. 15.

43 The 'output gap' is a macroeconomic variable indicating the difference between actual (observed) and potential (estimated) growth of the economy.

44 L. Kotecki defended this idea during VAT investigative commitee hearings in a mimeo coauthored with A. Bratkowski tittled 'Luka VAT w świetle analiz makroekonomicznych'. Its large parts had been included in chapters 6.2–6.5 of the Z. Konwiński, M. Pampuch,

elasticity' could offer explanation for overestimating VAT revenues during the budget planning process (see Figure 1.3)[45] as well as for declining VAT-to-GDP ratios (see Figure 1.4).

Moreover, despite the '*Green Island*' narrative (Poland was the only EU Member State who managed to avoid falling into a recession after 2008[46]), it was argued that '*the decline in the economic trends in Poland in the years 2012–2013 was one of the deepest in the EU, next to Cyprus, Greece, the Czech Republic and Italy*'[47].

In other words, the declining (by 2013, even in absolute terms, see Section 1.4.) VAT revenues were still interpreted as a product of exceptionally adverse macroeconomic conditions, not the compliance crisis requiring dedicated policy response.

This benevolent denial of the mounting compliance crisis seems visible in the analysis of the parliamentary discourse presented in Chapter 3 – as well as in laconic explanations provided during the lawmaking processes of the earliest tax law instruments aimed at curbing VAT frauds – namely reverse charge introduced in 2011 for scrap metal and in 2013 for steel.

G. Tokarska Separate opinion to the VAT investigative committee report, Parliamentary document no. 3805, VIII Term.

45 Simplifying a bit, such models employ historically estimated ratios ('elasticities') to short-term macroeconomic forecasts (like next year consumption and investments) to produce forecast of VAT revenues. If the next year 'elasticity' will be lower than historical 'elasticity' applied to generate forecasts, then revenues will turn out overestimated.

46 See Polanski Z. (2014). Poland During the Crisis: A 'Green Island' Approaching the Euro Area? [in:] Hölscher J. (ed.) *Poland and the Eurozone. Studies in Economic Transition*. Palgrave Macmillan, London, https://doi.org/10.1057/9781137426413_9

47 The Republic of Poland. (2014). Convergence Programme 2014 update, available at: https://commission.europa.eu/publications/2014-european-semester-national-plans_en (Accessed Oct. 31 2023), pp. 23–26. For readers with macroeconomic background it could be interesting to read the explanation of this apparent paradox: 'contrary to the aforementioned countries, the economic growth in Poland was positive. This non-typical development of cyclical conditions in Poland (the biggest observed deviation against the trend line representing the average dependence between the change in the output gap and the real GDP) indicates that in our country, in spite of the negative effects of the financial crisis, maintaining of the relatively high growth rate of the potential GDP was possible. In this context, the nevertheless observed positive economic growth in Poland, but at a low level, ab. 1.5 %, means a situation for the public finances which is similar to that observed in other countries in the period of economic recession' (Republic of Poland, 2014, p. 25).

It seems not an accident, that it took political leadership change in the Ministry of Finance (in Nov. 2013 M. Szczurek replaced J. Vincent-Rostowski, who hold the position since late 2007) to initiate more systematic policy response to VAT noncompliance (see legislative instruments like Single Control File, JPK, reviewed in the Chapter 5). Later on, as right-wing government of Law and Justice replaced center-liberal cabinet of Civic Platform and Polish People's Party, 2017 Convergence Programme update had been extended with an appendix entitled '*Measures increasing tax compliance in the years 2017–18*' – indicating the shift towards the narrative on vigorous campaign against the VAT frauds and shadow economy.

References

Bird R. (1993). Review of 'Principles and Practice of Value Added Taxation: Lessons for Developing Countries'. *Canadian Tax Journal*, 41(6), 1222–25.

Brondolo J. (2009). Collecting Taxes During an Economic Crisis. *IMF Staff Position Notes*, 2009(017), A001. Retrieved Oct 16, 2023, from https://doi.org/10.5089/9781462339440.004.

Dybka P., Kowalczuk M., Olesiński B., Rozkrut M., & Torój A. (2019). Currency Demand and MIMIC Models: Towards a Structured Hybrid Method of Measuring the Shadow Economy. *Int Tax Public Finance,* 26(2019), 4–40. https://doi.org/10.1007/s10797-018-9504-5.

European Commission, Directorate-General for Taxation and Customs Union. (2009). Study to Quantify and Analyse the VAT Gap in the EU-25 Member States: Report 2009. Publications Office of the European Union. https://data.europa.eu/doi/10.2778/018525.

European Commission, Directorate-General for Taxation and Customs Union. (2013). Study to Quantify and Analyse the VAT Gap in the EU-27 Member States: Report 2013. Publications Office of the European Union. https://data.europa.eu/doi/10.2778/456646

European Commission, Directorate-General for Taxation and Customs Union. (2014). 2012 Update Report to the Study to Quantify and Analyse the VAT Gap in the EU-27 Member States: Report 2014. Publications Office of the European Union. https://data.europa.eu/doi/10.2778/571352

European Commission, Directorate-General for Taxation and Customs Union. (2015). 2012 Update Report to the Study to Quantify and Analyse the VAT Gap in the EU Member States: Report 2015. Publications Office of the European Union. https://op.europa.eu/s/y16i

European Commission, Directorate-General for Taxation and Customs Union. (2016). Study and Reports on the VAT Gap in the EU-28 Member State: Report

2016. Publications Office of the European Union. https://data.europa.eu/doi/10.2778/417954

European Commission, Directorate-General for Taxation and Customs Union. (2017). Study and Reports on the VAT Gap in the EU-28 Member States: Report 2017. Publications Office of the European Union. https://data.europa.eu/doi/10.2778/371136

European Commission, Directorate-General for Taxation and Customs Union. (2018a). Study and Reports on the VAT Gap in the EU-28 Member States: Report 2018. Publications Office of the European Union. https://data.europa.eu/doi/10.2778/013500

European Commission, Directorate-General for Taxation and Customs Union. (2018b). The Concept of Tax Gaps – Report III – MTIC Fraud Gap Estimation Methodologies. Publications Office, https://data.europa.eu/doi/10.2778/418684.

European Commission, Directorate-General for Taxation and Customs Union, Poniatowski, G., Durán-Cabré, J., & Bonch-Osmolovskiy, M. (2019). Study and Reports on the VAT Gap in the EU-28 Member States: Report 2019. Publications Office of the European Union. https://data.europa.eu/doi/10.2778/04272

European Commission, Directorate-General for Taxation and Customs Union, Śmietanka, A., Bonch-Osmolovskiy, M., & Poniatowski, G. (2020). Study and Reports on the VAT Gap in the EU-28 Member States: 2020 Final Report. (G. Poniatowski, edito) Publications Office. https://data.europa.eu/doi/10.2778/2517.

European Commission, Directorate-General for Taxation and Customs Union, Poniatowski, G., Bonch-Osmolovskiy, M., & Śmietanka, A. (2021). VAT Gap in the EU: Report 2021. Publications Office. https://data.europa.eu/doi/10.2778/447556.

European Commission, Directorate-General for Taxation and Customs Union, Poniatowski, G., Bonch-Osmolovskiy, M., & Śmietanka, A. (2022). VAT Gap in the EU: Report 2022. Publications Office of the European Union. https://data.europa.eu/doi/10.2778/109823.

FISCALIS. (2016). The Concept of Tax Gaps Report on VAT Gap Estimations by FISCALIS Tax Gap Project Group (FPG/041). Available at: https://taxation-customs.ec.europa.eu/system/files/2016-08/tgpg_report_en.pdf (Accessed Oct. 31 2023).

Gajewski D. J., & Grzybowski T. (2018). *Nadużycie prawa w podatku od wartości dodanej, Zeszyty naukowe sądownictwa administracyjnego*, 5, 9-31,

Gajewski D. J., & Joński K. (2022). 'VAT Gap' Estimation: Distinguishing Between Informality and Fraud. *EC Tax Review*, 31(3), 124–130, https://doi.org/10.54648/ecta2022012.

IMF. (2015). Current Challenges in Revenue Mobilization – Improving Tax Compliance. *Policy Papers*, 2015(005), A001. Retrieved Oct 16, 2023, from https://doi.org/10.5089/9781498344890.007.

ISP. (2014). Raport podsumowujący najważniejsze doświadczenia 10-lecia podatku od towarów i usług oraz podatku akcyzowego w Polsce (lata 2004–2014). *Biuletyn Instytutu Studiów Podatkowych*, nr 7.

Jaras, T., Whittle, E., Patel, K. et al. (2015) Implementing the 'destination principle' to Intra-EU B2B Supplies of Goods – Feasibility and Economic Evaluation Study – Final Report. Publications Office, 2015, https://data.europa.eu/doi/10.2778/216975.

Keen M., & S. Smith. (2007). *VAT Fraud and Evasion: What Do We Know, and What Can be Done?*. IMF Working Paper, WP/07/31.

Knowles S. (2018). *Narrative by Numbers: How to Tell Powerful & Purposeful Stories with Data*. Abingdon, Oxon: Routledge.

Ministry of Finance, Ministry of Interior, Prosecution General. (2015). *Przestępczość związana z podatkiem od towarów i usług – propozycje rozwiązań systemowych*, preliminary report published as an Appendix to the VAT investigative committee report, Parliamentary document no. 3805, VIII Term.

Niemczyk P., Foryciarz K., & Kielan B. (2015). Nowe formy przestępczości zorganizowanej na przykładzie wybranych form przestępczości gospodarczej [in:] E. Pływaczewski, W. Filipkowski, & Z. Rau, (eds.), *Przestępczość w XXI wieku zapobieganie i zwalczanie. Problemy prawno-kryminologiczne*. Warsaw: Wolters Kluwer, pp. 736–754.

Polanski Z. (2014). Poland During the Crisis: A 'Green Island' Approaching the Euro Area? [in:] Hölscher J. (ed.), *Poland and the Eurozone. Studies in Economic Transition*. London: Palgrave Macmillan, https://doi.org/10.1057/9781137426413_9.

Supreme Audit Office. (2013). Analiza wykonania budżetu państwa i założeń polityki pieniężnej w 2012 r., available at: https://www.nik.gov.pl/analiza-budzetu-panstwa/archiwum/, (accessed Oct. 31 2023).

Supreme Audit Office. (2018). Przeciwdziałanie wyłudzeniom podatku VAT, available at: https://www.nik.gov.pl/plik/id,17650,vp,20231.pdf, (Accessed Oct. 31 2023).

Tait A. (1988). *Value Added Tax, International Practice and Problems*. International Monetary Fund, https://doi.org/10.5089/9781557750129.071.

Thackray M., & Ahmed K. (2018). Republic of Poland: Technical Assistance Report-Revenue Administration Gap Analysis Program – The Value-Added Tax Gap, IMF, Country Report No. 2018/357, available at: https://www.imf.org/en/Publications/CR/Issues/2018/12/07/Republic-of-Poland-Technical-Assistance-Report-Revenue-Administration-Gap-Analysis-Program-46445 (Accessed Oct. 31 2023).

The Republic of Poland. (2013). Convergence Programme 2013 Update, available at: https://commission.europa.eu/publications/2013-european-semester-national-plans_en (Accessed Oct. 31 2023).

The Republic of Poland. (2014). Convergence Programme 2014 Update, available at: https://commission.europa.eu/publications/2014-european-semester-national-plans_en (Accessed Oct. 31 2023).

The Republic of Poland. (2017). Convergence Programme 2017 Update, available at: https://commission.europa.eu/content/2017-european-semester-national-reform-programmes-and-stabilityconvergence-programmes_en (Accessed Oct. 31 2023).

The Republic of Poland. (2021). Wieloletni plan finansowy państwa na lata 2021–2024, available at: https://www.gov.pl/web/finanse/wieloletni-plan-finansowy-panstwa (Accessed Oct. 31 2023).

The Republic of Poland. (2023). Wieloletni plan finansowy państwa na lata 2023–2026, available at: https://www.gov.pl/web/finanse/wieloletni-plan-finansowy-panstwa (Accessed Oct. 31 2023).

Vaughan D. (2016). *The Challenger Launch Decision: Risky Technology*. Culture, and Deviance at NASA, Univ. of Chicago Press.

Appendix 1. Raw data on VAT collected, VAT reclaims and VAT revenues (cash and accrual recording, PLN billion)

	VAT revenues [PL: dochody budżetu państwa z tytułu VAT] - cash recording [ujęcie kasowe]	**VAT revenues [PL: dochody budżetu państwa z tytułu VAT] - accrual recording [ujecie memoriałowe, ESA 2010]**	**VAT collected [PL: wpływy VAT]**	**VAT reclaims [PL: zwroty VAT]**
2007	96,3	97,8		
2008	101,8	101,9	158,7	56,9
2009	99,5	99,6	154,4	55,0
2010	107,9	109,7	165,4	57,5
2011	120,8	122,6	190,0	69,1
2012	120,0	116,3	195,3	75,3
2013	113,4	116,6	192,6	79,2
2014	124,3	122,7	210,5	86,3
2015	123,1	125,9	210,7	87,6
2016	126,6	134,6	220,2	93,5
2017	156,8	154,7	244,5	87,7
2018	174,9	172,3	271,6	96,7
2019	180,9	182,1	294,0	113,1
2020	184,6	186,0	297,7	113,1
2021	215,7	225,1	354,6	138,9
2022	230,4	223,4	407,4	177,0

Sources: VAT revenues, cash recording – Statistics Poland [PL: Główny Urząd Statystyczny, GUS] annual macroeconomic indicators, available at https://stat.gov.pl/wskazniki-makroekonomiczne/ (accessed Oct. 31 2023)., alternatively, the same data had been reported also in Supreme Audit Office (NIK) annual reports on budget implementation, available at: https://www.nik.gov.pl/analiza-budzetu-panstwa/archiwum/, (accessed Oct. 31 2023).

VAT revenues, accrual recording – EUROSTAT, Government revenue, expenditure and main aggregates, General government, VAT, receivable
VAT collected & VAT reclaims – for 2008 – 2020, Gajewski and Jonski (2022) and sources listed therein, for 2020 MoF response to the request for public information dated Oct. 4th 2023 (No BMI1.0123.2521.2023).
VAT collected includes the following categories of Polish budgetary classification: 75652 – Pozostałe wpłaty z podatku od towarów i usług rozliczane przez urzędy skarbowe; 75648 – Wpłaty z podatku od towarów i usług od importu towarów rozliczane przez urzędy celno-skarbowe (do III 2017 r. VAT pobierany przez urzędy celne); 75658 – Wpłaty podatku od towarów i usług w przypadku wewnątrzwspólnotowego nabycia paliw silnikowych (VAT-14) (od VIII 2016 r.); 75650 – Wpłaty ze zryczałtowanego podatku od towarów i usług rozliczane przez urzędy skarbowe od usług taksówek osobowych; 75651 – Wpłaty z podatku od towarów i usług rozliczane przez urzędy skarbowe jako dodatkowe zobowiązanie podatkowe z tytułu nieprawidłowości popełnianych przez podatnika przy rozliczaniu podatku (sankcje); 75654 – Rozliczenia w podatku od towarów i usług z tytułu kas

Appendix 1. Continued

rejestrujących; 75659 – Wpłaty z podatku od towarów i usług w przypadku procedury szczególnej – schemat unijny (od sierpnia 2021 r.); 75660 – Wpłaty z podatku od towarów i usług w przypadku procedury szczególnej – schemat nieunijny (od sierpnia 2021 r.); 75661 – Wpłaty z podatku od towarów i usług w przypadku procedury szczególnej – schemat importu (od września 2021 r.).
VAT reclaims includes the following categories of Polish budgetary classification:75653 – Zwroty podatku od towarów i usług rozliczane przez urzędy skarbowe (tzw. zwroty systemowe); 75655 – Zwroty osobom fizycznym niektórych wydatków związanych z budownictwem mieszkaniowym

Dominik J. Gajewski (SGH Warsaw School of Economics),
Kamil Joński (SGH Warsaw School of Economics)

Chapter 2 Intra-community transactions involving Poland in the mirror statistic data

Abstract: This chapter employs discrepancies in the reporter-partner international trade data in order to draw a picture of Polish VAT frauds involving intra-community deliveries. MTIC frauds likely to produce discrepancies in the mirror statistics had been described, and 2007–2022 Eurostat data on Polish trade with other EU Member States analysed in to spot particularly high discrepancies (in absolute terms).

Keywords: MTIC fraud, 'Acquisition fraud', 'Carousel fraud', 'Diversion fraud', 'mirror statistics'

2.1. Genaral comments

As outlined in the previous chapter, the proliferation of *Missing Trader Intra Community* fraud (*MTIC fraud*) constituted important part of the Polish VAT compliance crisis. This chapter attempts to shed some light on the growth and patterns of MTIC fraud in Poland over 2007–2022 period. To this end, it presents inspection of so called mirror statistics of the international trade between Poland and the other EU Member States.

The idea of comparing mirror statistics of the international trade dates back to the ninety-sixties[1], however back then it served to gauge the reliability of statistical data. It was based on the observation, that single transaction involving sell of some good from country A to B is recorded in international trade statistics twice – first, as an export to country B, declared by country A and second, as an import from country A, declared by country B.

One can intuitively expect that these two should match each other – as they represents the very same transaction. In fact, there are numerous reasons for discrepancies in the mirror statistics: application of different criteria of partner attribution; use of CIF[2] values in import statistics and FOB[3] values in export statistics; or application of different trade systems[4].

1 Morgenstern O. (1963). *On the Accuracy of Economic Observations* (2nd ed.). Princeton University Press, New Jersey.
2 Imports are reported on a cost, insurance and freight (CIF) basis.
3 exports are reported on a free on board (FOB) basis.
4 General versus Special Trade System. UNSD. (2019). *IMTS Bilateral Asymmetries – How to Measure, Analyze, Reduce and Way Forward*. United Nations Publications, New York.

As a result, it turns out that the world runs a current account surplus with itself[5]. Also the EU has a trade surplus with itself – and there are reasons to believe that this statistical artefact have something to do with the proliferation of VAT frauds[6].

Unfortunately, discrepancies in mirror statistics could not be causally attributed to VAT frauds, neither they could deliver sound estimate of their overall volume. However, they could serve as an useful red flag, pointing to extraordinary events in some markets.

Thus, this chapter presents an attempt to draw a picture of Polish VAT frauds involving intra-community deliveries, building upon discrepancies in mirror statistics of Polish trade with other EU Member States. Its goal is purely descriptive, and empirical approach suited to provide the overall view – in order to suggest the directions for more rigorous inquiry into specific sectors.

2.2. VAT frauds and discrepancies in mirror-statistics

The departure point for the discussion of mirror statistics discrepancies will be the brief review of selected VAT fraud mechanisms, involving intra-community delivery – in particular those involving so called 'missing trader' (*MTIC fraud*). As observed by His Majesty's Revenues and Customs, '*fraud which affects asymmetries includes acquisition fraud, carousel fraud, diversion fraud and trade-based money laundering*'[7]. For clarity reasons, the very basic designs of each fraud will be presented, with particular emphasize on their impact on Intrastat reported export to (Intra-Community Supplies) and imports from (Intra-Community Acquisitions) the Member States involved. In practice, transaction chains assembled by the fraudsters tend to be much more complicated, nevertheless they are based on the same basic concepts.

---

5 Gros D. (2017). Is Germany's current account surplus bad for the world economy?, CEPS commentary, available at: https://www.ceps.eu/ceps-publications/germanys-current-account-surplus-bad-world-economy/ (Accessed Oct. 31, 2023), p. 1.

6 Braml M., & Felbermayr G. (2022). The EU Self-Surplus Puzzle: An Indication of VAT Fraud?. Int Tax Public Finance 29, 1075–1097, https://doi.org/10.1007/s10797-021-09713-x

7 See: UK trade in goods statistics: Reasons for trade in goods asymmetries. (2023). available at: https://www.gov.uk/government/publications/uk-trade-in-goods-statistics-reasons-for-trade-in-goods-asymmetries (Accessed Oct. 31, 2023).

2.2.1. Missing Trader Intra-Community Acquisition Fraud (ICA)

In its most basic form, the acquisition fraud requires three parties (of which at least one controlled by the fraudsters), located in two Member States.

The transaction chain begins with the supplier, located in the Member State A. Depending on the specific circumstances, the supplier could be – for example, a genuine industrial producer, offering real-world goods – or entity involved with trading activities. The supplier could be independent actor, but one cannot rule out situations where she is controlled by the fraudsters. Typically, she is an honest taxpayer in her country of residence. For the sake of our analysis we assume that as such, she will also fulfill its reporting obligations as far as international trade statistics are concerned (as long as it passes the reporting thresholds).

The second link in the chain is the first buyer, located in the Member State B. In case of acquisition fraud, the first buyer turns out to be a 'Missing Trader', controlled by the fraudsters.

Finally, the third link of the transaction chain is the final buyer, also located at the Member State B. Depending on the specific set-up, the final buyer could be (i) an honest enterprise, genuinely unaware that she became chain in fraudulent transaction, (ii) an enterprise suspecting that the price offered by the first buyer is suspiciously competitive, nevertheless willing to turn blind eye on that, instead of due diligence, or (iii) be coerced to participate in the transaction.[8]

Assuming no fraudulent activities, the transaction chain would look like follows:

The supplier sells goods to the first buyer, located in Member State B. He transfers goods and issues an invoice with net price, say 100 and 0 VAT (Intra-Community Supply). The first buyer has to declare an Intra-Community Acquisition – with net price 100 and, say, 20% VAT due in Member State B (i.e. the gross cost of goods was 120). Later on, the first buyer sells the goods to the domestic company – the final buyer. To remain competitive against the foreign supplier, she decides to charge lower net price, say 95, with 20% VAT. Thereby, the final buyer pays the first buyer the gross price 114, including VAT of 19 (note, the input VAT of 20 is deductible). Then, the first buyer is due to remit VAT of 20 to the domestic tax authorities in B.

---

8 In this case it would be victim of some sort of extortion scheme. Just like in 'good old days' organized crime groups blackmailed entrepreneurs to pay for 'protection', nowadays they could blackmail them to get supplies from particular companies. On the one hand, the enterprise pays to criminals (via extorted VAT), on the other, it nevertheless obtain desired good at competitive price.

Thereby, if the transaction would be carried out *lege artis*, the first buyer would record loss on this sell.

That would change with acquisition fraud involved. The only difference is that the first buyer turns out to be a 'Missing Trader' – thereby he carries out both Intra-Community Acquisition and the domestic sell to the final buyer as described above – however instead of remitting the VAT to domestic tax authority, it disappears. Thereby, the first buyer – a '*Missing Trader*' – generated a profit equaling the charged VAT that is not paid minus the loss on the sale (the example had been adapted from: European Commission[9]).

From the economic point of view, the loss of VAT in Member State B had been somehow split between the fraudsters (the profit of the missing trader) and the final buyer, who managed to buy goods cheaper than an honest supplier could allow (as it was non-paid VAT that financed the price rabat of 100-95=5).

Crucially for our analysis, the acquisition fraud is likely to generate discrepancies in the mirror statistics. The supplier is likely to report Intra-Community Supply in the Intrastat. However, the first buyer (i.e. the '*Missing Trader*') is unlikely to report her Intra-Community Acquisition. As a consequence, one can reasonably assume that the transaction would appear as export to Member State B, as declared by A. However it fail to appear as import form Member State A, as declared by B. Obviously, the silent assumption had been made that both the supplier and the first buyer passes the reporting thresholds, in other words they are expected to report their respective supplies and acquisitions.

2.2.2. Diversion fraud

In its most basic form, the diversion fraud (also referred to as a domestic sales designed as intra-Community supplies, see: European Commission[10]) requires three entities (of which at least two are controlled by the fraudsters), located in two Member States. First of them is a seller, located in the Member State A, carrying out the VAT fraud.

The second entity involved in the fraud is the fictitious buyer, located in the Member State B, and also controlled by the fraudsters. Alternatively, her VAT identification number '*could have been hijacked so that he is not even aware of*

9 European Commission, Directorate-General for Taxation and Customs Union. (2018b). The concept of tax gaps – Report III – MTIC fraud gap estimation methodologies, Publications Office, https://data.europa.eu/doi/10.2778/418684, p. 10.

10 European Commission, 18b, p. 14.

the fraud' (European Commission[11]). Finally, the third entity is the real buyer, located at the Member State A.

Contrary to the Acquisition fraud, in case of diversion fraud the 'flow' of goods and the 'flow' of invoices diverges. In other words, transactions documented on paper differs from – and are generated to conceal – those occurring in the real life.

On the paper, the seller located in the Member State A performs Intra-Community Supply to the fictitious buyer applying the zero VAT rate. As he is allowed to deduct the input VAT from earlier stages, he is now entitled to receive a refund of VAT from the tax authority in Member State A.

At the same time, as the fictitious buyer carried out an Intra-Community Acquisition, she ought to pay deductible VAT according to the rate in Member State B (which she has not, acting like a 'Missing Trader').

In the reality, the fictitious buyer (or her VAT identification number) is not part of the transaction whatsoever (or, alternatively, receives just a tiny fraction of the goods actually sold, to maintain appearances). Instead, the goods are sold on the domestic market, to the real buyer. As simulated Intra-Community Supply allowed the seller to avoid paying VAT, he is able to offer lower prices than his honest competitors. Depending on the specific set-up, the domestic supply could occur within the shadow economy (i.e. without invoicing), or pretend to be legitimate, VAT taxed transaction.

Again, from the economic point of view, the loss of VAT in Member State A had been somehow split between the seller and the real buyer.

Crucially for our analysis, the diversion fraud could possibly generate discrepancies in the mirror statistics. The seller is likely to report his simulated Intra-Community Supply in the Intrastat. However, there is no guarantee that the fictitious buyer would report her Intra-Community Acquisition (if she is a 'Missing Trader' or even a hijacked VAT identification number). As a consequence, one can expect that the transaction would appear as export to Member State B, declared by Member State A. However it fail to appear as import form Member State A, as declared by B. Obviously, the silent assumption had been made that both the supplier and the first buyer passes the reporting thresholds, in other words they are expected to report their respective supplies and acquisitions.

11 European Commission, 18b, p. 14.

2.2.3. Carousel fraud

In the acquisition fraud and diversion fraud described above, fraudulent companies were parts of the transaction chains providing supply of goods either to the official or shadow economy. The carousel fraud described in this section lack this property. In this case, the entire transaction chain – organized in circular form – aims at extorting VAT. Carousel fraud could be based either on the real flow of goods, or just flow of invoices (simulating flow of goods). In the former case, the goods applied tend to exhibit high value-to-volume ratio (to minimize costs of transportation) and be difficult to individual identification (to make it harder to prove that there are the very same goods, running around over and over again[12]).

In its simplest form, involving just three entities (European Commission[13]), carousel fraud begins like an acquisition fraud – with Intra-Community Supply from seller located in Member State A to the 'Missing Trader' located in the Member State B. Just like in the example in Section 2.1.1., the Intra-Community Supply have net price 100 with zero VAT applicable. The Intra-Community Acquisition, made by the 'Missing Trader' with net price 100 is taxed with, say, 20% deductible VAT (obviously the 'Missing Trader' have no intention to ever pay it).

The extension – as compared to acquisition fraud – is that instead of supplying the goods on the market to presumably honest final buyer, the 'Missing Trader' sells them to the 'broker company', also controlled by the fraudsters. Thereby, there is no need to compete with price – 'Missing Trader' could sell the goods to the 'broker' at net price of 100, with 20% of VAT applicable in domestic supply in Member State B.

The role of a 'broker' is to close the circular transaction chain – just like in simulated transaction of diversion fraud – he carries out VAT exempt Intra-Community Supply, back to the initial supplier in Member State A. Since 'broker' paid input VAT of 20 to the 'Missing Trader' he is allowed to receive a refund of VAT from the tax authority in Member State B.

In other words, the goods came the full circle – sold from entity to entity at price 100 – and the profit of fraudsters (i.e. non remitted VAT of 20) had been paid from the Member State B treasury, via VAT reclaim.

---

12 Although it is not an absolute rule, as there are well-known examples of carousel frauds involving mobile phones, individually identifiable by IMEI number.

13 European Commission, 2018, pp. 11–12.

As the goods came back to the seller in Member State A (called the 'conduit company'), the cycle could be repeated, creating economic *perpetuum mobile* – at least to the until the 'Missing Trader' would have to disappear.

From the economic point of view, the loss of VAT in Member State B (VAT refunded to the 'broker' and not remitted by the '*Missing Trader*') equals the gain of the fraudsters.

Crucially for our analysis, the carousel fraud is likely to generate discrepancies in the mirror statistics. As assumed in CASE[14] the 'conduit company' selling goods to B report it in Intrastat system, while 'Missing Trader' in B is unlikely to do this. As a consequence, '*The observed substantial and persistent differences between registered import in a MS of import and export to the MS of import, reported by EU MS of export, may indicate existence of VAT carousels*' (as reported in: European Commission[15]). The only way for carousel fraud not to affect mirror statistics discrepancies is when either all participants – or none of them – would report their respective sales and purchases in Intrastat, which is assumed quite unlikely situation given different roles played by 'Missing Traders', 'brokers' and the 'conduit companies' (CASE, 2015, appendix 3).

2.3. The '*grid search*': Discrepancies in mirror statistics of Poland-EU trade, 2007–2022

Unfortunately, discrepancies in mirror statistics could not be causally attributed to VAT frauds, neither they could deliver sound estimate of their overall volume. However, in the literature on VAT fraud, they had been employed in two roles.

First, they served as an alarm bell, pointing to extraordinary developments in specific market. The example of such usage is offered by a series of reports, commissioned by steel business associations and prepared by Ernst & Young

14 CASE. (2015). Ocena czy poprzez wprowadzenie od dnia 1 października 2013 r. odwróconego obciążenia VAT na niektóre wyroby stalowe ograniczono nadużycia w rozliczaniu odatku VAT w obrocie tymi towarami oraz czy warunki funkcjonowania przedsiębiorstw w branży objętej zmianami uległy poprawie, report in Polish, commissioned by the Ministry of Finance, available as a appendix to the OSR Ex-post (evaluation) of the act of July 26th 2013 available at: https://legislacja.rcl.gov.pl/projekt/12282103 (Accessed Oct. 31, 2023), p. 37.

15 European Commission, 18b, pp. 20–21.

consultancy[16] or by (Olczykowski, Kassel[17]). Also, they could provide useful insights to customs administrations[18].

Second, the changes in the mirror statistics discrepancies had been employed in order to estimate the size of MTIC frauds. Specifically, the econometric methodology had been used to link introduction of the *reverse charge* in the specific markets, with changes in the respective mirror statistics[19].

This chapter attempts to use mirror statistics in slightly different way, in an attempt to draw a birds' eye picture of Polish VAT frauds involving intra-community deliveries over 2007–2022 period.

To this end, EUROSTAT data on the *EU trade since 1988 by HS2-4-6 and CN8 – former content – (ds-045409)* had been employed, to examine discrepancies in reporting of import and export to and from Poland and the remaining 27 EU Member States (including UK before 2020).

As a result, two tables had been constructed: the first one (Table 2.1) present discrepancies in declared inflow of goods from other Member States to Poland[20]. The second one (Table 2.2) present discrepancies in declared outflow of goods from Poland to these Member States.[21]

Typically, in the literature, discrepancies in the mirror statistics are provided in the relative terms. However, given the goal of the described empirical exercise, the absolute figures seems to be more telling.

---

16 Ernst & Young. (2012). Opodatkowanie VAT obrotu niektórymi wyrobami stalowymi. Analiza możliwych kierunków zmian legislacyjnych w świetle narastających wyłudzeń podatku VAT w Polsce, Warszawa, 31 sierpnia 2012 r.; 59 Ernst & Young. (2013). Opodatkowanie VAT obrotu niektórymi wyrobami stalowymi. Wnioski w zakresie skali szarej strefy w Polsce, Warszawa, 16 stycznia 2013 r.; Ernst & Young. (2014). Analiza wpływu zmian administracyjnych na wielkość szarej strefy na rynku prętów zbrojeniowych i sytuację sektora finansów publicznych, Warszawa, marzec 2014 r.

17 Olczykowski K., & Kassel T. (2017). The battle may be won, but the war goes on: The latest dispatches from the front, mBank – CASE Seminar Proceedings No. 147/2017.

18 Grigoriou Ch., Kalizinje F., & Raballand G. (2019). How Helpful Are Mirror Statistics for Customs Reform? Lessons from a Decade of Operational Use. World Customs Journal, 13(2), pp. 105–113.

19 See: CASE (2015); Bussy A. (2020). Cross-border Value Added Tax Fraud in the European Union, available at SSRN: http://dx.doi.org/10.2139/ssrn.3569914.

20 I.e. the differences between import from each of those countries – as declared by Poland – and export to Poland, as declared by these countries.

21 I.e. the differences between export to each of those countries – as declared by Poland – and import from Poland, as declared by these countries.

Table 2.1. Discrepancies in the mirror statistics of goods inflow to Poland: the difference between import from each Member State – as declared by Poland – and export to Poland, as declared by these Member States (EUR billion, negative values imply that Poland reports lower import from given country, then this country's declared export to Poland)

	2007	2008	2009	2010	2011	2012	2013	2014	2015	2016	2017	2018	2019	2020	2021	2022
Austria	- 0,58	- 0,26	- 0,29	- 0,26	- 0,24	- 0,32	- 0,33	- 0,25	- 0,38	- 0,37	- 0,41	- 0,50	- 0,75	- 0,50	- 0,67	- 0,81
Belgium	- 0,59	- 0,68	- 0,51	- 0,46	- 0,80	- 0,53	- 0,70	- 0,68	- 0,83	- 0,56	- 0,60	0,09	- 0,08	- 0,28	- 0,97	- 0,44
Bulgaria	- 0,04	- 0,04	- 0,03	- 0,03	- 0,05	- 0,07	- 0,06	- 0,07	- 0,06	- 0,07	- 0,07	- 0,03	- 0,05	- 0,00	- 0,07	0,39
Cyprus	0,06	0,11	0,04	0,07	0,19	0,20	0,25	0,35	0,25	0,10	0,11	0,12	0,07	0,14	0,09	0,36
Czechia	**- 0,63**	**- 0,67**	**- 0,34**	**- 0,57**	**- 1,18**	**- 1,04**	**- 0,87**	**- 1,05**	**- 1,42**	**- 1,14**	**- 1,30**	**- 1,27**	**- 1,36**	**- 1,70**	**- 2,15**	**- 2,72**
Germany	**- 1,08**	**- 0,19**	**- 1,00**	**0,07**	**- 1,55**	**- 1,30**	**- 1,37**	**- 2,25**	**- 3,14**	**- 3,82**	**- 1,06**	**- 0,54**	**- 1,93**	**- 1,97**	**- 2,01**	**1,59**
Denmark	0,08	0,06	0,01	0,03	- 0,02	- 0,05	- 0,02	0,03	- 0,08	- 0,14	- 0,03	0,03	- 0,23	- 0,41	- 0,44	- 0,41
Estonia	0,00	- 0,00	- 0,01	0,00	- 0,01	- 0,03	- 0,05	- 0,03	- 0,07	- 0,03	- 0,01	- 0,01	- 0,03	0,02	- 0,03	- 0,12
Spain	0,01	0,21	- 0,17	- 0,23	- 0,56	- 0,28	- 0,56	- 0,67	- 0,90	- 0,83	- 0,76	- 0,64	- 0,90	- 0,60	- 0,81	- 0,94
Finland	- 0,03	- 0,05	- 0,11	- 0,13	- 0,17	- 0,11	- 0,15	0,05	0,04	- 0,01	- 0,03	- 0,04	- 0,05	- 0,06	- 0,12	- 0,18
France	- 0,18	- 0,01	- 0,25	- 0,09	- 0,36	- 0,52	- 0,46	- 0,43	- 0,55	- 0,64	- 0,68	- 1,01	- 0,78	- 0,64	- 1,01	- 1,50
UK	0,21	0,28	0,32	- 0,28	- 0,66	- 0,20	0,10	- 0,18	0,17	0,02	0,01	- 0,03	- 0,12			
Greece	- 0,02	- 0,02	- 0,01	- 0,04	0,10	0,04	- 0,02	- 0,01	0,09	0,03	- 0,06	- 0,09	- 0,09	- 0,11	- 0,22	- 0,21
Croatia	- 0,01	0,01	0,02	- 0,02	- 0,02	- 0,03	- 0,02	- 0,04	- 0,01	0,02	- 0,02	- 0,04	- 0,05	- 0,05	- 0,06	- 0,05
Hungary	- 0,29	- 0,30	- 0,22	- 0,27	- 0,22	- 0,30	- 0,34	- 0,39	- 0,53	- 0,50	- 0,42	- 0,23	- 0,23	- 0,30	- 0,23	- 0,45
Ireland	- 0,09	0,13	0,11	0,19	0,12	0,16	0,12	0,13	0,11	- 0,08	0,17	0,25	0,24	0,40	0,19	0,29
Italy	**- 1,00**	**- 0,84**	**- 0,84**	**- 1,09**	**- 1,45**	**- 1,30**	**- 1,28**	**- 1,12**	**- 1,54**	**- 1,34**	**- 1,50**	**- 1,88**	**- 1,59**	**- 1,44**	**- 1,74**	**- 2,41**
Lithuania	- 0,05	- 0,11	- 0,23	- 0,36	- 0,31	- 0,45	- 0,69	- 0,80	- 1,10	- 0,72	- 0,42	- 0,32	- 0,28	- 0,20	- 0,42	0,16
Luxembourg	- 0,03	- 0,02	- 0,01	0,04	0,21	0,26	0,19	0,16	0,13	0,09	0,19	0,10	0,02	0,02	0,06	0,01
Latvia	- 0,01	- 0,03	- 0,03	- 0,11	- 0,22	- 0,31	*- 0,43*	- 0,25	- 0,23	- 0,11	- 0,05	0,18	- 0,01	- 0,03	- 0,05	- 0,09
Malta	0,00	0,01	- 0,00	0,00	0,01	0,00	- 0,00	0,03	0,02	0,02	0,04	0,05	0,04	0,03	0,07	0,08
Netherlands	**- 0,27**	**- 0,23**	**- 0,52**	**- 0,59**	**- 0,90**	**- 0,86**	**- 1,30**	**- 1,23**	**- 1,41**	**- 1,55**	**- 1,75**	**- 2,56**	**- 2,34**	**- 2,66**	**- 2,76**	**- 3,02**
Portugal	0,01	- 0,04	- 0,02	- 0,04	- 0,10	- 0,08	- 0,09	- 0,05	- 0,06	- 0,08	- 0,04	- 0,03	- 0,01	- 0,07	- 0,03	- 0,02
Romania	- 0,15	- 0,16	- 0,15	- 0,12	- 0,19	- 0,24	- 0,19	- 0,16	- 0,20	- 0,21	- 0,23	- 0,25	- 0,40	- 0,28	- 0,32	- 0,40
Sweden	0,20	0,14	- 0,04	- 0,04	0,02	0,13	0,39	0,41	0,49	0,37	0,76	0,52	0,43	0,14	- 0,06	- 0,06
Slovenia	- 0,08	- 0,09	- 0,08	- 0,16	- 0,21	- 0,14	- 0,20	- 0,19	- 0,25	- 0,27	- 0,23	- 0,30	- 0,27	- 0,23	- 0,20	- 0,24
Slovakia	- 0,29	- 0,22	- 0,21	- 0,25	- 0,42	- 0,84	- 0,92	- 1,04	- 1,19	- 0,46	- 0,79	- 0,82	- 0,52	- 0,50	- 0,49	- 0,49

*Sources:*Own calculation based on EUROSTAT data on the EU trade since 1988 by HS2-4-6 and CN8 – former content – (ds-045409).

Table 2.2. Discrepancies in the mirror statistics of goods outflow from Poland: the difference between export to each Member State – as declared by Poland – and import from Poland, as declared by these Member States (EUR billion, positive values imply that Poland reports higher export to a given country, then this country's declared import from Poland)

	2007	2008	2009	2010	2011	2012	2013	2014	2015	2016	2017	2018	2019	2020	2021	2022
Austria	0,34	0,39	0,42	0,60	0,40	0,40	0,41	0,43	0,37	0,18	0,61	0,66	0,56	0,08	0,36	0,22
Belgium	0,14	0,14	- 0,11	0,02	- 0,02	0,01	0,05	0,04	0,16	0,12	0,26	0,44	0,30	0,05	0,41	0,36
Bulgaria	- 0,03	- 0,03	- 0,03	0,01	- 0,02	- 0,03	0,02	0,02	0,07	- 0,02	0,07	0,01	- 0,03	0,01	0,07	0,06
Cyprus	0,05	0,06	0,14	0,06	0,19	0,18	0,18	0,27	0,32	0,13	0,10	0,13	0,12	0,17	0,11	0,14
Czechia	0,28	0,39	0,50	0,60	0,69	0,63	0,61	0,77	0,43	- 0,35	0,17	- 0,05	0,18	0,83	0,47	1,88
Germany	**2,23**	**2,09**	**1,99**	**1,96**	**1,44**	**1,29**	**0,84**	**1,85**	**1,18**	**0,86**	**2,05**	**3,11**	**2,49**	**3,23**	**4,13**	**4,09**
Denmark	0,21	0,20	0,22	0,38	0,38	0,17	0,13	0,22	0,41	0,23	0,49	0,43	0,18	0,06	0,11	0,22
Estonia	0,07	0,11	0,01	- 0,02	- 0,09	0,01	- 0,25	0,06	0,06	0,04	0,09	0,11	0,12	0,21	0,17	0,13
Spain	0,14	0,09	0,07	0,01	- 0,04	0,04	- 0,16	- 0,31	- 0,24	- 0,54	- 0,36	- 0,78	- 0,66	0,16	0,23	0,13
Finland	0,04	0,05	- 0,05	- 0,04	- 0,13	- 0,06	- 0,07	- 0,03	0,02	- 0,02	- 0,04	0,02	0,10	0,06	0,05	- 0,02
France	0,38	0,29	0,52	0,56	0,23	0,43	0,59	0,89	0,86	0,51	1,09	1,13	1,47	1,14	1,77	2,90
UK	0,72	1,34	1,09	0,48	0,59	0,67	0,83	1,03	0,92	1,00	1,31	1,70	1,42			
Greece	0,02	0,09	0,08	0,15	0,22	0,15	0,11	0,15	0,22	0,18	0,09	0,06	0,12	0,12	0,11	0,08
Croatia	- 0,02	- 0,05	- 0,02	- 0,04	- 0,02	- 0,03	- 0,04	- 0,03	0,03	0,00	- 0,05	- 0,03	- 0,02	- 0,00	0,02	0,00
Hungary	0,23	0,31	0,38	- 0,07	0,09	0,06	0,30	0,28	0,25	0,25	0,29	0,20	0,51	0,30	0,44	0,09
Ireland	0,14	0,12	- 0,00	0,18	0,14	0,15	0,16	0,15	0,18	0,21	0,31	0,44	0,24	0,16	0,54	0,29
Italy	0,34	0,22	0,05	- 0,08	- 0,28	- 0,13	0,03	0,30	0,10	- 0,02	0,27	0,50	0,13	0,77	0,84	1,53
Lithuania	- 0,22	- 0,24	- 0,12	- 0,17	- 0,16	- 0,15	- 0,15	- 0,12	- 0,10	- 0,12	- 0,08	- 0,21	- 0,13	- 0,21	0,27	- 0,08
Luxembourg	0,02	0,02	- 0,00	0,02	0,03	0,01	0,02	0,02	0,05	0,05	0,09	0,14	0,09	0,06	0,10	0,15
Latvia	0,02	0,04	- 0,01	0,01	- 0,06	- 0,11	0,05	0,19	0,07	- 0,01	0,05	- 0,01	- 0,07	- 0,08	- 0,07	- 0,12
Malta	0,00	0,01	- 0,00	0,00	0,03	0,01	0,03	0,04	0,01	0,02	0,02	0,04	0,02	0,04	0,06	0,03
Netherlands	0,33	0,63	0,32	0,37	0,56	0,78	0,42	0,64	0,11	0,19	0,37	0,47	0,37	0,27	0,33	- 0,08
Portugal	0,05	0,03	0,06	0,08	0,07	0,05	0,06	0,07	0,09	0,01	0,04	0,08	0,11	0,14	0,20	0,11
Romania	- 0,15	- 0,14	- 0,07	- 0,10	- 0,09	- 0,16	- 0,16	- 0,12	- 0,08	- 0,18	- 0,26	- 0,06	0,04	0,06	- 0,16	- 0,29
Sweden	0,08	- 0,06	0,00	0,29	0,28	0,24	0,29	0,76	0,62	0,66	0,55	0,44	0,69	0,82	0,55	0,84
Slovenia	- 0,01	0,04	0,01	0,01	- 0,01	- 0,01	- 0,02	0,03	0,00	- 0,02	0,00	0,03	- 0,01	0,02	0,07	0,03
Slovakia	0,04	0,36	0,20	0,43	0,10	0,18	0,19	0,28	0,25	- 0,01	0,27	0,30	0,16	0,30	0,29	0,53

Sources: Own calculation based on EUROSTAT data on the EU trade since 1988 by HS2-4-6 and CN8 – former content – (ds-045409).

For example, Poland's declared import from Latvia in 2013 represented only 41 % of Latvia's declared export to Poland – the highest relative difference of this sort[22] observed in the examined period. The fact that nearly 60% of Latvian export failed to be reported to Intrastat by Polish buyers indicated a substantial anomaly – indeed, involving fraudulent activity (see Section 2.4.).

However, in absolute terms, discrepancies in trade between Poland, Latvia and Cyprus are hardly noticeable, when compared with persistent discrepancies in trade with Czechia, Germany, Italy or Netherlands. Thus, it seems reasonable to assume that these are the countries that could be the most important pieces in the Polish MTIC fraud puzzle.

2.4. Anecdotal example: *Liepajas Metalurgs*, construction rods and the mirror statistics

The example of Latvia, mentioned in the previous section due to its extraordinarily high discrepancy (as expressed in relative terms), offers opportunity to illustrate the value of mirror statistics in spotting problematic developments on the markets – as well as to demonstrate the idea behind empirical exercise reported in this chapter.

The story goes back to 2012, as Polish enterprises involved in steel production observed, that despite construction boom (linked to the EU funded infrastructural project and UEFA Euro 2012 co-hosted by Poland and Ukraine) the demand for – and prices of – construction rods declined[23]. The reason was that some companies had been able to offer construction rods with few percent discount, winning public procurements based exclusively on the lowest price criterion.[24] As steel business associations commissioned Ernst & Young consultancy to examine the situation on the market, mirror statistics had been used. It turned out that construction rods export from Latvia to Poland vastly outnumbered

22 On the other extreme, the import from Cyprus – as declared by Poland – was 63,5 times larger than export to Poland as declared by Cyprus.

23 See testimonies of I. Dybał and R. Talarek before VAT investigative committee.

24 See testimony of I. Dybał and R before VAT investigative committee. Polish quotation: ' Oczywiście brało się to m.in. stąd, że jeżeli są przetargi, których jest warunek 100 % cena, to firmy budowlane szukały przede wszystkim towaru bardzo taniego. Nie byliśmy w stanie z tym towarem konkurować…*ja się spotykałam z takimi pytaniami: to jak był taki tani towar, to można się było zorientować. On czasem nie był wcale aż tak tani. Te firmy jeszcze zarabiały, nie oddawały całego tego VAT-u, tak że czasem ta różnica była 2–3 %, co w naszej branży już jest bardzo dużo*'.

their declared import from Latvia to Poland. Further analysis revealed that extraordinarily competitive construction rods are provided by fraudsters using acquisition fraud (see Section 2.2.1) schemes.[25]

As *reverse charge* mechanism had been introduced in the construction rods market in 2013, the discrepancy between mirror statistics of rods export/import shrunk immediately. Moreover, Liepajas Metalurgs – Latvian steel producer, widely believed to be the key supplier for construction rods acquisition frauds, bankrupted shortly afterwards.[26]

When EUROSTAT data presented in the Table 2.1. are broken down to still quite broad – albeit much more informative – level of 96 chapters of Combined Nomenclature (SN – for the list see appendix. 1), it turns out that the noticeable part of 2010–2011 overall discrepancy is related to the 'Iron and steel' market (see Figure 2.1). However, in subsequent years, there were 'mineral fuels' market where discrepancy emerged (on developments in Polish liquid fuels market see Figure 1.4. in Chapter 1, Section 1.4. and UN Global Compact[27]).

---

25 Ernst & Young. (2014). Analiza wpływu zmian administracyjnych na wielkość szarej strefy na rynku prętów zbrojeniowych i sytuację sektora finansów publicznych, Warszawa, marzec 2014 r, see press release at: https://web.archive.org/web/20140804082711/http://www.ey.media.pl/pr/281379/analiza-ey-ponad-300-mln-rocznie-tyle-zyska-skarb-panstwa-dzieki-likwidacji-szarej-strefy-w-handlu-pretami-zbrojeniowymi (Accessed Oct. 31, 2023), p. 7; UN Global Compact. (2016). Przeciwdziałanie szarej strefie w Polsce 2015/2016, UN Global Compact, available at: https://mf-arch2.mf.gov.pl/documents/764034/5123644/20160407_GCNP_raport_szara_strefa.pdf (Accessed Oct. 31, 2023), pp. 74–76. Testimonies before VAT investigative committee revealed, that initially it was thought that construction rods are supplied by fraudsters engaged in the acquisition fraud, however later on it turns out that also diversion fraud had been carried out. See Polish quotation from the testimonies of I. Dybał: '*Pamiętam, że w pewnym momencie najpierw byliśmy przekonani, że dotyczy to tylko dostaw unijnych. Nie zdawaliśmy sobie sprawy, że również wywozu z naszego kraju*' and P. Niemczyk '*myśmy, pamiętam, w tym okresie też prowadzili kilka obserwacji hurtowni prętów zbrojeniowych w taki sposób, że jeżeli hurtowania z różnych tam swoich rynkowych zachowań deklarowała, że np. te pręty są eksportowane np. do Czech, to myśmy obserwowali, czy ciężarówki wożące pręty zbrojeniowe z tej hurtowni, rzeczywiście jadą do Czech. … to były metody detektywistyczne … pamiętam taką hurtownię, która, deklarując, że wywozi te do Czech, to w okresie czasu, w którym miała dokonać dużej transakcji, pamiętam, że jedna ciężarówka pojechała rzeczywiście w stronę Czech, to było na Dolnym Śląsku, a pozostałych tam kilkanaście w stronę Poznania*'.

26 See: https://xml.metalbulletin.com/Article/3375460/industry-all/Bankrupt-Liepajas-Metalurgs-continues-talks-with-two-bidders.html (Accessed Oct. 31, 2023)

27 UN Global Compact, 2016, pp. 77–86.

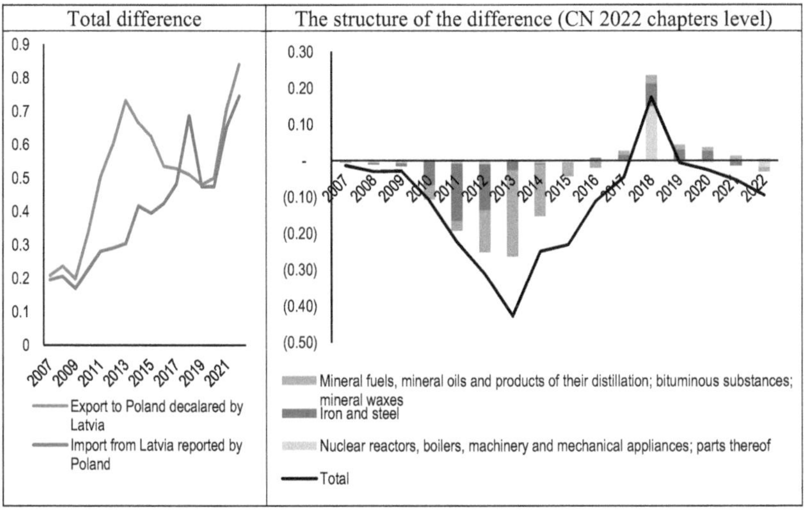

Figure 2.1. Discrepancies between mirror statistics of Latvian export to Poland and Polish import from Latvia, 2007–2022 (EUR billion)

On the right panel, categories of goods accounting for the biggest part of the overall discrepancy in mirror statistics had been selected for presentation (color bars). The other categories of goods – out of 96 CN 2022 chapters analyzed – accounts for the remaining part of the total discrepancy (black line).

Source: Own calculation based on EUROSTAT data on the EU trade since 1988 by HS2-4-6 and CN8 – former content – (ds-045409).

This example proves that mirror statistics of trade with EU partners can be productively used in order to trace markets vulnerable to the MTIC fraud, and gauge their dynamic (growth or contraction). Nevertheless, one have to keep in mind several caveats. First, as already explained, there are numerous reasons for mirror statistics discrepancies that have nothing to do with VAT fraud[28]. Of them, differences in the reporting thresholds could prove particularly important. However, (i) growth in mirror statistics discrepancy, (ii) in the market known for its 'sensitivity', and (iii) at the time consistent with other signals of fraudulent activity should serve as an important red flag for policymakers.

28 UNSD. (2019). *IMTS Bilateral Asymmetries – How to Measure, Analyze, Reduce and Way Forward*. New York, United Nations Publications.

2.5. Exploring the biggest (absolute) discrepancies in the mirror trade statistics

Drawing on the approach presented in the previous chapter, five EU Member States with the highest persistent discrepancies in the mirror statistics with Poland (as identified in the Tables 2.1. and 2.2.) had been examined in greater detail, using disaggregation to the level of 96 chapters of Combined Nomenclature (SN – for the list see Appendix. 1).

2.5.1. Inflows of goods from Czechia underreported in Poland

Contrary to the example of Latvia, the discrepancy between export to Poland declared by Czechia – and import from Czechia declared by Poland – depicted on Figure 2.2 turns out (i) much smaller, (ii) quite persistent, lacking sudden peaks, and (iii) before 2020 distributed among many SN chapters analyzed, not concentrated in just few key categories of goods.

On the one hand, one can reasonably argue that closer trade relationships – including SME – could produce such discrepancies in the mirror statistics due to the Intrastat reporting thresholds. On the other hand, the discrepancy suddenly emerging in 2011 (and disappearing in 2014) in '*Iron and steel*' category could indicate similar fraudulent activity as the one described in Section 2.4.

Noteworthy the rise of discrepancy in '*Electrical machinery and equipment and parts thereof; sound recorders and reproducers, television image and sound recorders and reproducers, and parts and accessories of such articles*' observed after 2019 justifies hypothesis, that it could reflect some sort of MTIC activity. While in 2022 trade in this category represented 21% of exports to Poland as declared by Czechia – and just 15% of imports from Czechia as declared by Poland – it accounted for nearly half of the overall discrepancy between the mirror statistics of the two countries.

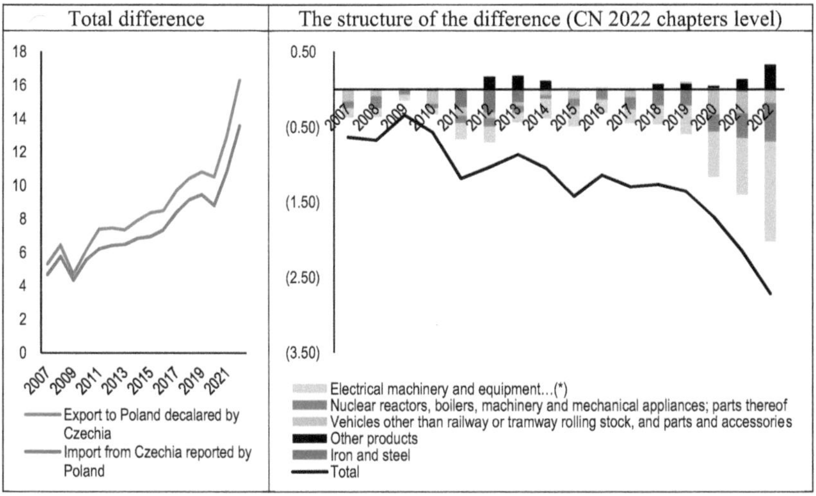

Figure 2.2. Discrepancies between mirror statistics of Czech export to Poland and Polish import from Czehia, 2007–2022 (EUR billion)

*-for full name of the category see Appendix 1.

On the right panel, categories of goods accounting for the biggest part of the overall discrepancy in mirror statistics had been selected for presentation (color bars). The other categories of goods – out of 96 CN 2022 chapters analyzed – accounts for the remaining part of the total discrepancy (black line).

Source: Own calculation based on EUROSTAT data on the EU trade since 1988 by HS2-4-6 and CN8 – former content – (ds-045409).

2.5.2. Inflows of goods from Germany underreported in Poland

As compared with Latvia and Czechia, the discrepancies between export to Poland declared by Germany – and import from Germany declared by Poland – seems very small in relative terms. However, the sheer volume of the trade between the two countries makes these discrepancies the largest ones in absolute terms. Also, the size of the overall discrepancy varied in time, peaking in 2016.

The more detailed analysis uncover, that in some categories of goods the export reported by Germany exceeds the import declared by Poland (for example: mineral fuels, inorganic chemicals, reactors, boilers, machinery) while in another it goes the other way around (for example Articles of apparel and clothing accessories – knitted and not knitted).

The discrepancy in mineral fuels over 2013–2016 looks particularly interesting given the developments in Polish liquid fuels market (see Figure 1.4. in Chapter 1, Section 1.4. and UN Global Compact[29]),[30].

Interestingly, after 2019, the discrepancies grew for '*inorganic chemicals; organic or inorganic compounds of precious metals, of rare-earth metals, of radioactive elements or of isotopes*' and '*natural or cultured pearls, precious or semi-precious stones, precious metals, metals clad with precious metal, and articles thereof; imitation jewellery; coin*' (German export exceeds Polish import) as well as cryptic '*other products*' (Polish import exceeds German export).

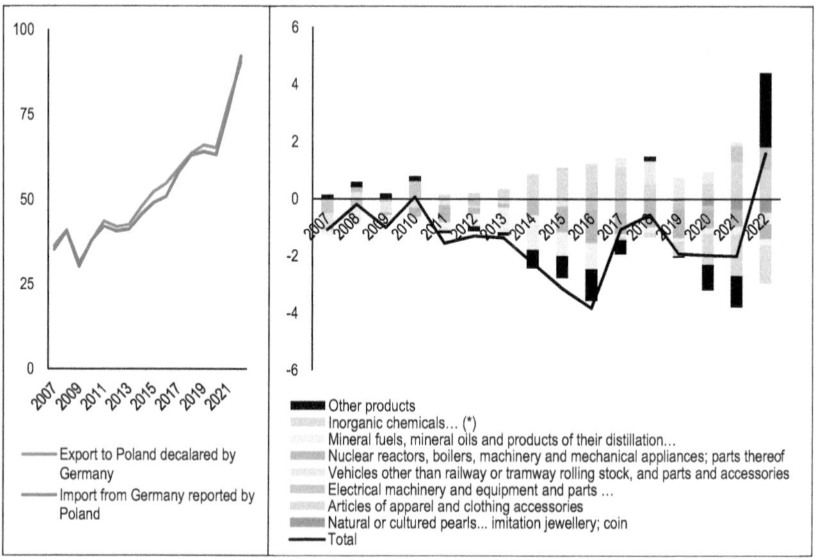

Figure 2.3. Discrepancies between mirror statistics of German export to Poland and Polish import from Germany, 2007–2022 (EUR billion)

*-for full name of the category see Appendix 1.

On the right panel, categories of goods accounting for the biggest part of the overall discrepancy in mirror statistics had been selected for presentation (color bars). The other categories of goods – out of 96 CN 2022 chapters analyzed – accounts for the remaining part of the total discrepancy (black line).

Source: Own calculation based on EUROSTAT data on the EU trade since 1988 by HS2-4-6 and CN8 – former content – (ds-045409).

29 UN Global Compact, 2016, pp. 77–86.

30 Before VAT investigative committee, P. Niemczyk recalled on-the-ground counting of tank trucks, carried out as part of consulting job on liquid fuel market VAT frauds.

2.5.3. Outflows of goods from Poland underreported in Germany

Also in case of the Polish export to Germany (and German import from Poland) relative discrepancies in mirror statistics are comparably very small – however the volume of trade makes them substantial in absolute terms (see Table 2.2).

Again, more detailed analysis uncover, that in some categories of goods the export reported by Poland exceeds the import declared by Germany (for example: vehicles and parts, plastics, electrical machinery) while in another it goes the other way around (cryptic '*other products*').

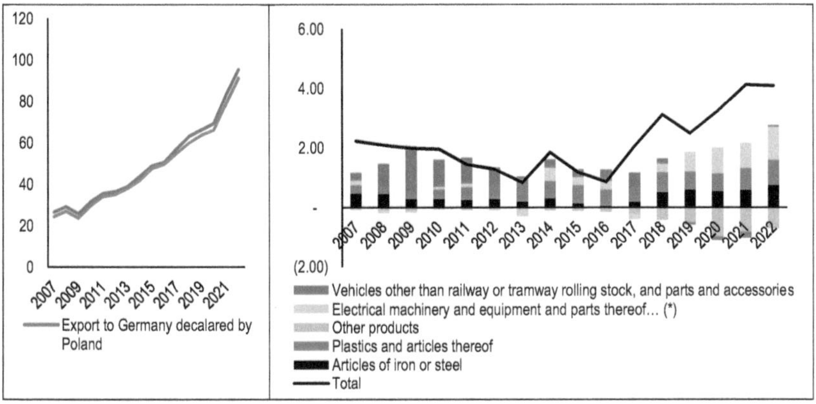

Figure 2.4. Discrepancies between mirror statistics of Polish export to Germany and German import from Poland, 2007–2022 (EUR billion)

*-for full name of the category see Appendix 1.

On the right panel, categories of goods accounting for the biggest part of the overall discrepancy in mirror statistics had been selected for presentation (color bars). The other categories of goods – out of 96 CN 2022 chapters analyzed – accounts for the remaining part of the total discrepancy (black line).

Source: Own calculation based on EUROSTAT data on the EU trade since 1988 by HS2-4-6 and CN8 – former content – (ds-045409).

The goal was to examine which of the countries – Belarus or Germany – is the primary supplier. Polish quotation: '*liczyliśmy ciężarówki albo cysterny, które przekraczały polską granicę przez granicę polsko-litewską albo polsko-niemiecką, i zastanawialiśmy się, czy liczba tych cystern jest adekwatna do danych statystycznych, wynikających z Eurostatu, które mówiły, ile np. paliw Polska importuje z tych kierunków, prawda?... pamiętam, że myśmy weryfikowali taki pogląd, czy więcej paliwa nielegalnego pochodzenia trafi na polski rynek z rafinerii białoruskich czy niemieckich, prawda? To wcale nie było takie proste, to wymagało właśnie dosyć dużo takiej pracy np. liczenia tych cystern, co może się wydać zabawne, że to mogło być ciekawe źródło informacji, a jednak było*' .

It seems that the overreported export of '*vehicles other than railway or tramway rolling stock, and parts and accessories thereof*' could indicate some sort of fraudulent activity (like diversion fraud) starting as early as 2008. However it seems plausible that the most of the discrepancies had been caused by other factors, including reporting thresholds.

2.5.4. Inflows of goods from Italy underreported in Poland

The discrepancies in Italian export to Poland – and Polish import form Italy – are relatively comparable to these of Czech export to Poland. Broken down by CN 2022 chapters, they looks diverse (i.e. substantial changes in total discrepancy are not driven by specific category of goods as in case of Latvia) and quite stable – with exception of '*pharmaceutical products*', where discrepancy grew after 2019.

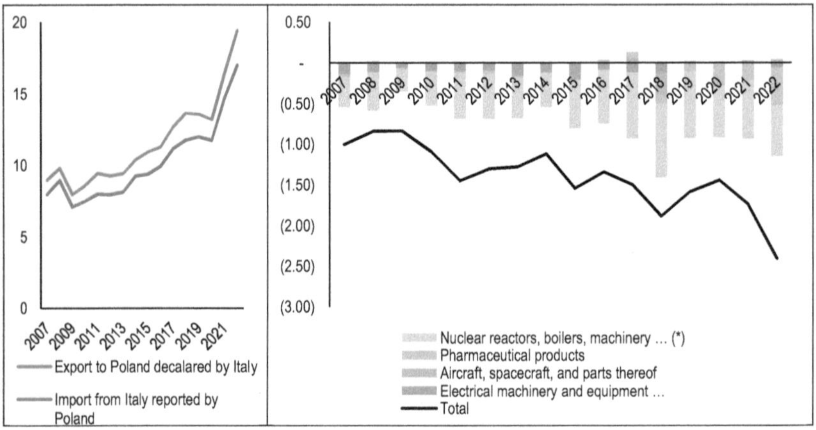

Figure 2.5. Discrepancies between mirror statistics of Italian export to Poland and Polish import from Italy, 2007–2022 (EUR billion)

*-for full name of the category see Appendix 1.

On the right panel, categories of goods accounting for the biggest part of the overall discrepancy in mirror statistics had been selected for presentation (color bars). The other categories of goods – out of 96 CN 2022 chapters analyzed – accounts for the remaining part of the total discrepancy (black line).

Source: Own calculation based on EUROSTAT data on the EU trade since 1988 by HS2-4-6 and CN8 – former content – (ds-045409).

2.5.5. Inflows of goods from Netherlands underreported in Poland

The discrepancies in Dutch export to Poland – and Polish import form the Netherlands – in relative terms are comparable to these between Poland and Czechia or Italy. However, the two groups that generates the largest part of the total discrepancy – '*nuclear reactors, boilers, machinery and mechanical appliances; parts thereof*' and '*electrical machinery and equipment and parts thereof; sound recorders and reproducers, television image and sound recorders and reproducers, and parts and accessories of such articles*' – could hypothetically be linked to some sort of MTIC activities. Interestingly, when the discrepancy in the former category of goods evaporated in 2017, the discrepancy in the latter category – comparable in size – emerged. In the subsequent years, the discrepancy in '*electrical machinery*' narrows gradually, while the one in '*reactors, boilers and machinery*' rebuilds.

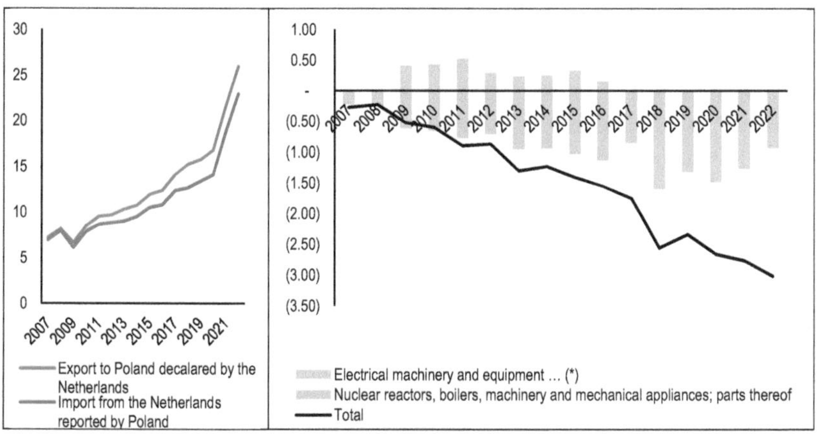

Figure 2.6. Discrepancies between mirror statistics of Dutch export to Poland and Polish import from Netherlands, 2007–2022 (EUR billion)

*-for full name of the category see Appendix 1.

On the right panel, categories of goods accounting for the biggest part of the overall discrepancy in mirror statistics had been selected for presentation (color bars). The other categories of goods – out of 96 CN 2022 chapters analyzed – accounts for the remaining part of the total discrepancy (black line).

Source: Own calculation based on EUROSTAT data on the EU trade since 1988 by HS2-4-6 and CN8 – former content – (ds-045409).

References

Braml M., & Felbermayr G. (2022). The EU Self-Surplus Puzzle: An Indication of VAT Fraud?. *Int Tax Public Finance* 29, 1075–1097, https://doi.org/10.1007/s10797-021-09713-x.

Bussy A. (2020). Cross-Border Value Added Tax Fraud in the European Union, available at SSRN: http://dx.doi.org/10.2139/ssrn.3569914.

CASE. (2015). Ocena czy poprzez wprowadzenie od dnia 1 października 2013 r. odwróconego obciążenia VAT na niektóre wyroby stalowe ograniczono nadużycia w rozliczaniu odatku VAT w obrocie tymi towarami oraz czy warunki funkcjonowania przedsiębiorstw w branży objętej zmianami uległy poprawie, report in Polish, commissioned by the Ministry of Finance, available as a appendix to the OSR Ex-post (evaluation) of the act of July 26th 2013 Journal of Law ref. No. (Dz.U.2013.1027). Available at: https://legislacja.rcl.gov.pl/projekt/12282103 (Accessed Oct. 31, 2023)

Ernst & Young. (2014). *Analiza wpływu zmian administracyjnych na wielkość szarej strefy na rynku prętów zbrojeniowych i sytuację sektora finansów publicznych*. Warszawa, marzec 2014 r. see press release at: https://web.archive.org/web/20140804082711/http://www.ey.media.pl/pr/281379/analiza-ey-ponad-300-mln-rocznie-tyle-zyska-skarb-panstwa-dzieki-likwidacji-szarej-strefy-w-handlu-pretami-zbrojeniowymi (Accessed Oct. 31, 2023).

European Commission, Directorate-General for Taxation and Customs Union. (2018b). The Concept of Tax Gaps – Report III – MTIC Fraud Gap Estimation Methodologies. Publications Office, https://data.europa.eu/doi/10.2778/418684.

Grigoriou Ch., Kalizinje F., & Raballand G. (2019). How Helpful Are Mirror Statistics for Customs Reform? Lessons from a Decade of Operational Use. *World Customs Journal*, 13(2), 105–113.

Gros D. (2017). Is Germany's Current Account Surplus Bad for the World Economy?. CEPS commentary, available at: https://www.ceps.eu/ceps-publications/germanys-current-account-surplus-bad-world-economy/ (Accessed Oct. 31, 2023).

Morgenstern O. (1963). *On the Accuracy of Economic Observations* (2nd ed.). New Jersey: Princeton University Press.

Olczykowski K., & Kassel T. (2017). The Battle May Be Won, But the War Goes On: The Latest Dispatches from the Front, mBank – CASE Seminar Proceedings No. 147/2017

UN Global Compact. (2016). Przeciwdziałanie szarej strefie w Polsce 2015/2016. UN Global Compact, available at: https://mf-arch2.mf.gov.pl/documents/764034/5123644/20160407_GCNP_raport_szara_strefa.pdf (Accessed Oct. 31, 2023).

UNSD. (2019). *IMTS Bilateral Asymmetries – How to Measure, Analyze, Reduce and Way Forward.* New York: United Nations Publications.

Appendix 1. Combined Nomenclature (CN 2022) chapters applied to the analysis

Sect	Chapter	
I	1	Live animals
	2	Meat and edible meat offal
	3	Fish and crustaceans, molluscs and other aquatic invertebrates
	4	Dairy produce; birds' eggs; natural honey; edible products of animal origin, not elsewhere specified or included
	5	Products of animal origin, not elsewhere specified or included
II	6	Live trees and other plants; bulbs, roots and the like; cut flowers and ornamental foliage
	7	Edible vegetables and certain roots and tubers
	8	Edible fruit and nuts; peel of citrus fruit or melons
	9	Coffee, tea, mate and spices
	10	Cereals
	11	Products of the milling industry; malt; starches; inulin; wheat gluten
	12	Oil seeds and oleaginous fruits; miscellaneous grains, seeds and fruit; industrial or medicinal plants; straw and fodder
	13	Lac; gums, resins and other vegetable saps and extracts
	14	Vegetable plaiting materials; vegetable products not elsewhere specified or included
III	15	Animal or vegetable fats and oils and their cleavage products; prepared edible fats; animal or vegetable waxes
IV	16	Preparations of meat, of fish or of crustaceans, molluscs or other aquatic invertebrates
	17	Sugars and sugar confectionery
	18	Cocoa and cocoa preparations
	19	Preparations of cereals, flour, starch or milk; pastrycooks' products
	20	Preparations of vegetables, fruit, nuts or other parts of plants
	21	Miscellaneous edible preparations
	22	Beverages, spirits and vinegar
	23	Residues and waste from the food industries; prepared animal fodder
	24	Tobacco and manufactured tobacco substitutes
V	25	Salt; sulphur; earths and stone; plastering materials, lime and cement
	26	Ores, slag and ash
	27	Mineral fuels, mineral oils and products of their distillation; bituminous substances; mineral waxes

Appendix 1. Continued

Sect	Chapter
VI	28 Inorganic chemicals; organic or inorganic compounds of precious metals, of rare-earth metals, of radioactive elements or of isotopes
	29 Organic chemicals
	30 Pharmaceutical products
	31 Fertilisers
	32 Tanning or dyeing extracts; tannins and their derivatives; dyes, pigments and other coloring matter; paints and varnishes; putty and other mastics; inks
	33 Essential oils and resinoids; perfumery, cosmetic or toilet preparations
	34 Soap, organic surface-active agents, washing preparations, lubricating preparations, artificial waxes, prepared waxes, polishing or scouring preparations, candles and similar articles, modelling pastes, 'dental waxes' and dental preparations with a basis of plaster
	35 Albuminoidal substances; modified starches; glues; enzymes
	36 Explosives; pyrotechnic products; matches; pyrophoric alloys; certain combustible preparations
	37 Photographic or cinematographic goods
	38 Miscellaneous chemical products
VII	39 Plastics and articles thereof
	40 Rubber and articles thereof
VIII	41 Raw hides and skins (other than furskins) and leather
	42 Articles of leather; saddlery and harness; travel goods, handbags and similar containers; articles of animal gut (other than silkworm gut)
	43 Furskins and artificial fur; manufactures thereof
IX	44 Wood and articles of wood; wood charcoal
	45 Cork and articles of cork
	46 Manufactures of straw, of esparto or of other plaiting materials; basketware and wickerwork
X	47 Pulp of wood or of other fibrous cellulosic material; recovered (waste and scrap) paper or paperboard
	48 Paper and paperboard; articles of paper pulp, of paper or of paperboard
	49 Printed books, newspapers, pictures and other products of the printing industry; manuscripts, typescripts and plans

(*continued*)

Appendix 1. Continued

Sect	Chapter
XI	50 Silk
	51 Wool, fine or coarse animal hair; horsehair yarn and woven fabric
	52 Cotton
	53 Other vegetable textile fibres; paper yarn and woven fabrics of paper yarn
	54 Man-made filaments; strip and the like of man-made textile materials
	55 Man-made staple fibres
	56 Wadding, felt and nonwovens; special yarns; twine, cordage, ropes and cables and articles thereof
	57 Carpets and other textile floor coverings
	58 Special woven fabrics; tufted textile fabrics; lace; tapestries; trimmings; embroidery
	59 Impregnated, coated, covered or laminated textile fabrics; textile articles of a kind suitable for industrial use
	60 Knitted or crocheted fabrics
	61 Articles of apparel and clothing accessories, knitted or crocheted
	62 Articles of apparel and clothing accessories, not knitted or crocheted
	63 Other made-up textile articles; sets; worn clothing and worn textile articles; rags
XII	64 Footwear, gaiters and the like; parts of such articles
	65 Headgear and parts thereof
	66 Umbrellas, sun umbrellas, walking sticks, seat-sticks, whips, riding-crops and parts thereof
	67 Prepared feathers and down and articles made of feathers or of down; artificial flowers; articles of human hair
XIII	68 Articles of stone, plaster, cement, asbestos, mica or similar materials
	69 Ceramic products
	70 Glass and glassware
XIV	71 Natural or cultured pearls, precious or semi-precious stones, precious metals, metals clad with precious metal, and articles thereof; imitation jewellery; coin

Appendix 1. Continued

Sect	Chapter	
XV	72	Iron and steel
	73	Articles of iron or steel
	74	Copper and articles thereof
	75	Nickel and articles thereof
	76	Aluminium and articles thereof
	78	Lead and articles thereof
	79	Zinc and articles thereof
	80	Tin and articles thereof
	81	Other base metals; cermets; articles thereof
	82	Tools, implements, cutlery, spoons and forks, of base metal; parts thereof of base metal
	83	Miscellaneous articles of base metal
XVI	84	Nuclear reactors, boilers, machinery and mechanical appliances; parts thereof
	85	Electrical machinery and equipment and parts thereof; sound recorders and reproducers, television image and sound recorders and reproducers, and parts and accessories of such articles
XVII	86	Railway or tramway locomotives, rolling stock and parts thereof; railway or tramway track fixtures and fittings and parts thereof; mechanical (including electromechanical) traffic signalling equipment of all kinds
	87	Vehicles other than railway or tramway rolling stock, and parts and accessories thereof
	88	Aircraft, spacecraft, and parts thereof
	89	Ships, boats and floating structures
XVIII	90	Optical, photographic, cinematographic, measuring, checking, precision, medical or surgical instruments and apparatus; parts and accessories thereof
	91	Clocks and watches and parts thereof
	92	Musical instruments; parts and accessories of such articles
XIX	93	Arms and ammunition; parts and accessories thereof
XX	94	Furniture; bedding, mattresses, mattress supports, cushions and similar stuffed furnishings; lamps and lighting fittings, not elsewhere specified or included; illuminated signs, illuminated nameplates and the like; prefabricated buildings
	95	Toys, games and sports requisites; parts and accessories thereof
	96	Miscellaneous manufactured articles
XXI	97	Works of art, collectors' pieces and antiques
		Other products

Source: Combined Nomenclature, 2022 (CN 2022); available at: https://op.europa.eu/s/y3nw (Accessed Oct. 31, 2023).

Artur Bogucki (SGH Warsaw School of Economics),
Kamil Jońska (SGH Warsaw School of Economics)

Chapter 3 Noticing the VAT compliance crisis: The analysis of VAT-related Parliamentary speeches

Abstract: This chapter analyzes VAT compliance narratives in Polish Parliament speeches from 2007–2023, identifying three main views – systemic flaws, criminal fraud, and economic cycles. Natural language processing of 4,665 speeches reveals politicization of VAT issues, with varying emphasis by political parties.

Keywords: VAT Compliance, EU Tax Policy, Policy of Law, Computational Law, Tax Law

3.1. General comments

In Chapter 3 three distinct narratives circulated in the policy-making circles had been described. The 'inherent flaw' view focused on the weaknesses at the heart of the harmonized EU VAT design – Intra-Community Supply and Intra-Community Acquisition taxation making MTIC fraud possible.

The 'gangster' view focused on the organized crime behind VAT frauds – in particular large-scale MTIC frauds in vulnerable sectors like steal or liquid fuels, and praised policing techniques of criminal law enforcement apparatus as a key solution to the problem.

Finally, the 'automatic stabilizer' view – apparently rooted in the focus on cyclical fluctuations of economy in the aftermath of 2008 Global Financial Crisis – viewed 'VAT gap' as a form of fiscal stimulus to the economic growth.

These narratives – discerned from the qualitative data – offer quite sensible generalization allowing further analysis of the formulation and implementation of policy response to VAT compliance crises. However, the goal of this chapter is to systematically examine the narratives on VAT-related topic, using parliamentary speeches delivered over 2007–2023 period (VI, VII, VIII and IX parliamentary terms).

Although the position of Polish parliament vis a vis other centers of political power admittedly declined[1], it nevertheless offered a space where politicians

1 Nalepa M. (2020). Poland: The Road to Authoritarianism Is Paved by Gradual Majoritarian Shifts [in:] I. Khmelko, R. Stapenhurst, M. L. Mezey (eds.) *Legislative*

from rivaling camps could argue with each other (or at least appeal to each other's information bubbles).

Moreover, the parliamentary debates over the draft laws submitted by the cabinet (i.e. drafted in the Ministry of Finance – on the role of executive in creation of Polish statutory law[2]) includes elaborate speeches and Q&A sessions with cabinet officials, providing the opportunity to contrast views of MPs with those of the government bureaucracy.

3.2. VAT-related issues in the parliamentary speeches – Descriptive statistics

The departure point for further analysis presented in this chapter is a query of the searchable minutes of deliberations in the Lower Chamber of Polish Parliament ('Sejm')[3] which – according to the constitution – exercise control over the activities of the Council of Ministers and plays key role in the lawmaking process, considering bills (i.e. statutory legislation) in the course of three readings (the Upper Chamber – 'Senat' – considers it only once).

The query employed 'VAT' keyword, in order to pinpoint wide range of speeches related to the Value Added Tax in general and the 'VAT gap' in particular. All in all, the original dataset included 4 665 speeches[4] over four consecutive Parliamentary terms. During the first two (VI and VII, 2007–2015) the center-liberal coalition of Civic Platform (PO) and People's Party (PSL) maintained majority and formed the Cabinet, with right-wing Law & Justice (PiS) the biggest opposition party. During the second two terms (VIII and IX, 2015–2023) the Law & Justice (PiS) commanded the majority and formed the Cabinet, with Civic Platform (PO – later on, Civic Coalition – KO) the major opposition party.

Decline in the 21st Century: A Comparative Perspective, Milton, Taylor et Francis Group.

2 Joński K., & Rogowski W. (2022). Legislative Inflation in Poland: Bird's Eye View on Three Decades after the the 1989 Breakthrough. The Journal of Legislative Studies, DOI: 10.1080/13572334.2022.2052465.

3 The web links for these are the following: VI term: https://orka2.sejm.gov.pl/Debata6.nsf; VII term: https://www.sejm.gov.pl/sejm7.nsf/wypowiedzi.xsp?view=S; VIII term: https://www.sejm.gov.pl/sejm8.nsf/wypowiedzi.xsp?view=S; IX term: https://www.sejm.gov.pl/sejm9.nsf/wypowiedzi.xsp?view=S (Accessed Oct. 31, 2023).

4 Those included speeches that had been submitted in written, but not delivered during the debates. Of them 990 in VI term, 1229 in VII term, 1403 in VIII term and 1043 in IX term.

Figure 3.1. plots the annual number[5] of Lower Chamber speeches including 'VAT' keyword, broken down by the type of the speaker (government representatives included the Prime Minister, the cabinet ministers and deputy ministers[6]).

Although some could feel puzzled by the apparent lack of any pattern in this data, consistent with the dynamics of the crisis as gauged by 'VAT gap' metrics. However, one has to keep in mind that over the examined period the Parliament proceeded numerous laws (including budget laws) somehow related to VAT. What is visible however, is that VAT related speeches were more frequent over 2012–2013 – and later on, 2016–2017 – than during 2014–2015.

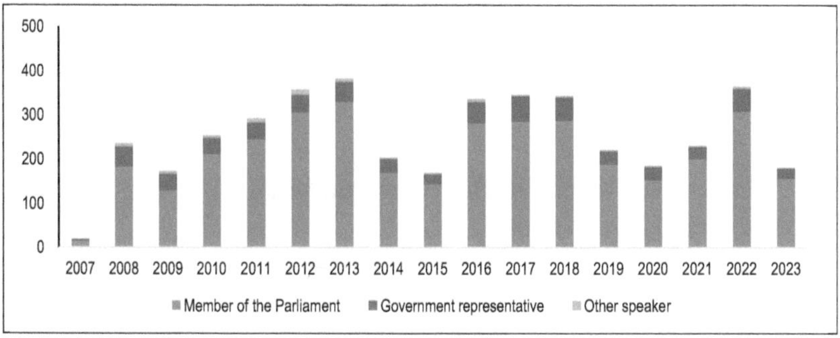

Figure 3.1. Parliamentary speeches mentioning 'VAT', broken down by the type of speaker, VI-IX parliamentary terms

Source: Own analysis using data compiled from www.sejm.gov.pl

Additional insights can be gleaned from breaking down the data on MP's speeches including 'VAT' keyword (Figure 3.2.). Apparently, the topic was more likely to be raised by the actual opposition (PiS in VI and VII, and PO/KO in VIII and IX term) than by the government majority.

5 Multiple speeches delivered (i) by the same MP, (ii) on the same issue (as recorded in the description), and (iii) in the same day had been counted as a single speech (if MP is interrupted by the Speaker, parts of his speech are recorded in these minutes as separate speeches). That led to total of 4 276 speeches, of them 913 in VI term, 1107 in VII term, 1282 in VIII term and 974 in IX term.

6 Polish: 'sekretarz stanu' and 'podsekretarz stanu'.

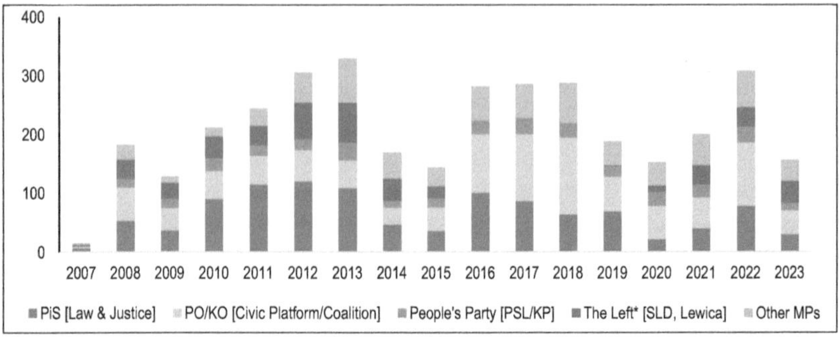

Figure 3.2. Parliamentary speeches mentioning 'VAT', broken down by the type of speaker, VI-IX parliamentary terms

*- Left was not represented in the VIII term.

Source: Own analysis using data compiled from www.sejm.gov.pl

3.3. VAT-related issues in the parliamentary speeches – Keywords

Descriptive analysis of the selected sample of VAT-related parliamentary speeches presented in the previous section provide rather limited information. Thereby, keywords had been used in order to demonstrate the changing pattern of statements, likely to be related to VAT compliance crisis.

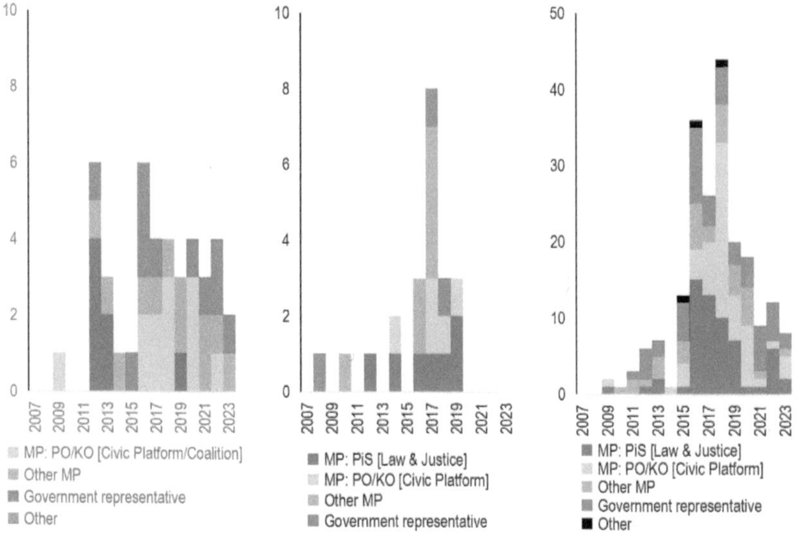

Figure 3.3. Parliamentary speeches mentioning 'VAT' as well as selected keywords, broken down by the type of speaker, VI–IX parliamentary terms

Source: Own analysis using data compiled from www.sejm.gov.pl

The assembled data presented on Figure 3.3 suggests, that the issue of 'VAT gap' became substantially 'politicized' in the VIII term (2016–2019) with relatively frequent usage by Law & Justice (PiS) MPs and L&J cabinet representatives. Interestingly, in 2018 the opposition Civic Platform MPs became the most frequent users of 'VAT gap' in their speeches - an event clearly linked with the establishment of VAT investigative committee in the Parliament.[7]

7 Uchwała Sejmu Rzeczypospolitej Polskiej z dnia 5 lipca 2018 r. w sprawie powołania Komisji Śledczej do zbadania prawidłowości i legalności działań oraz występowania zaniedbań i zaniechań organów i instytucji publicznych w zakresie zapewnienia dochodów Skarbu Państwa z tytułu podatku od towarów i usług i podatku akcyzowego w okresie od grudnia 2007 r. do listopada 2015 r. (Journal of Law reference no. M.P. 2018 poz. 687).

3.4. VAT-related issues in the Parliamentary speeches – Text mining

The identified speeches were retrieved using the Beautiful Soup package and further processed to remove administrative data that can bias classifications. The data was pre-processed for further analysis. Capital letters were removed, words were lemmatized and special tokens as well as stop words were removed. Polish stop words were retrieved from Github[8] and used for tokenization. The pre-processed texts are vectorized using TF-IDF, a common method to assign importance to words in a text.

The concordance of a group of keywords were checked for 150 characters before and after the keywords. We compare the government representatives for the VI and VII term (first) and VIII and IX term (second). Results are plotted on Figure 3.3.

The second government mentioned scam (oszustwo) 13 times vs 2 times for the first government. When gap (lukę) was mentioned, the second government mentioned VAT 21 times vs 9 times for the first government. Luka was mentioned 127 times by the second government vs 20 times by the first.

Contrary, growth (wzrost) was mentioned 571 times by the first government and 378 by the second. The first government focused more on European: 77, union: 82, expenses: 54, employment: 38 and market: 38. The second on tax: 40, income: 51, gas: 34.

8 https://github.com/bieli/stopwords/blob/master/polish.stopwords.txt

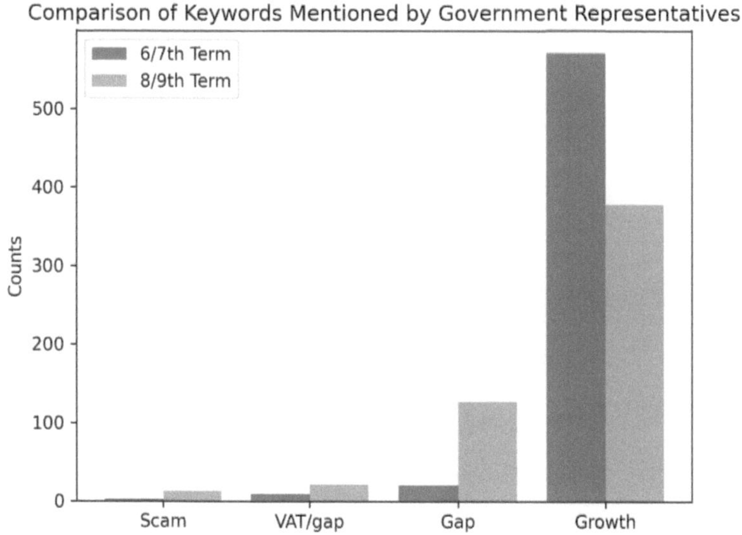

Figure 3.4. Comparison of keywords mentioned by Government Representatives (Cabinet Ministers and the deputy ministers)

Source: Own analysis using data compiled from www.sejm.gov.pl

Also, the Law & Justice (PiS) MPs had been compared for the 1st and 2nd period (terms VI and VII vs VIII and IX). Results are plotted on Figure 3.4. When talking about growth (wzrost), they mentioned VAT more in the first period (134 times over 80 times the second period) and income (dochodów) less (48 and 133 times respectively)

They also focused on VAT/gap much more the second period: 91/102 times the second period and 4/5 times the first.

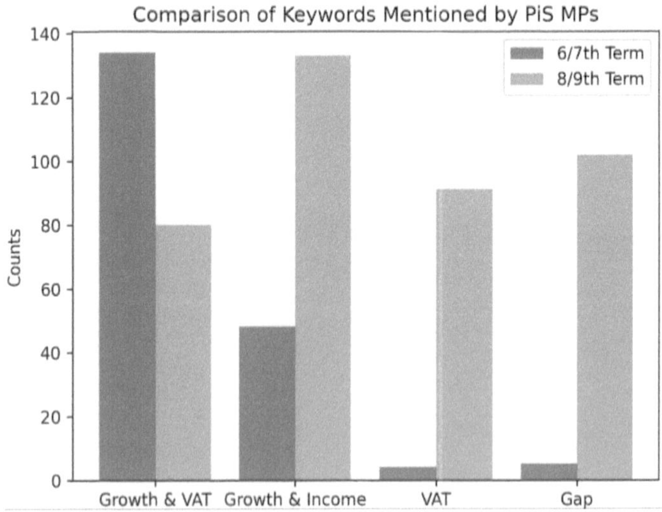

Figure 3.5. Comparison of keywords mentioned by Law & Justice (PiS) MPs
Source: Own analysis using data compiled from www.sejm.gov.pl

Use of the words scam ('oszustwo'), carousel ('karuzela') and mafia ('mafia') stand out as being said more often in the second period (VIII and IX terms), especially by the opposition.

Table 3.1 lists the usage of selected keywords by speakers from three groups: government representatives (Cabinet Ministers and deputy ministers), majority MPs and opposition MPs. Since the governing majority shifted in 2015, two periods have been distinguished, the first spanning VI and VII parliamentary terms, and the second spanning VIII and IX terms.

Table 3.1. Usage of selected keywords by government representatives (Cabinet Ministers and deputy ministers) and majority and opposition MPs during the first (VI and VII term) and second period (VIII and IX term)

	Fraud ('oszustwo')	**Embezzlement ('defraudacja')**	**Carousel ('karuzela')**	**Mafia ('mafia')**	**Mob ('mob')**	**VAT tax ('podatku', 'vat')**	**VAT gap ('luka', 'vat')**	**Number of documents**
1st government	2	0	2	0	0	238	2	343
2nd government	9	0	3	2	0	200	7	343
1st majority MP	1	0	0	0	0	376	0	506
2nd majority MP	1	0	4	9	0	365	3	528
1st opposition MP	5	0	0	0	0	918	0	1305
2nd opposition MP	26	0	7	13	0	591	3	1514

Source: Own analysis using data compiled from www.sejm.gov.pl

While Table 3.1 traces keywords selected as likely to appear in the 'VAT gap' related speeches, Appendix 1 lists 30 most occurring words and their frequencies for these three groups during the first (VI and VII term) and second period (VIII and IX term). Perhaps surprisingly, none of them can be reasonably identified as linked to any narrative regarding VAT fraud or VAT compliance.

References

Nalepa M. (2020). Poland: The Road to Authoritarianism is Paved by Gradual Majoritarian Shifts [in:] I. Khmelko, R. Stapenhurst, M. L. Mezey (eds.), *Legislative Decline in the 21st Century: A Comparative Perspective*. Milton: Taylor et Francis Group.

Joński K., & Rogowski W. (2022). Legislative Inflation in Poland: Bird's Eye View on Three Decades after the 1989 Breakthrough. *The Journal of Legislative Studies*, https://doi.org/10.1080/13572334.2022.2052465.

Appendix 1. The 30 words that appear most frequently and the number of times they appear for the different groups listed in the Table 3.1.

1st government	2nd government	1st majority	2nd majority	1st opposition	2nd opposition
chodzi: 1407	poseł: 1735	ustawy: 1578	poseł: 1805	vat: 2569	ustawy: 4108
r: 1386	ustawy: 1109	r: 1380	ustawy: 1660	ustawy: 2339	poseł: 3772
podatku: 943	chodzi: 988	podatku: 1363	podatku: 1212	podatku: 2192	panie: 2631
poseł: 901	państwo: 917	vat: 1090	r: 1206	r: 1988	vat: 2622
ustawy: 863	państwa: 912	budżetu: 1022	państwa: 1126	panie: 1740	podatku: 2556
vat: 820	r: 845	państwa: 828	vat: 1016	państwa: 1727	państwo: 2025
państwa: 739	vat: 836	mld: 827	mld: 917	rząd: 1515	nr: 1698
finansów: 660	podatku: 755	finansów: 798	panie: 794	mld: 1382	r: 1647
europejskiej: 639	finansów: 714	komisji: 713	komisji: 786	finansów: 1348	państwa: 1613
zakresie: 634	mld: 699	publicznych: 685	państwo: 776	budżetu: 1287	mld: 1546
oczywiście: 619	mamy: 567	panie: 675	nr: 695	minister: 1186	dziękuję: 1531
mln: 573	sali: 560	projekt: 573	finansów: 648	wysoka: 1155	projektu: 1506
mamy: 547	panie: 552	mln: 567	sali: 642	chodzi: 1151	komisji: 1426
powiedzieć: 534	oczywiście: 534	chodzi: 544	budżetu: 641	ministrze: 1096	finansów: 1303
przypadku: 526	mln: 527	europejskiej: 527	dziękuję: 617	izbo: 1095	zmianie: 1238
polsce: 513	dziękuję: 499	unii: 516	publicznych: 591	projekt: 1074	wysoka: 1147
unii: 502	zakresie: 486	towarów: 514	projektu: 515	dziękuję: 1051	rząd: 1145
tys: 499	ministerstwie: 452	wydatków: 512	wysoka: 509	państwo: 1044	izbo: 1103
związku: 497	europejskiej: 451	usług: 509	izbo: 498	marszałku: 1023	pierwsze: 1079
budżetu: 477	projekt: 421	marszałku: 496	głos: 455	komisji: 935	projekt: 1046
pracy: 452	głos: 420	wysoka: 493	proszę: 448	poseł: 912	chodzi: 1017
pytanie: 445	powiedzieć: 411	poseł: 493	zmianie: 439	publicznych: 895	sali: 1012

(continued)

Appendix 1. Continued

1st government	2nd government	1st majority	2nd majority	1st opposition	2nd opposition
mld: 443	pytanie: 407	zmiany: 482	rząd: 414	pytanie: 852	mamy: 976
projekt: 433	stanu: 405	wzrost: 481	towarów: 414	polsce: 849	towarów: 973
działania: 432	proszę: 404	zakresie: 481	europejskiej: 395	projektu: 846	budżetu: 964
rząd: 421	tys: 373	projektu: 466	usług: 387	mamy: 810	usług: 949
rynku: 419	przedsiębiorców: 373	dziękuję: 465	szanowni: 380	mln: 803	marszałku: 922
zmiany: 409	przypadku: 368	izbo: 452	projekt: 379	praca: 776	druk: 913
wysoka: 409	komisji: 364	1: 387	prawo: 371	europejskiej: 732	publicznych: 902
usług: 397	zmiany: 363	wydatki: 376	2015: 365	oczywiście: 719	ministrze: 899

Dominik J. Gajewski (SGH Warsaw School of Economics),
Kamil Joński (SGH Warsaw School of Economics)

Chapter 4 Policy response – Tax administration activities

Abstract: The chapter reviews the activities of the broadly defined tax administration apparatus in Poland – the first line of defence against the VAT fraud. It reviews the structure of the Polish tax administration and its 2017 reshuffling, as well as statistical data summarizing its effectiveness. Backward-looking control activities had been distinguished from real-time blockages of VAT reclaims and bank accounts.

Keywords: Tax Controls, Fiscal Controls, National Revenue Administration (KAS), VAT fraud

4.1. General comments

After analysing data on the '*VAT Gap*' in Poland and the spread of VAT-related narratives, this chapter begins the review of policy response to the Polish VAT compliance crisis. To this end, three areas of policy response had been distinguished – the first covers the day-by-day activities of the tax authorities tasked with enforcing tax law – in particular tax audits. The second involved legislative response, namely new tax policy instruments developed and implemented as a remedies for the ongoing compliance crisis. While these two remain in the realm of the administrative law, the third area refers to the criminal law instruments deployed against VAT fraud.

The day-by-day activities of the tax administration offer the natural departure point for analysis of the policy response to the VAT compliance crisis. They involve continuous processes aimed at enforcing tax compliance, like scrutiny of the documents provided by the taxpayers, targeting and carrying out tax audits and issuing administrative decisions establishing tax liabilities. It was the kind of activities that could be reasonably expected to rang alarm bells as the crisis developed. Also, they could be expected to provide first line of defence against VAT frauds in the administrative law realm. The goal of this chapter is to examine how Polish tax authorities performed these tasks.

The rest of the chapter is organized as follows. Section 2 provides the institutional background on the Polish tax administration apparatus and its 2017 reorganization. Section 3 argues, that our understanding of the tax administration reaction to the VAT compliance crisis can be informed by earlier experience with massive excise duty frauds – and reviews this episode. After such introduction, Section 4 provides statistical data summarizing the performance of tax administration in the area of VAT. It puts particular emphasis on the 'efficiency' of their activities – namely the relation of efforts made to their (monetary) effects. Finally, Section 5 reviews data on blocked VAT reclaims and blockages implemented as one of the instruments aimed at curbing VAT fraud (STIR – described in details in Chapter 5).

4.2. Institutional background[1]

4.2.1. Pre-2017 organization of the tax administration in Poland

Prior to the 2017 establishment of the National Revenue Administration (Polish: '*Krajowa Administracja Skarbowa*', *KAS*), what we broadly refers to as a 'tax administration'apparatus' had been organized into three distinct institutional structures, assigned with specific missions and regulated in separate legal acts.

The first structure, tasked with day-by-day running of the taxation process and guaranteeing reliability of the documentation provided by the taxpayers, had been regulated in the *Act of 29 August 1997 Tax Ordinance*[2]. The structure involved the 400 **Tax Offices** (Polish '***Urząd Skarbowy***') as a first instance entities, and 16 **Tax Chambers** (Polish '*Izba Skarbowa*'). Among others, they carried out so called Tax Controls (Polish: '*Kontrola Podatkowa*') aimed at verifying the consistency between tax declarations submitted by the taxpayers and the underlying accounting data and the real-life business activities. As Tax Offices encountered every taxpayer in the country, their activities were expected to be rather supportive then repressive (at least as long as the state apparatus believes in the integrity of the majority of the taxpayers).

The second structure, tasked with countering tax fraud, had been regulated in the *Act of 28 September 1991 on Fiscal Control.*[3] The structure involved the 16 **Fiscal Control Offices** (Polish '*Urząd Kontroli Skarbowej*') – with their field offices – as a first instance entities, and the **General Inspector of Fiscal Control** (Polish '*Generalny Inspektor Kontroli Skarbowej*'). They carried out Fiscal Controls

1 The section draws on Gajewski D. J. (ed.) (2022). *Funkcjonowanie sądownictwa administracyjnego na tel koniunktury gospodarczej: perspektywa ekonomicznej analizy prawa*, Warsaw, SGH University Press (in Polish), pp. 41–74.
2 Journal of laws reference no. (Dz.U.1997.137. 926 with ammendments).
3 Journal of laws reference no. (Dz.U.1991.100.442 with amendments).

(Polish: '*Kontrola Skarbowa*') aimed at targeting tax fraud. Interestingly, there was a special service called 'Fiscal Investigation' (Polish '*Wywiad Skarbowy*') located within this structure, authorized to use intrusive policing techniques[4] like monitoring and wiretapping to uncover fraudulent activities.

Finally, the third structure, dealing primarily with cross-border movement of goods, had been regulated by the *Act of 27 August 2009 on Customs Service*.[5] The structure involved 16 **Customs Chambers** (Polish: '*Izba Celna*'), 45 **Customs Offices** (Polish '*Urząd Cenly*') and 143 custom units (Polish: '*Oddział Celny*').

4.2.2. National Revenue Administration (KAS) reform

As 'VAT Gap' crisis gain political traction, and right-wing Law & Justice cabinet embarked the narrative of countering VAT frauds in order to fund ambitious social spending agenda (see Chapter 3), broadly defined tax administration apparatus undergone substantial institutional reshuffling.

According to the *Act of 16 November 2016 on National Revenue Administration*[6] the new institutional structure had been built upon the existing one. *The Chief of the National Revenue Administration* (deputy Minister of Finance) supervises the 16 **Revenue Administration Chambers** (Polish '*Izba Administracji Skarbowej*'). The lower tier of the structure involves 400 **Tax Offices** (Polish 'Urząd Skarbowy') and 16 **Custom-Fiscal Offices** (Polish: 'Urząd Celno-Skarbowy'). The Custom-Fiscal Offices oversees subordinate structure involving 45 Custom-Fiscal Offices field offices (Polish: '*Degelatura Urzędu Celno-Skarbowego*') and 143 custom units (Polish: '*Oddzial Celny*').

The basic distinction between the Tax Controls – regulated in *Tax Ordinance* – and Custom-Fiscal Controls (Polish: '*Kontrola Celno-Skarbowa*') – now regulated in the *Act on National Revenue Administration* – remained.

4 So called 'operational and exploratory activities' (Polish: '*czynności operacyjno-rozpoznawcze*').

5 Journal of laws reference no. (Dz.U.2009.168.1323 with amendments).

6 Journal of laws reference no. (Dz.U.2016.1947 with amendments).

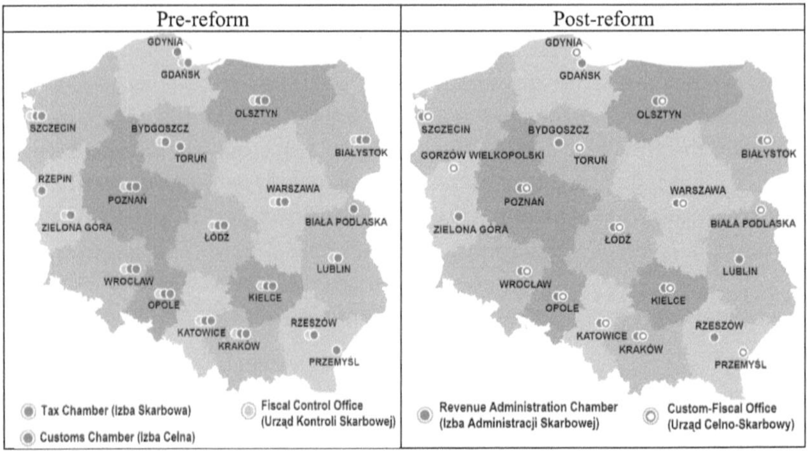

Figure 4.1. Organizational structure of Polish tax administration apparatus

Source: Adapted from the Ministry of Finance slides available at: https://www.gov.pl/attachment/4d35e6d4-7fbc-4c3a-82bc-a9e158868381 (accessed Oct. 31 2023).

4.3. The prologue: Excise duty compliance problems in early two-thousands

Before discussing the tax administration apparatus – and, in particular, the pre-2017 Fiscal Control Offices – reaction to the deepening VAT compliance crisis, it is revealing to examine another episode of tax compliance crisis, that had occurred a decade earlier.

Back in the mid-two-thousands, as Poland entered the EU (2004), it was cross-border smuggling and excise duty that became symbols of weakness of the Polish tax apparatus[7] – just like the 'VAT gap' and cross-border carousel frauds a decade later.

7 Back in 2006, the tax liabilities in excise duty, as established by Fiscal Control Offices, exceeded those in VAT, see (Ministry of Finance, 2009, p. 14). For details on the mechanisms of excise duty frauds at that time, see Appendix 22 to the VAT investigative committee (2019), *Opracowanie Koordynatora Krajowej Grupy Zadaniowej ds. Wyrobów alkoholowych dotyczące uwarunkowań, które generowały bądź ułatwiały w okresie 2004–2007 oszustwa akcyzowe w obrocie alkoholem etylowym, w tym alkoholem przeznaczonym do wytwarzania produktów przemysłowych (chemikaliach) wraz z podaniem rzeczywistego przykładu oszustwa akcyzowego, styczeń 2009 r.*

These schemes involved what was dubbed in Poland 'a strawmen' – companies serving as a junction between the outlawed and the ordinary economy. To this end, they pretended to be honest businesses – however, they were officially run by quite extraordinary figures (like homeless people recruited by crime groups) and lack any recoverable assets. Once illicit activities had been uncovered, the perpetrators tended to disappear, leaving 'strawmen' behind.[8]

From tax administration's point of view, it was relatively easy to reach an left behind 'strawmen' – a legal person trading with the ordinary businesses. Typically, it was precisely the entity that, according to law, had the obligation to pay tax. Thereby, Fiscal Control Offices carried out their Fiscal Controls against 'a strawmen', painstakingly documented the amounts of their tax liabilities and issued the administrative decisions establishing them. The monetary amounts specified in these decisions had been reported as 'results' of controls (Polish '*ustalenia kontroli skarbowej*'). The flip side was that 'a strawmen' – lacking sellable assets and led by accidental people – were unlikely to ever pay.

The reality on the ground was vividly exposed by the new supervisor of the Fiscal Control Offices, A. Parafianowicz, appointed by the Centrist cabinet of Civic Platform and People's Party. Instead of focusing on the monetary amount of tax liabilities established in the decisions issued by his subordinates, he examined the sums actually cashed-in as a result of the Fiscal Controls.

Not only they turned out an order of magnitude lower than tax liabilities established in the decisions. They appeared lower than the budget costs of the Fiscal Control apparatus itself.

As recounted by Parafianowicz in his testimony before VAT investigative committee, in Fiscal Control Offices '*empty decisions*' had been rewarded, as monetary benefits had been linked to the '*paper outcomes*'. As a consequence, Fiscal Control Offices issued '*frequently absurd*' decisions, like those establishing multimillion tax liabilities of 'strawmen' that are '*unenforceable, and never will be collected*'.[9] Indeed, Financial Control 2008 annual report (Ministry of

8 In this respect they somehow resembled the 'Missing Traders' in VAT frauds. As a consequence, the word – 'słup' in Polish – remains popular as reference to the 'Missing Traders' in VAT frauds.

9 Polish quotation: '*Odeszliśmy od premiowania w UKS-ach pustych decyzji, … w latach wcześniejszych (tam, do 2008 roku) system premiowania polegał na tym, że premiowano za wyniki na piśmie a nie za wyniki efektywnej ściągalności, czy egzekucji, czy zabezpieczenia. Więc sytuacja polegała na tym, że UKS-y wydawały te decyzje (często absurdalne) … chociażby wielomilionowe decyzje na słupy, tak, wiadomo przecież, że to jest nie do ściągnięcia i nigdy nie będzie, … natomiast skupiliśmy się na efektywności – co*

Finance – 2009[10]) reported 30% decline in tax liabilities established in excise duty – as a result of, among others, 'changed control methodology, resulting in abandonment of issuing decisions against "strawmen". Currently, in such cases *criminal-financial proceedings* (Polish: *"Postępowanie karno-skarbowe") are initiated*'.[11]

However, the new approach was far from clear-cut. Financial Control 2009 annual report (Ministry of Finance, 2010[12]) praised '*substantial increase*' in amount of issued decisions – including 33% growth in case of VAT and 14% in case of excise duty.[13]

Finally, in a passage deeply rooted in the *New Public Management* philosophy of Reagan and Thatcher era (the one illuminating early Civic Platform) – and in what can be read as an example of quite bitter irony – the Financial Control 2011 annual report (Ministry of Finance – 2012[14]) proclaimed that '*since few years the total amount cashed-in exceeds the costs of Financial Control. Thereby, one can conclude that currently Financial Control fully covers its operations*'.[15] The conclusion was accompanied with chart summarising sum of the tax liability established in Financial Control decisions over 2009–2011, amounts actually cashed-in and the costs of Financial Control operation (see Figure 4.2).

---

realnie te kontrole dają, jak one są planowane, koordynowane, przede wszystkim typowane'.

10 Ministry of Finance. (2009). Sprawozdanie Kontrola Skarbowa w 2008 r., p. 15.

11 Polish quotation: '*Trzecim powodem systematycznego spadku ustaleń jest zmiana metodologii kontroli, która skutkowała odstąpieniem od wydawania decyzji na podmioty tzw. „słupy". Obecnie w przypadku stwierdzenia nieprawidłowości dokonywanych przez takie podmioty przeprowadzane są postępowania karne-skarbowe*'.

12 Ministry of Finance. (2010). Sprawozdanie Kontrola Skarbowa w 2009 r., p. 15.

13 Polish quotation: 'porównaniu z 2008r. nastąpił znaczący wzrost ustaleń podatkowych, w tym: w zakresie podatku od towarów i usług o 33 %, w zakresie podatku dochodowego od osób prawnych o 48 %, w zakresie podatku dochodowego od osób fizycznych o 4 %, w zakresie podatku akcyzowego o 14 %'.

14 Ministry of Finance. (2012). Sprawozdanie Kontrola Skarbowa w 2011 r., p. 16.

15 Polish quotation: '*W kontroli skarbowej obserwujemy korzystne tendencje. Przy utrzymujących się na tym samym poziomie kosztach działalności urzędów kontroli skarbowej, wzrasta wysokość wpłat do budżetu państwa, dokonywanych w efekcie przeprowadzonych kontroli. Jednocześnie od kilku lat łączna kwota wpłat przewyższa kwotę ponoszonych przez kontrolę skarbową kosztów. Można zatem powiedzieć, że obecnie kontrola skarbowa w pełni „zarabia na swoje utrzymanie*'.

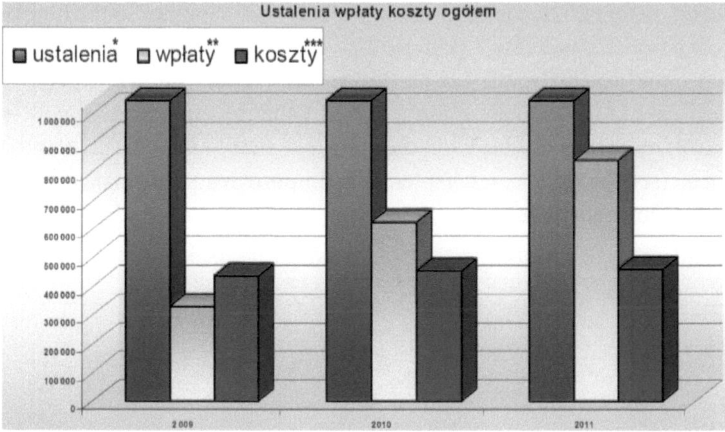

Figure 4.2. Effectiveness of Financial Control over 2009–2011 as reported in Ministry of Finance (2012)

*- Tax liability established by Financial Control. Vertical axis ranges from 0 to PLN 1 billion. In fact, the sums reached: in 2009 – 2,43 billion PLN, in 2010 – 2,11 billion PLN and in 2011 – 2,53 billion PLN.

**- sums cashed-in as a result of Financial Control

***- costs of Financial Control

Source: Reprinted from Ministry of Finance (2012, pp. 16).

4.4. Old dog's old tricks: Tax administration and the 'VAT gap' crisis

Figure 4.3. summarizes the number of Tax Controls[16] (carried out by Tax Offices – Polish 'Urząd Skarbowy') and Fiscal Controls (later on Custom-Fiscal Controls)[17] in the area of VAT over 2014–2022 – the period associated with the countering with 'VAT gap'.

Three observations can easily be made. First, consistently with their different purpose, the number of Tax Controls remains substantially higher than these of Fiscal Controls (Custom-Fiscal Controls). However, the sum of established VAT liabilities is noticeably lower.

16 Carried out by Tax Offices – Polish 'Urząd Skarbowy'.

17 Carried out by Fiscal Control Offices (Polish '*Urząd Kontroli Skarbowej*') and – after 2017 reshuffling – Custom-Fiscal Offices (Polish: '*Urząd Celno-Skarbowy*').

Second, before 2021, the ratio of established VAT liabilities to the number of controls tended to increase – pattern that, under some assumptions discussed later on – could be interpreted as improvement in the targeting process.

Third, over 2014–2016 the amount of VAT liabilities established in both kinds of controls more than doubled. On the one hand, that could reflect both growing 'VAT gap' (see Figure 1.1. in Chapter 1) and improving performance of the tax administration apparatus.

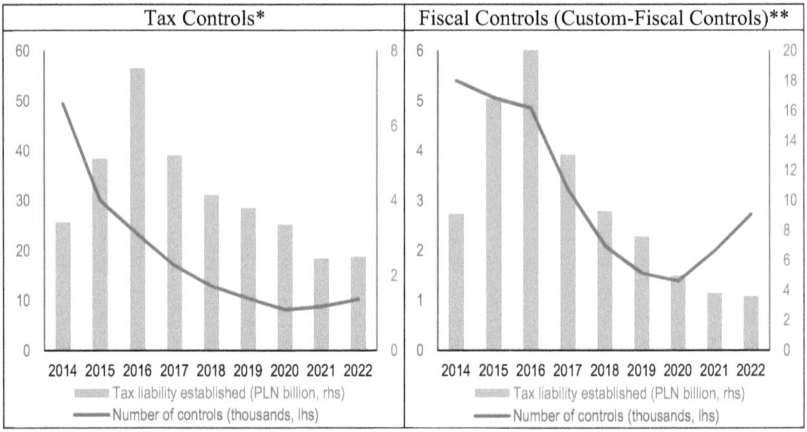

Figure 4.3. Number of controls and amount of established tax liability: VAT, 2014–2022

*- Polish: 'Liczba zakończonych kontroli podatkowych zrealizowanych przez urzędy skarbowe w latach 2018–2022 w zakresie VAT oraz kwoty uszczupleń ww. kontroli'

**- Polish: 'Łączna liczba kontroli zakończonych celno-skarbowych (KCS) i postępowań kontrolnych (PK) zrealizowanych przez urzędy celno-skarbowe w latach 2018–2022 w zakresie VAT oraz łączne kwoty ustaleń kontroli celno-skarbowych i postępowań kontrolnych'.

Sources: Data provided by the Ministry of Finance: in response to MP I. Leszczyna inquiry no. 31643, VIII Term (June 27th 2019, DNK7.054.20.2019), and in response to author's public information request (Oct 4th 2023, BMI1.0123.2521.2023).

On the other hand, growth in established VAT liabilities could indicate the return to '*empty decisions*' and '*paper outcomes*'.

In 2013 annual report (Ministry of Finance – 2014b[18]) signed by Parafianowicz successor, A. Królikowska, there is still chart resembling the one in Figure 4.2. It is also noted that '*another year, the amount cashed-in exceeds the costs of*

18 Ministry of Finance. (2014). Sprawozdanie Kontrola Skarbowa w 2013 r., pp. 7–8.

Fiscal Control activities'. However, the very next sentence praises the amount of established tax liability of 6,45 PLN billion – 70,6% increase as compared to 2012[19]. Similar summary was presented in the next year report.

Data presented in the Figure 4.4. documents that – despite lessons learned over 2008–2010 period – in the apogee of VAT compliance crisis, VAT liabilities established by Fiscal Control spectacularly failed to translate into amounts actually cashed in.

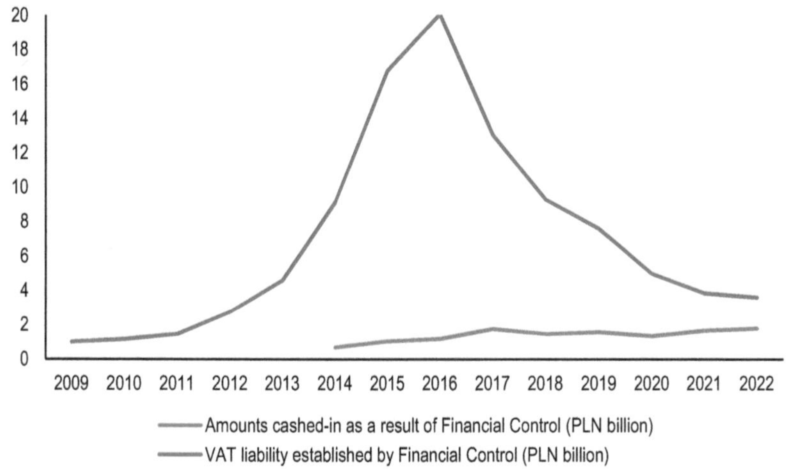

Figure 4.4. Fiscal Control effectiveness over VAT compliance crisis

Sources: Data provided by the Ministry of Finance: in response to MP I. Leszczyna inquiry no. 31643, VIII Term (June 27th 2019, DNK7.054.20.2019), and in response to author's public information request (Oct 4th 2023, BMI1.0123.2521.2023), and data reported in the Annual Reports of the Financial Control.

As deputy Minister of Finance J. Neneman explained in Sep. 2015, '*the targeting accuracy in Fiscal Control Offices in ninety percent – every shot is success*'. However, '*this success fail to translate into the money*' as '*at the end, or at the beginning of the chain, there is so called 'strawmen*' (i.e. 'Missing Trader').[20] Moreover one

19 Polish quotation: '*Kolejny już rok łączna kwota dokonanych wpłat przewyższa kwotę ponoszonych przez Kontrolę Skarbową kosztów działalności. W 2013r. kwota ustaleń wyniosła 6.446,7 mln zł – co stanowi wzrost ustaleń ogółem w stosunku do roku 2012 o 70,6 %, w tym kwota ustaleń wynikających z wydanych decyzji wzrosła aż o 78,3 %*'.

20 Deputy Minister of Finance J. Neneman parliamentary speach, Sep. 10th 2015 (99 session of VII Term). Polish quotation: '*Oszustwa dotyczące podatku VAT są absolutnym*

could expect, that delays between the underlying economic activity and the decision of Financial Control, establishing VAT liability further complicates the enforcement and recovery process. According to Gajewski and Joński[21] analysis of VAT-related judgments of Polish Administrative Courts, for decisions issued in 2017 typical lag had been 4,5 years (see also anegdotal evidence[22]).

In her testimony before VAT investigative committee, A. Królikowska – who replaced A. Parafianowicz as supervisor of Financial Control Offices – had been asked about 2015 Supreme Audit Office[23] findings on decisions against the 'strawmen'.[24] In her view, issuing decisions establishing VAT liability against

priorytetem. Co się udaje? Udaje się dość dobrze typować. Skuteczność typowań w UKS-ach wynosi 90 %, czyli co strzał, to sukces. Ten sukces nie przekłada się na pieniądze, bo jak państwo z pewnością wiecie, biznes przestępczy dotyczący podatku VAT działa tak, że na końcu czy też na początku łańcucha jest tzw. słup, który nie ma majątku. Zatem możemy zrobić ustalenia, ale z tych ustaleń nie ma pieniędzy. Przestępcy również się wycwanili, w cudzysłowie, to jest cały łańcuch transakcji'.

21 Gajewski D., & Joński K. (2020). Country Note: Procedures of the Polish Tax Authorities and the VAT Gap: Evidence from Administrative Court Files. Intertax, 48(11), pp. 1012–1019, https://kluwerlawonline.com/journalarticle/Intertax/48.11/TAXI2020102.

22 In Waśko J. (2017). Wszczynanie postępowań karnych skarbowych w trakcie postępowań kontrolnych – analiza praktyki wybranych urzędów kontroli skarbowej, Przegląd Podatkowy, 2017(2), pp. 44–49.

23 Supreme Audit Office, NIK. (2016). Analiza wykonania budżetu państwa i założeń polityki pieniężnej w 2015 roku, available at: https://www.nik.gov.pl/analiza-budzetu-panstwa/archiwum/ (Accessed Oct. 31 2023).

24 In 2015 report on budget implementation the Supreme Audit Office (NIK, 2016, pp. 110–111) reported, that tax authorities failed to established the genuine perpetrators of the VAT frauds – as well as collect the established tax liabilities. They pointed out specifically to the decisions based on the article 108 of the Act of March 11th 2004 on Goods and Services Tax (Journal of Laws reference no Dz.U.2004.54.535 with amendments) – '*Where a legal person, an organisational unit without legal personality or a natural person issues an invoice in which he shows the amount of the tax, he shall pay that amount*'. Over 2013–2015 period the amounts cashed in amounted to 1,3% of the VAT liabilities established in the decisions issued on the basis of article 108. Polish quotation: '*od podmiotów uczestniczących w oszukańczym procederze, głównie firm „słupów", nie wyegzekwowano wymierzonych w wyniku działań kontrolnych podatków. W większości badanych przypadków organy kontroli skarbowej nie ustaliły także faktycznych organizatorów oszustw podatkowych … Na podstawie art. 108 ustawy o podatku od towarów i usług organy kontroli skarbowej wymierzyły należny podatek w kwotach: 2,3 mld zł w 2013 r., 5,2 mld zł w 2014 r., 4,9 mld zł w I półroczu 2015 r., a 12,0 mld zł w całym 2015 r. Wpłaty do budżetu w latach 2013–2014 i w I półroczu 2015 r. wyniosły zaledwie 162,3 mln zł, tj. 1,3 %*'

the '*Missing Traders*' constituted a necessarily step to go further down the chain of fraudulent transactions. To question legality of 'buffer's' VAT reclaim, Fiscal Control had to prove that the 'Missing Trader' failed to fulfill her obligation, or issued 'empty invoice'. In her view, Supreme Audit Office '*failed to grasp the mechanism of controlling VAT fraudulent chains*'.[25]

4.5. Real-time countermeasures: VAT returns and STIR blockages

Tax controls and financial controls remain – by design – backwards looking, in a sense that they aim at exposing frauds that had been already carried out, with a hope to recover the VAT liability from those involved. However, tax administration apparatus could also act in the real time, for example by blocking bogus claims for VAT reclaims – the cornerstone of the MTIC frauds. According to the (Ministry of Finance – 2014[26]), the data on VAT reclaims blocked as a result of Fiscal Controls had been recorded since 2011 (see Figure 4.5).

As visible on the chart, there was unprecedented action of VAT reclaims blockages in 2016 – as over PLN 1 billion of undue VAT reclaims had been blocked (according to the Appendix 1 Chapter 1, the overall VAT reclaims paid in 2016 amounted 93,5 PLN billion).

25 Polish quotation: '*stoósemki są potrzebne, ich wydanie, dla rozpracowania całego łańcucha. Bo to nie jest kontrola u pojedynczego podmiotu, tylko w momencie, kiedy robimy cały łańcuch, to musimy wydać stoósemkę, żeby pójść do kolejnego podmiotu i udowodnić mu wyłudzenie VAT-u … dla mnie było to krzywdzące* [konkluzje NIK]. *Tak to odbierałam – że to jest pewne niezrozumienie mechanizmu rozpracowywania i kontrolowania łańcuchów VAT-owskich … pierwsza decyzja jest wydawana u „słupa", … potem idziemy do bufora … Art. 108 jest wystawiany w przypadku pustych faktur. … on jest konieczny dla celów dowodowych, … Bufor zwraca się… o zwrot VAT-u w swoim rozliczeniu … żeby wykazać, że jego zwrot VAT-u jest nienależny, to ja muszę pokazać, że na tym pierwszym poziomie… była fałszywa faktura … One* [decyzje wobec 'słupów'] *są trudno ściągalne albo nieściągalne, ale dzięki temu jesteśmy w stanie przejść dalej do buforu w tym procesie*'.

26 Ministry of Finance, 2014, p. 3.

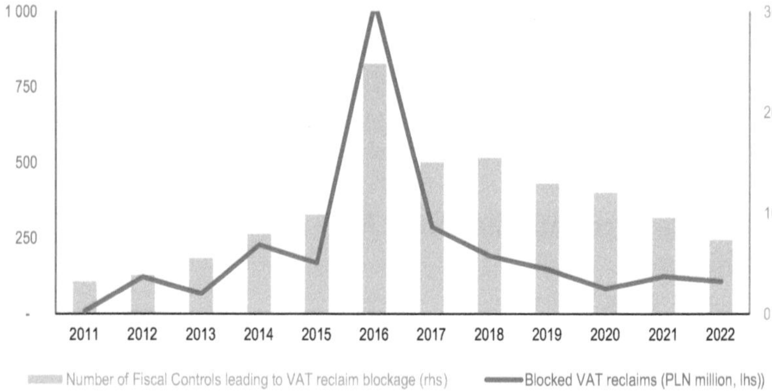

Figure 4.5. VAT reclaims blockages as a result of Fiscal Controls, 2011–2022

Sources: Data provided by the Ministry of Finance: in response to MP J. Cichoń inquiry no. 32784, VIII Term (Aug 29th 2019, DNK7.054.23.2019), and in response to author's public information request (Oct 4th 2023, BMI1.0123.2521.2023).

Another tool allowing tax administration apparatus real-time reaction to fraudulent activities is an ICT system maintained by the clearing houses – so called STIR system (Polish: '*System Teleinformatyczny Izby Rozliczeniowej*'). The mechanism aims at analysing the risk of using the activity of banks and credit unions for purposes associated with crime, in particular, VAT fraud by organised criminal groups and related crime (The Republic of Poland, 2017[27]). Importantly, it was introduced as part of legislative/ICT response to the 'VAT gap' crisis (see Chapter 5). Thereby it was unavailable to tax authorities prior to 2018, as MTIC frauds proliferated.

27 The Republic of Poland. (2017). Convergence Programme 2017 update, available at: https://commission.europa.eu/content/2017-european-semester-national-reform-programmes-and-stabilityconvergence-programmes_en (Accessed Oct. 31 2023), p. 66.

Table 4.1. STIR system blockages of bank/credit union accounts

	2018	2019	2020	2021	2022
Number of blockages*	23	120	196	261	267
Blocked monetary amount (PLN million)	10,2	69,7	96,2	100,9	77,4

*- In the Ministry of Finance in response to MP J. Cichoń inquiry no. 32784, VIII Term (Aug 29th 2019, DNK7.054.23.2019) the 2018 data on STIR had been described as follows 'W 2018 roku ustanowiono blokadę łącznie na 41 rachunkach bankowych należących do 23 podmiotów kwalifikowanych, na łączną kwotę 10 230 947,30 zł.'
Source: Data provided by the Ministry of Finance in response to author's public information request (Oct 4th 2023, BMI1.0123.2521.2023).

References

Gajewski D. J. (ed.) (2022). *Funkcjonowanie sądownictwa administracyjnego na tle zmian koniunktury gospodarczej: perspektywa ekonomicznej analizy prawa.* Warsaw: SGH University Press (in Polish).

Gajewski D. J., & Joński K. (2020). Country Note: Procedures of the Polish Tax Authorities and the VAT Gap: Evidence from Administrative Court Files, *Intertax*, 48(11), 1012–1019, https://kluwerlawonline.com/journalarticle/Intertax/48.11/TAXI2020102

Ministry of Finance. (2009). Sprawozdanie Kontrola Skarbowa w 2008 r.

Ministry of Finance. (2010). Sprawozdanie Kontrola Skarbowa w 2009 r.

Ministry of Finance. (2012). Sprawozdanie Kontrola Skarbowa w 2011 r.

Ministry of Finance. (2014). Sprawozdanie Kontrola Skarbowa w 2013 r.

Supreme Audit Office, NIK. (2016). Analiza wykonania budżetu państwa i założeń polityki pieniężnej w 2015 roku, available at: https://www.nik.gov.pl/analiza-budzetu-panstwa/archiwum/ (Accessed Oct. 31 2023).

The Republic of Poland. (2017). Convergence Programme 2017 Update, available at: https://commission.europa.eu/content/2017-european-semester-national-reform-programmes-and-stabilityconvergence-programmes_en (Accessed Oct. 31 2023).

Waśko J. (2017). Wszczynanie postępowań karnych skarbowych w trakcie postępowań kontrolnych – analiza praktyki wybranych urzędów kontroli skarbowej. *Przegląd Podatkowy*, 2017(2), 44–49.

Dominik J. Gajewski (SGH Warsaw School of Economics),
Marcin Kotlarz (SGH Warsaw School of Economics),
Adam Olczyk (SGH Warsaw School of Economics)

Chapter 5 Policy response – Legislative initiatives in the area of tax law

Abstract: When introducing tools for reducing the VAT gap, the legislator responded in different ways to the demands, made during and after the legislative process. The extent to which their interests and the goals of the normative changes made were actually coordinated, significantly affected the quality of the law and the stability of the imposed regulations.

Key words: VAT gap, tightening the tax system, legal instruments, legislation process, quality of tax law.

5.1. General comments

The growing problem of the VAT gap forced the legislature to adopt far-reaching changes to the tax system. These involved the introduction of tools both of a general nature (GAAR, MDR) and aimed only at correcting the existing solutions in the VAT. Some of them reached the structural foundations of VAT, others consisted of a significant modification of the rules for taxpayers to meet the obligations imposed on them, another involved the introduction of new obligations to use IT tools specifically designed to seal the tax system. The article shows how to implement four of these instruments, the most relevant considering the importance for the amount of budget revenues and their impact on the way taxpayers meet their VAT obligations.

The implementation of the tools discussed: split payment, fuel package, VAT sanctions and reporting in the format of a single control file (JPK), did not result from the obligation of minimum harmonization and did not require extensive coordination with EU authorities. However, these solutions are also not specifically Polish. Instruments with similar legal and economic characteristics operate in numerous EU member states, including countries in the Central and Eastern European region. Thus, the problems associated with their implementation in Poland have, in principle, a universal dimension, resulting from the importance of the decisions of the Court of Justice of the European Union (VAT sanction, fuel package), the guidelines of the European Commission (split payment), as well as related to the general specificity of the use of modern IT tools (JPK).

Some of these problems were identified even during the consultations held with the addressees of the tax law, resulting in varying responses from the legislature. The manner in which the legislature responded to the demands made during the legislative process and the extent to which it coordinated the interests of its participants significantly affected the quality of the law enacted as well as the need for its subsequent correction through the courts.

5.2. Split payment

5.2.1. Legal mechanism of split payment

The split payment mechanism stands out among the legal solutions to counter the VAT gap. For this regulation directly responds to particularly important occurrences, which were perceived as those that indeed led to the existence of such a large VAT gap in Poland over the years. This is because split payment responds to the basic type of VAT fraud, which is when a taxpayer does not pay VAT tax.

How does this mechanism work? Split payment is based on the fact that the tax paid by the buyer of a good or service goes into such a recipient's bank account, which that recipient cannot freely dispose of. The payment of the price for the good or service is split. The net amount goes directly to the seller, of course. On the contrary, the amount of tax is separated and transferred precisely to a special account. The situation of an untrustworthy taxpayer who is prevented from operating the received tax amount is much more difficult (if not impossible) in regard to the potential fraud he could commit.

Before indicating what a taxpayer can do with the amount in his VAT account, it is necessary to explain the essence of the bank account itself, into which tax payments are made. It is linked to the main bank account of the entrepreneur. The buyer of a good or service does not need to know this number, moreover, the VAT account does not need to be listed on the invoice or contract at all. The overbooking takes place in the bank's system itself. This additional tax account is created automatically when the entrepreneur sets up a main account in the Polish banking system. It is not paid additionally, there is no need to apply for it, it is created automatically. Already here the main concern associated with the adopted solution becomes evident – does it not restrict the EU prohibition on restricting the freedom to provide services, as specified in Article 56 TFEU[1]? This will be discussed later.

In whose interest is it to pay for transactions through split payment? To answer this question, it should be noted that the Polish legislator distinguishes two situations under which the split payment mechanism is used:

1. voluntary
2. mandatory.

Re. 1.

In the first case, the use of payment of tax through split payment, may give certain benefits primarily to the buyer of the good or service. This is because the payment of tax using this mechanism will confirm that the buyer has taken steps to fulfill due diligence. In the event that the tax authority questions the right to reduce input VAT, the reference to the fact that the payment was made using split payment will be important evidence confirming due diligence.

Re. 2.

Mandatory split payment, on the other hand, is in the interest of the general public, or, more precisely, in the interest of the state treasury. This is because it is part of the tightening of the tax system.

In this context, it should be noted that the special role of mandatory split payment is manifest in the fact that it applies to those sectors that are considered particularly 'sensitive' when it comes to tightening the tax system. It covers transactions of the kind for which studies have shown that the risk of vat fraud is particularly high. This is precisely the measure that strikes directly at 'suspicious' sectors. In such a case, the application of split payment is mandatory. Importantly, it does not apply to all transactions, but those whose value exceeds PLN 15,000. Such a legislative decision is a manifestation of the use of safe harbour, which is in general characteristic of the processes of tightening the tax system and fighting the VAT gap. The Polish legislator unequivocally refrains from taxing those transactions that are of little significance in the perspective of the entire budget (as well as the VAT gap). A similar decision was made regarding the transfer pricing regulation, where the obligation to prepare transfer pricing documentation and conduct a transfer pricing analysis depends on whether the

---

1 European Union, *Consolidated version of the Treaty on the Functioning of the European Union*, 26 October 2012, OJ L. 326/47-326/390; 26.10.2012 (hereinafter cited as 'TFUE').

value of the controlled transaction exceeds the required amount, or whether it is related to loans.

What types of transactions are listed in the regulations that obligate transactions through split payment? The regulation[2] lists here, for example, the following types of benefits related to:

- trade in steel
- trade in fuels
- construction services
- coal and coal products
- electrical machinery and equipment
- parts and accessories for motor vehicles.

If the split payment system is not applied, the participants in the transaction risk the application of a vat sanction, which leads to the determination of an additional amount of tax liability.

5.2.2. Legislative process

In the case of split payment, we had a particularly interesting legislative process, during which a number of issues related to its implementation were taken into account.

First of all, it should be noted that the legislative process required the approval of EU bodies, since the split payment mechanism is a derogation from the legal regulation provided for by the EU Council Directive[3]. Remarkably, the application of the split payment method itself did not require a derogation decision. This is because there is no treaty norm that would explicitly prohibit such a method of booking. However, the following issues turned out to be disputed:

(a) the imposition of an obligation on the supplier of goods or services to enter on the invoice information that the tax must be paid to a special VAT account;
(b) the question of the prohibition of restrictions on the freedom to provide services under Article 56 TFEU in connection with the obligation to establish a bank account with a Polish bank.

2 Annex No. 15 to the VAT Act (Journal of Laws of 201, item 1751).
3 Council Directive 2006/112/EC of 28 November 2006 on the common system of value added tax ('VAT Directive').

Secondly, extensive consultations were held in the legislative process, which led to the fact that, as a result, the final wording of the regulation took into account the voices of representatives of various industries who spoke out during the drafting of the legislation.

Third, the legal regulation of split payment affected not only tax law, but also banking law. Therefore, it required prior action, which would adequately respond to the problems raised in this industry.

The above resulted in the need to coordinate the legislative process on split payment in different spaces.

5.2.3. Coordination at the EU level

The Polish legislator has recognized that the implementation of split payment into the national legal system is a derogation from Article 395 of the VAT Directive, which states that 'The Council, acting unanimously on a proposal from the Commission, may authorise any Member State to introduce special measures for derogation from the provisions of this Directive, in order to simplify the procedure for collecting VAT or to prevent certain forms of tax evasion or avoidance'.

While the separation of the price into two amounts by itself does not contradict the Directive, the use of split payment leads to the obligation to include a special note on the invoice about the need to pay VAT into a separate and blocked VAT bank account of the supplier/service provider opened in Poland (if the transaction involves goods and services that are listed in the Annex). Article 226 of the VAT Directive, meanwhile, lists the mandatory elements of an invoice. The addition of an obligatory element, which taxpayers will always have to include on the invoice, required the approval of the Council of the European Union.

In view of the above, in May 2018 Poland submitted a derogation request. By Council Executive Decision 2019/310 of February 18, 2019, Poland received the necessary approval. At the same time, Poland was required to submit a report on the impact of split payment 18 months after its implementation. Poland submitted the report on April 29, 2021. The above Decision was effective until February 28, 2022. By Council Executive Decision 2022/559 of April 5, 2022, the deadline was extended to February 28, 2025.

Remarkably, paragraph 8 of the February 18, 2019 Decision stated that suppliers/service suppliers will not bear the cost of opening and operating a VAT bank account, as the VAT account is to be maintained by the bank without any commission or fees.

This objection corresponds to the concerns expressed by the European Commission in the process of coordination. In a letter dated June 27, 2018. The European Commission stated: 'the obligation for the non-established taxable persons supplying goods subject to the SPM to open a bank account with a bank in Poland would constitute a restriction of the freedom to provide services and, thus, would be contrary to Article 56 TFEU. Even though such a requirement would apply to both, taxable persons established in Poland and non-established taxable persons, it would lead to an indirect discrimination of non-established taxable persons because they would not be allowed to indicate their foreign accounts for the payments of the VAT amounts by their customers'[4].

In a letter dated July 4, 2018, the Polish Ministry of Finance sent a letter to the European Commission confirming the absence of fees that would be required of taxpayers. Moreover, in the same letter, it was the Ministry that proposed to enter an appropriate reservation in this regard in the derogation decision.

5.2.4. Coordination at the national level

5.2.4.1. Discourse with taxpayers

The introduction of mandatory split payment into the Polish legal system was preceded by a long process, which included extensive consultations. This process should be considered positively. First, the response from those interested in the change in question was widespread. Second, many of these views were taken into account.

During the consultation process, some parties involved pointed, for example, to the lack of regulation of the system of offsetting mutual claims (the question was if it is possible to simply set off the counter-claim in case the law provides for the mandatory application of split payment)[5]. As six independent entities representing various industries pointed out, this was very important to clarify because in sectors where split payment is mandatory (e.g., the construction industry), it is a very common method of payment. This issue was clarified by the Polish legislator in the final version of the introduced regulation, generally excluding the obligation to use split payment in such a process.

---

4 Own materials sourced from the Ministry of Finance.

5 *Justification of the draft law amending the VAT law*, dated July 9, 2019, Print no. 3602, orka.sejm.gov.pl/Druki8ka.nsf/0/AD1A072C72B0F1CCC1258432005D0DBA/%24File/3602.pdf, p. 17 (Accessed Oct. 31, 2023).

Entrepreneurs also pointed to the common practice of issuing advance invoices, which the draft regulation did not stipulate. The legislator took these demands into account and included in the draft law a provision allowing advance payments to be made under the split payment system even before receiving the invoice.

It was interesting to see how the legislator reacted to the postulates concerning the limit on joint and several liability of the buyer, initially set at PLN 12,000 in the first draft. In view of the doubts pointed out in this regard by the business community – including such voices that called for raising this limit to the amount of, for example, PLN 50,000 – the legislator decided to abandon any limits in this field. Accordingly, the split payment regulation is applicable, in cases of joint and several liability of the buyer, at any amount.

A few considerations concerned sanctions related to the application (or non-application) of split payment. In this case, also some of the comments were taken into account. The most important issue concerns the amount of the sanction. In fact, in the process of working on the law, the amount of the sanction was reduced from being 100 % to 30 % of the transaction. The legislator also took into account the voices of the business community and introduced a catalog of situations in which the sanction will not apply.

The last change we want to point out concerned linking the split payment obligation to an invoice and not a transaction. A large number of participants pointed out the problems that could arise if the legal regulation would use the term 'transaction' – as originally planned – and not an 'invoice'. The question arose how to treat the situation when a taxpayer makes transactions with one business partner, in which he sells the same goods, 3 times in one month, and the total amount exceeds the limit of PLN 15,000? In the context of sanctions, implemented as part of the tightening of the tax system, this type of doubt was strongly justified. In addition, the situation was not facilitated by the fact that the concept of 'transaction' has for years caused various practical problems, including on the basis of other laws (for example, in the transfer pricing regulation). Therefore, the law on split payment introduced requirements that are related to the amount appearing on the invoice.

5.2.4.2. Discourse with banks

The taxpayer's obligation to have a VAT account in a Polish bank is corresponded to the obligation of Polish banks to create such a mechanism. The creation of the possibility to keep such an account had to be free of charge for entrepreneurs. As we have noted, such an obligation resulted from the arrangements made with the

European Commission and was also included in paragraph 8 of the Derogation Decision.

It should therefore come as no surprise that banks have reacted critically to being given such an obligation[6]. The Union of Polish Banks has presented extensive arguments in this regard. The union argued that the implementation of such an obligation on the part of banks is incompatible with the Constitution of the Republic of Poland. In its view, the adoption of such a regulation violates the principle of economic freedom and introduces obligations for banks that are not justified by valid reasons. The union's arguments even indicate that such action by the legislature reflects an action that is characteristic of a socialist economy, in which the market is centrally controlled. The union also stressed that the regulation in question does not take into account the fact that banks are autonomous economic entities, independent of the state, which cannot shoulder the burden of fighting the VAT gap. It pointed out that in the case of other countries that use the split payment mechanism, the account is state-owned and run by state authorities. In addition, the planned regulation was also expected to conflict with the Banking Law itself. This is because the Polish law explicitly indicates that banks are authorized to charge commissions on activities, and the split payment regulation circumvents this requirement.

The answer posted in the draft law was very brief, but at the same time very meaningful. The draftsman stated: 'Note taken into account. The justification will be modified on the constitutionality of the proposed regulations'[7].

The draft law briefly refers to the problem of costs that banks will bear in connection with the introduction of split payment. The relevant section of the draft law, which requires such information, states: 'Taking into account the huge diversity of IT systems operating in financial institutions, the different level of their expansion and, for example, the ability of some of these institutions to adapt them to the projected requirements within their own resources, and additionally, in the case of making changes to the systems by external entities, it is not possible to accurately estimate the cost of adaptation to the obligations indicated in the

---

6 These comments were made at an earlier stage than the sections of the draft cited earlier, which concerned mandatory split payment. The banks' comments on the obligation to create VAT accounts were already expressed at the level of the creation of the law, which introduced optional split payment. *Justification of the draft law amending the VAT law,* dated September 7, 2017, Print no. 1864, https://orka.sejm.gov.pl/Druki8ka.nsf/0/1F1EC57451D0A351C12581A90046A10E/%24File/1864.pdf. (Accessed Oct. 31, 2023).

7 Idem, p. 103.

draft law. Therefore, without knowing the scale of such costs, assuming that the average one-time cost of adapting IT systems is in the order of PLN 3 million for each financial institution, it can be indicated that financial institutions will incur total costs in the order of PLN 1905 million'[8].

At the same time, it was pointed out that it is not possible to estimate in monetary terms the costs of financial institutions associated with the day-to-day handling of VAT accounts.

Comments regarding the cost of making transfers have been taken into account. The project proponent assumed that the draft would be modified so that making transfers from VAT accounts would not involve fees higher than traditional transfers.

During the legislative process on mandatory split payment, various parties – including those representing Polish banks – raised concerns about ensuring adequate vacatio legis for the law. It was pointed out that banks must reprocess according to their internal regulations, have time to inform customers of the change in regulations, etc. All such comments were met with a response indicating that the effective date indicated in the draft law is due to the need to urgently implement Council Implementing Decision (EU) 2019/310 of February 18, 2019, which was issued for a particular period (from March 1, 2019 to February 28, 2022).

5.3. Fuel package

5.3.1. The requirement to consult on introduced laws

An telling example that demonstrates how a lack of proper coordination of the legislative process can lead to the introduction of a regulation that ultimately turned out to be flawed is how the so-called fuel package was introduced into Polish law. It was introduced by a government draft, and therefore did not require arrangements at the consultation level. It should be noted that the lack of consultation of draft laws has been criticized in Poland for years as a sign of very bad lawmaking practices.

It is worth noting that over the years the Constitutional Court has created in Poland standards of appropriate form for legislative acts[9]. Among the rulings of

---

8 Idem, p. 8.

9 Urbańska K., *Diagnoza systemu stanowienia prawa w Polsce z punktu widzenia organizacji pracodawców*, prezydent.pl, https://www.prezydent.pl/storage/file/core_files/2021/8/9/6c90b00587f734f247a6ce46bd9b0a78/02urbanska_katarzyna_slabosc_systemu_diagnoza.pdf. (Accessed Oct. 31, 2023).

the Constitutional Court, there were considerations of allegations that indicated that there was a violation of the statutory procedure for issuing a normative act in that the opportunity for the expression of opinions by relevant, interested parties was not provided. Such an obligation rests, according to the Constitutional Court, on the lawmaking authority[10]. In its rulings, the Court stressed that consultation must not be formal, but must be real. Consultation should take place first and foremost at the level of work on the bill, before it even gets to the Parliament.

Creating a law through a project that comes from the government avoids the process of consulting with those who may be concerned by the changes. Meanwhile, as the consultation process on split payment has shown, such agreements are often crucial for the resulting regulation to present an appropriately high level.

5.3.2. Regulation of the fuel package

Pursuant to Article 103(5a) of the Law on Tax on Goods and Services of 11.3.2004 (i.e., Journal of Laws of 2022, item 931; hereinafter: VATU), in the case of the intra-Community acquisition of fuels, the taxpayer is obliged, without a summons from the head of the tax office, to calculate and pay the amounts of tax to the account of the tax office competent for the payment of excise tax, within 5 days from the date on which the goods were introduced into the place of receipt or into the tax warehouse specified in the relevant permit. According to Article 17a of VATU, the payer of tax on The intra-Community acquisition of fuels is the registered recipient or tax warehouse operator, respectively, making the intra-Community acquisition of such fuel on behalf of another entity.

This regulation was introduced into Polish law as part of the so-called fuel package. The regulations came into force on August 1, 2016. It should be emphasized here the speed at which the regulation in question was introduced. The draft was submitted to the Sejm on May 31, 2016. – i.e. it became mandatory 3 months after it was unveiled in the Parliament.

The purpose of this regulation was to tighten the VAT system in Poland with regard to the fuel industry, in which carousel fraud was particularly prevalent[11].

---

10 These include the following judgments of the Constitutional Court: of June 16, 1986, U 3/86; of April 20, 1993, U 12/92; of October 19, 1993, K 14/92; of November 30, 1993, K 18/92; of April 4, 1995, K 10/94; of November 19, 1996, K 7/95.

11 Kieszkowski W., *Płatnik ma obowiązek zapłaty VAT z tytułu WNT paliwa*, Legalis.pl. (Accessed Oct. 31, 2023).

As the authors dealing with this problem pointed out, this topic was also widely discussed in the rulings of the Supreme Administrative Court[12]. In its ruling of December 11, 2018, I FSK 1919/16, this court mentioned the requirements for special diligence to be exercised when entering into transactions in this industry: 'In the opinion of the Supreme Administrative Court, the Company at least could have anticipated the occurrence of fraud. The court of first instance rightly noted that the Company had experienced personnel in the production and commercial, financial and economic, and tax fields, in which appropriate procedures governing the rules of obtaining contractors and entering into transactions had been developed and were in force, and at the very least could have anticipated the occurrence of tax fraud risks occurring in the fuel industry'[13].

The justification for the draft of this law extensively pointed to frauds in the fuel industry. It was pointed out, for example, that the size of the zone in which taxes are not paid in fuel trading is estimated at 10–18 %, and losses to the state budget at PLN 2.5–5 billion per year[14]. The following excerpt from the justification of the project (available under the so-called Government Legislation Center) is significant: after indicating the above amounts, which confirm that the fuel package could indeed affect part of the budget, the draftsman listed the following entities concerned by the regulation:

- entities trading liquid fuels with foreign countries
- tax warehouses and registered consignees making service purchases of motor fuels on behalf of other entities under the excise duty suspension procedure
- customs offices.

While in point 5 of the project's explanatory memorandum there is a section 'Information on the scope, duration and summary of the results of the consultations'[15]. It is noted here that: 'The draft law was subjected to a separate procedure, excluding inter-ministerial consultations'[16].

12 Idem.

13 Available at https://orzeczenia.nsa.gov.pl/.

14 *Justification of the draft law amending the VAT law,* dated May 31, 2016, Print no. 554, https://orka.sejm.gov.pl/Druki8ka.nsf/0/6B73214F66D4EA16C1257FC5003BAD98/%24File/554.pdf, p. 1. (Accessed Oct. 31, 2023).

15 Idem, p. 3.

16 Idem.

5.3.3. CJEU judgment 9.9.2021 in case C-855/19

In the aforementioned judgment, the CJEU stated that regulations of EU law do not allow the imposition in national law of such an obligation to pay VAT on the intra-Community acquisition of goods, which would occur before the due date of the tax itself:

> *Consequently, in view of the fact that the possibility of collecting interim payments pursuant to the second sentence of Article 206 of the VAT Directive allows Member States to bring forward not the date on which VAT becomes chargeable, but only the date of payment of VAT that has already become chargeable, that provision must be interpreted as precluding a provision of the law of a Member State which requires payment of VAT before it has become chargeable pursuant to Article 69 of that directive.*
>
> *That conclusion cannot be called into question by Article 273 of the VAT Directive, which states that, subject to compliance with certain conditions listed in that provision, Member States may impose any other obligations which they deem necessary to ensure the correct collection of VAT and to prevent evasion. While Member States enjoy a discretion as to the means of achieving those objectives, they are nevertheless required to exercise their powers in this area in accordance with EU law (see, to that effect, judgment of 15 April 2021, Grupa Warzywna, C-935/19, EU:C:2021:287, paragraphs 25 and 26 and the case-law cited).*

It should be noted that the judgment did not discourage the Polish legislator, who introduced legal changes effective as of December 28, 2021 with regard to the regulation that was negatively considered by the CJEU.

According to the current wording of the regulation, if the deadline for payment of tax determined in a manner appropriate to the intra-Community acquisition of fuel is on a date earlier than the date of issuance of an invoice by a taxpayer of value added tax, documenting the supply of goods which are the subject of intra-Community acquisition, the deadline expires on the day following the date of issuance of this invoice, but no later than the 16th day of the month following the month of making the supply of goods which are the subject of intra-Community acquisition.

Towards this regulation, it is also pointed out that it shows some deficiencies and is not clear in its interpretation.

The question is whether such 'partial' fixing of the regulation by the Polish legislator corresponds to the high standards of legislation set by the CJEU.

5.4. VAT sanction

5.4.1. The essence of the solution and the legal status

The so-called VAT sanction (mechanism of additional tax liability) consists in linking the burden of the sanction to the amount of tax not shown in the tax return and not paid, or to the amount of the difference between the amount of tax due and the tax resulting from the amounts erroneously declared. The occurrence of any of the above circumstances is associated with the determination by the authority of the amount of additional liability. In Polish legal order, this sanction is primarily intended to serve a preventive function and influence the correctness of taxpayers' compliance with their reporting obligations.

According to the current regulations, the basic rate according to which the size of the sanction is determined is 30 % of the difference between the amount that should be shown in the return and paid to the budget and the amount not shown and not paid, or erroneously shown in the return. The legislator also specified the prerequisites for waiving the VAT sanction or determining its amount according to increased and reduced rates. Thus, sanctions are not applied when the error in the declaration is the result of an obvious mistake or the declaration was self-corrected and the tax due was paid before the initiation of control proceedings. Reduced rates of up to 15 % and up to 20 % will apply in cases where the taxpayer takes into account the results of the audit, submits the correct declaration or its correction, and pays the missing amount of tax due before and after the completion of the audit proceedings, respectively. On the other hand, if intentional irregularities are found, the authority will apply a 100 % rate.

The VAT sanction is not an obligatory instrument in the EU member states. Its validity is based on Article 273 of the VAT Directive[17], according to which Member States may impose such other obligations as they deem necessary to ensure the correct collection of VAT and to prevent tax fraud, provided that domestic transactions and transactions between Member States by taxpayers are treated equally, and provided that these obligations, in trade between Member States, do not lead to border-crossing formalities.

The validity of the instrument of additional tax liability in national legislation is therefore not directly dependent on the specific regulations of European law and the extent to which they are modified by the European legislator. Nevertheless, the functioning of the VAT sanction raised far-reaching doubts in Poland as to its compliance with European regulations, related to the assessment of its legal nature and the compliance of detailed regulations with the basic principles of European law. Consequently, the functioning of this instrument in Poland was subject to significant changes, resulting, among other things, from the reaction of the Polish legislator to the anticipated and actual rulings of the Court of Justice

---

17 Council Directive 2006/112/EC of 28 November 2006 on the common system of value added tax (*OJ L 347, 11.12.2006, p. 1–118*).

of the European Union, which in subsequent rulings clarified the prerequisites for the admissibility of this solution. The boundary conditions thus defined may affect the laws of numerous member states, which use tools of similar economic importance and similar legal characteristics.

5.4.2. The origins of the VAT sanction and the rationale for its removal from the tax law

The VAT sanction was introduced in the provisions of the Polish VAT Act back in 1993. Its functioning raised numerous objections from the beginning, among others in connection with the amount of the additional liability (which initially reached 500 %) as well as because of the automaticity, with which taxpayers were charged with the sanction. Indeed, the construction of this instrument obliged tax authorities to establish VAT sanctions regardless of the reasons for irregularities in tax returns. Determination of sanctions was obligatory also in the case of errors that did not bear the signs of fraud, but resulted, for example, from frequent changes in tax regulations. Despite the fact, that the amount of the sanction was significantly reduced after several years, and from 1997 it was already 30 %[18], the legislator did not change the rules for its determination, and still its imposition was independent of the circumstances behind the irregularities. The peculiar radicalism of this solution caused the appearance of equally far-reaching initiatives, aimed at the complete removal of VAT sanctions from the legal order. The government's project to completely remove this tool from the tax law was submitted in 2006, along with a package of solutions aimed at removing regulations hindering entrepreneurship and simplifying the tax system[19]. The legislative process that began was interrupted with the shortening of the term of the then parliament.

The postulate to abolish VAT sanctions returned in the next parliamentary term, with the emergence of new jurisprudential arguments, linked to the need to adapt the Polish legal system to the provisions of European law. The justification of the parliamentary project for the liquidation of the additional tax liability of March 2008 is very laconic in this regard and *de facto* only describes

18 Kańtor K., & Wróblewska K., *Powrót sankcji w VAT*, Przegląd Podatkowy 2017/1, pp. 20–27, Lex/el. (Accessed Oct. 31, 2023).

19 Explanatory Memorandum of the government draft of June 26, 2006 on amendments to the Law on Goods and Services Tax and certain other laws, print 734, p. 12; Information of July 7, 2019, on the results of the audit 'Supervision of the Minister of Finance over the collection of goods and services tax', Supreme Audit Office, p. 28

the subject of the changes, without referring to their *ratio legis*[20]. Nevertheless, the actual reasons for this initiative were seen in the fact that in July 2007, the Supreme Administrative Court referred a preliminary question to the Court of Justice of the European Communities, which indicated numerous doubts about the compatibility of this solution with EU law[21]. In justifying its conclusion, the referring court noted that a tax liability, despite being a certain type of sanction, has all the characteristics of a tax liability under Polish law. Classification of the VAT sanction in this way, as a type of turnover tax, on the other hand, makes it possible to assess the admissibility of this tool through the prism of the features of an additional liability, determined by the tax authority. The doubts that arose in this regard seemed to support the imminent removal of the VAT sanction from legal circulation. This is because the sanction burdened not the consumer, but the taxpayer, and was not proportional to the price of the goods or services. Its determination also did not take into account the nature and gravity of the violation, including the basic circumstance – whether there was a depletion of tax revenues and whether it could be said that a tax crime had been committed in the case. The weight and scope of the cassation court's doubts, as well as the court's position, which did not raise a significant interpretive controversy, *de facto* favoring the recognition of the VAT sanction as a type of tax, caused the legislature to react and remove this tool from the law, under the Law of November 7, 2008[22].

Meanwhile, in its Judgment C-502/07 from January 15, 2009, the ECJ classified the additional tax liability differently, considering it an administrative sanction rather than a type of tax or fee. Indeed, according to the ECJ, an error in the tax return is not an activity of the taxpayer, the subject of which are goods or services, nor is the amount of the additional liability determined in proportion to the price received by the taxpayer. Thus, the VAT sanction does not have the necessary characteristics of VAT, and therefore does not contradict the principle of a common VAT system and can be imposed on value-added taxpayers, pursuant to Article 22(8) of the Sixth VAT Directive[23].

---

20 Explanatory Memorandum to the parliamentary bill of March 12, 2008 on amendments to the Law on Value Added Tax and certain other laws, print 661, p. 11.

21 Kańtor K., & Wróblewska K., *Powrót sankcji…*; *op.cit.*; Supreme Administrative Court's order of July 31, 2007 to refer a preliminary question in case I FSK 1062/06.

22 Pursuant to the Law of November 7, 2008 amending the Law on Value Added Tax (Journal of Laws of 2008, No. 209, item 1320).

23 ECJ Judgment of January 15, 2009, C-502/07, *K-1*, ECLI:EU:C:2009:11, pts 19, 20 and 28.

Preventive adjustment of legislation to the expected content of the Court's ruling is a rare way, in any case in tax law, of harmonizing national laws. Its result did not turn out to be satisfactory, due to the legislature's acceptance of the arguments of one of the parties to the dispute over the legal nature of this instrument, despite the existing controversies, including the divergent positions of the judicature[24]. As a result, the doubts expressed by the cassation court were too hastily considered as a proxy for the European court's decision and the existing legislative solutions were withdrawn. Such action of the legislator, as it seems, can be explained by the then tendency to liberalize regulations, formed in developed countries in the period preceding the financial crisis of 2008, and by the corresponding direction of political changes in Poland[25]. In subsequent years, however, the legislator has already shown much greater assertiveness in the face of judicature's views and the objections of direct participants in the legislative process, involved in the work on the reintroduction of VAT sanctions.

5.4.3. Sealing the tax system and returning to VAT sanctions

The reinstatement of VAT sanctions in the provisions of the Value Added Tax Law came along with the adoption of a number of other legislative solutions aimed at sealing the tax system and curbing fraud. In particular, the priority was to combat the problem of so-called carousel transactions, significantly affecting the amount and stability of tax revenues. The VAT sanction, introduced into the Value Added Tax Law on January 1, 2017, was intended to complement the basic solutions for countering abuses related to the use of the so-called 'disappearing taxpayer' mechanism (especially the reverse charge mechanism). To this end, in addition to the reinstatement of the previously used instrument of VAT sanction, applicable in the case of incorrect filing of the tax return or failure to file it, a new type of sanction of 100 %, determined in cases of the taxpayer's participation in certain types of tax fraud, was introduced. Both of the above solutions became the subject of criticism even at the stage of project work.

---

24 In its judgment of April 29, 1998, K 17/97, Polish Constitutional Court considered additional tax liability to be a type of administrative sanction. The Supreme Administrative Court took a similar position in Resolution (7) I FPS 2/06 of October 16, 2006.

25 In 2007, a party declaring a retreat from statist tendencies and the deregulation of the economy took political power in Poland following snap elections.

5.4.4. Increased rate of VAT sanctions

In the course of the legislative process, objections were raised especially with regard to the new type of sanction, burdening taxpayers with very harsh consequences in the event of showing in the tax return an invoice documenting fictitious turnover: issued by a non-existent entity, documenting actions not carried out, sham actions or containing amounts inconsistent with reality. This is because the proposed, and subsequently adopted, provisions in the VAT law provided for the establishment of an additional liability of 100 % of the value of the improperly reported tax, regardless of the taxpayer's lack of awareness that he was participating in an illegal transaction. This resulted in imposing the negative consequences of the transaction also on taxpayers who are, in fact, victims and not perpetrators of tax fraud. In such a situation, the functioning of the market is significantly disrupted. Indeed, taxpayers may choose solutions less favorable to themselves and more favorable to the interests of the Treasury, for fear of sanctions[26]. In the course of legislative work, business sector organizations even alleged that such far-reaching solutions are the result of indolence of the tax authorities, which, unable to hold accountable the actual organizers of carousel scams, shift the responsibility to honest taxpayers who had the misfortune of unknowingly becoming a participant in the chain of empty transactions[27]. Avoiding such a situation, on the other hand, is particularly difficult when operating on a large scale[28]. For the above reasons, the authors of the objections called for the introduction of an explicit provision that the proposed sanction will not be applied to taxpayers acting without fraudulent intent, in good faith.

These demands were implemented by the legislator at best half-heartedly, in an unusual and additionally flawed legislative technique. This is because the proposed legislation was not amended, but the non-legislative explanatory memorandum of the law was. As stated in response to one of the objections, the justification '*has been supplemented, as a result of which it has been indicated unequivocally, as this was the intention of the drafters from the beginning, that (…) increased sanctions will not be applied to taxpayers participating in such transactions unknowingly, i.e. acting in good faith. The jurisprudence of national*

26 Comments on the draft amendment law, submitted by the Polish Union of Steel Distributors, 3.10.2016, p. 2.

27 Comments on the draft amendment law, submitted by Związek Cyfrowa Polska, 19.10.2016, pp. 7–8.

28 Comments on the draft amendment law, submitted by the 'Lewiatan' employers' organizations, 3.10.2016, p. 12.

courts and the CJEU in this area will be fully applicable. Hence, allegations of violation of the principle of proportionality or automatism of the proposed solution should be considered unjustified'[29]. The way in which the justification of the draft was modified, including the declarations to adapt the tax authorities' interpretation of the provision to the jurisprudence of national courts and the CJEU, was undoubtedly consistent with the demands of business organizations. Nevertheless, this detached the letter of the provision from the purpose of the regulation, as described in the justification of the draft law. Such a method of lawmaking is contrary to the applicable regulations, according to which the provisions of a law are drafted in such a way that they express the intentions of the legislator accurately and in a manner understandable to the addressees of the norms they contain[30]. The above violation of the principles of legislative technique was not only formal. Leaving the letter of the provision unchanged while at the same time introducing new key criteria for determining VAT sanctions in the justification of the bill, reduced the transparency of the law being created and did not remove sources of uncertainty as to how it would be applied. Such a result is due to the obvious fact that the addressees of the solutions in question are not (only) qualified specialists, but taxpayers in general, most of whom usually do not have an in-depth knowledge of the documents, produced in the course of the legislative process, and which do not constitute a source of law. The majority of taxpayers are also usually not willing to challenge the decisions of tax authorities in court. For the above reasons, the described method of lawmaking may even indicate an intention to subjectively limit the repressiveness of the created regulations to as narrow a circle of addressees as possible, effectively extending the regulation more relative to taxpayers only to the circles most aware of the actual state of the law.

It is also noteworthy that in the amended explanatory memorandum to the bill, the drafters equated the category of the taxpayer's good faith not with the absence of fraudulent intent, but with the lack of awareness of participating in a fictitious transaction. The reason for the taxpayer's lack of awareness, on the other hand, may also be the lack of due diligence in verifying and assessing the legal nature of the transaction he is entering into. Indeed, such a premise for the determination of the increased sanction was adopted and approved by

29 Response of the Ministry of Finance of 15.11.2016 to the comments of the Business Centre Club, p. 4.

30 Article 6 of the Regulation of the Prime Minister of June 20, 2002 on 'Principles of Legislative Techniques' (Journal of Laws of 2016, item 283).

numerous courts, including the court of cassation[31]. Thus, the reason for the determination of an increased and highly obnoxious sanction could also be errors resulting from insufficient attention, or poor knowledge of the taxpayer, and not necessarily intentional actions. Such a result, it seems, can be considered as intended by the legislator. Indeed, leaving the restrictive letter of the provision, which does not contain the prerequisites for a more relative assessment of the taxpayer's actions, is an additional and clear signal to the judicature that the intention of the legislator is relevant to the content of the provision to make the introduced solutions repressive.

5.4.5. Basic VAT sanction rate

Regardless of the new tool of increased VAT sanction to 100 %, the proposed legislation reinstated the mechanism for sanctioning cases of erroneous filing of the tax return or failure to file the return and pay the amount of the tax liability. As before, the amount of the basic VAT sanction was 30 %. This time, however, provision was also made for the introduction of tools to differentiate the severity of this sanction from the taxpayer's behaviour. The possibility of differentiating the amount of additional tax liability was intended to stimulate taxpayers to quickly correct errors. This was to express the preventive role of this instrument in combating the growing number of irregularities and their negative fiscal consequences. To this end, it was envisaged to reduce the base amount of the sanction from 30 % to 20 % and then also to 15 %[32], when the taxpayer corrects the VAT return on his own and eliminates the irregularities, after the completion of the tax inspection and after the commencement of the inspection and before its completion, respectively. Also excluded is the setting of sanctions in cases of obvious errors, i.e., especially accounting and clerical mistakes: resulting, for example, from improper completion of the declaration fields or the omission or

---

31 In its December 8, 2022 ruling I FSK 1561/22, the Supreme Administrative Court stated that the prerequisite for the application of the increased sanction is the conscious use of an invoice documenting actions not performed, or the use of such an invoice when knowledge of such a nature of the document can be obtained with reasonable diligence. Otherwise, ruled the Regional Administrative Court in Warsaw in its judgment III SA/Wa 66/20 of September 30, 2020, that the sanction in question should not be applied to taxpayers who were merely caught up in a tax fraud (the authorities did not prove their conscious participation in the fraud, but only their failure to exercise due diligence in verifying the counterparty).

32 Article 112b paragraph 2a added by Article 1 item 25(b) of the Act of July 4, 2019 (Journal of Laws of 2019, item 1520), amending the present act as of September 1, 2019.

substitution of digits in the declared figures[33]. Sanctions are also not applied if the taxpayer corrects the errors himself before the tax audit begins.

Despite the relatively greater flexibility of the new solutions, the instrument of the basic VAT sanction also became the subject of reservations raised during the legislative process. This is because the introduced solutions allowed to adjust the weight of the sanctions to the manner and speed of the taxpayer's reaction to the ongoing audit proceedings, while they did not allow to individualize the sanctions imposed by the tax authority and take into account the circumstances of a given case, including the reasons for the erroneous completion of the tax return. Exceptions were made for obvious minor errors made by the taxpayer or for the taxpayer's own correction of irregularities. Thus, the relative automaticity of this solution put a question mark over the possibility of preserving the principle of proportionality and the realization of the intentions declared by the legislator, who introduced the VAT sanction not as an instrument of repression, but of prevention, with the aim of increasing the degree of diligence of taxpayers in fulfilling their reporting obligations. Both the principle of proportionality and the above ratio legis, on the other hand, require that the burden of the sanction be adjusted to the circumstances of the particular case and that the tax authorities be able to take into account, when determining the amount of the sanction, the fact that the error may be of an excusable nature, such as the degree of complexity of the regulations. As has been pointed out, such mistakes can occur especially in cases that are juridically ambiguous, subject to interpretation or resolution by the tax authority or court proceedings. In international transactions, the risk of mistakes involves reporting tax on activities that are either exempt or not subject to VAT in other countries. Especially in these cases, caused by an error as to the legal status, the amount of the mandatory sanction imposed by the authority will not affect the achievement of the legislator's goal, will not convince taxpayers of greater diligence in completing returns and will not increase the degree of reliability of the data received by the authority.

Stakeholders participating in the legislative process aptly pointed out that the above-mentioned ECJ ruling C-502/07 of January 15, 2009, indicated by the proponent as one of the premises justifying the reinstatement of the VAT sanction[34], by no means closes the discussion on the admissibility of this

33 Letter from the Ministry of Finance PTI.8100.4.2016.LJU.200, dated November 15, 2016, responding to comments made on the draft law.

34 Draft of 22.09.2016 on amendments to the Law on Value Added Tax and some other laws, p. 24.

instrument, taking into account the need to take into account the principle of proportionality[35]. Moreover, since the new solutions are to refer to the previously applied ones, it would be appropriate to consider taking into account the jurisprudence issued on the basis of the previous legislation[36]. Meanwhile, the failure to take into account the reasons for the irregularity in determining the additional tax liability (even if it arose as a result of mistake, negligence, misinterpretation of the provision) has been questioned in case law as violating the principle of proportionality. These theses were formulated already in the first decade of the 21st century. For example, in the judgment III SA/Wa 159/07 of 29.05.2007, the administrative court abandoned its application on the grounds that this VAT sanction, imposed in connection with errors in declaring tax, does not meet the requirements of the principle of proportionality, which is a general principle of European Community law[37]. Reservations regarding the lack of compliance with the principle of proportionality were also raised by the Minister responsible for the Republic of Poland's membership in the European Union, who participated in the legislative process[38]. Despite all these reservations, the proposed legislation was adopted unchanged[39].

5.4.6. Alignment of the rules for determining the reintroduced VAT sanction with the norms of European law

The provisions reintroducing the instrument of additional tax liability into the VAT Act became the subject of evaluation by Polish administrative courts, which took divergent positions on this issue. Some of them, recognizing the

35 Comments on the draft amendment bill submitted by the Polish Union of Steel Distributors by letter dated 3.10.2016, p. 2.

36 Comments on the draft amendment law submitted by the Business Centre Club, dated 16.11.2016, p. 8.

37 Judgment of the Regional Administrative Court in Warsaw III SA/Wa 159/07 of 29.05.2007.

38 Opinion of the Minister of Foreign Affairs of 16.10.2016 on the compliance with the law of the European Union of the draft law on amendments to the Law on tax on goods and services and certain other laws, expressed by the Minister responsible for the Republic of Poland's membership in the European Union, p. 2.

39 Article 112b of the VAT Law, defining the prerequisites for the application of the basic and reduced VAT sanction, and Article 112c of the VAT Law, defining the prerequisites for the application of the increased VAT sanction, adopted as of January 1, 2017 by the provisions of the Law of December 1, 2016 amending the Law on Value Added Tax and certain other laws (Journal of Laws of 2016, item 2024).

need to evaluate the regulation in question through the prism of the principle of proportionality, refused to apply the VAT sanction in cases where it was determined in isolation from the circumstances under which the VAT liability was understated. Other courts, relying on the literal wording of the regulations, held that it was not possible to limit or waive the sanction in its basic amount, regardless of the reasons for the appearance of irregularities in the filed return[40].

The above discrepancies were resolved by the CJEU, which, in its judgment C – 935/19 of April 15, 2021, questioned the compatibility of the provisions constituting the instrument of the standard VAT sanction with Article 273 of the said VAT Directive and the principle of proportionality[41]. As raised by the Court, they stand in the way of national legislation that obliges to set the VAT sanction at 20 % of the amount of the overstatement without distinguishing between situations caused by an error, which is characterized by the absence of indications of fraud and depletion of revenue to the state treasury, and situations in which there are no such special circumstances. The automatically applied method of determining the sanction in question does not give the authorities the opportunity to individualize the sanction imposed to ensure that it does not go beyond what is necessary to achieve the objectives of ensuring proper tax collection and preventing tax fraud.[42]

The CJEU's dispositions also became the rationale for the Polish Court of Cassation's decision on the increased (100 %) sanction provisions. This court assessed the provisions in question in an analogous manner, as resulting in a violation of the principle of proportionality and Article 273 of the cited directive. This is because the establishment of an increased sanction in any situation, automatically, without taking into account such factual circumstances as, for example, the fact that the taxpayer violated tax regulations as a result of a failure to observe acts of diligence, without deliberate and conscious participation in the tax fraud, by his behaviour striving to prevent tax evasion, undertaking cooperation with the tax authorities and law enforcement agencies, leads to such incorrect results[43]. At the same time, the justification of the ruling

---

40 Bernat M., *VAT sanction again incompatible with EU law*, Center for Analysis and Tax Studies of the Warsaw School of Economics, https://casp.sgh.waw.pl/blog/sankcja-vat (Accessed Oct. 31, 2023).

41 CJEU judgment of April 15, 2021, C-935/19, Grupa Warzywna sp. z o.o., ECLI:EU:C:2021:287

42 Ibidem, pp. 35–37.

43 Judgment of the Supreme Administrative Court of 22.10.2021. I FSK 489/21, paragraph 6.6.

pointed out the important consequences, resulting from the literal wording of the provisions: the cassation court did not find an error in the ruling of the court of first instance, which, approving the imposition of an increased VAT sanction, relied on the linguistic content of the provision, without reaching to the purposive interpretation and justification of the bill. Since the taxpayer must have clarity and certainty in the tax burden, the norms of tax law should be unambiguous in their content in terms of the essential elements of taxation, so that there is no need for purposive interpretation[44]. This settlement confirms the defectiveness of the legislature's action in the course of legislative work. Changing the justification of the bill without changing the linguistic layer of the provision is undoubtedly an insufficient procedure.

As a consequence of the above decisions, further changes were made to the construction of the VAT sanction[45], postulated in the course of legislative work by numerous stakeholders, including the government body responsible for Polish membership in the European Union. As a result of the changes made, the current regulations allow for flexibility in the application of VAT sanctions, define not rigid but maximum amounts of additional tax liability and contain enumeratively indicated premises, which the authority is obliged to take into account when assessing the reasons for irregularities[46]. Regulations specifying the prerequisites for the application of an increased sanction have also been clarified. According to the new wording of the provision, the most severe sanction (100 %) applies only if it is found that the irregularity was the result of a deliberate act of the taxpayer or his counterparty, of which the taxpayer had knowledge.

---

44 Ibidem, pkt 6.3.

45 Articles 112b and 112c of the VAT Law, as amended by the Law of May 26, 2023, amending the Law on Goods and Services Tax and certain other laws (Journal of Laws of 2023, item 1059).

46 Under Article 112b paragraph 2b (1) – (5) of the amended VAT Law, in determining the additional tax liability, the authority shall take into account: the circumstances under which the irregularities arose; the type and degree of violation of the taxpayer's obligation that resulted in the irregularities; the type, degree and frequency of irregularities found to date regarding tax obligations that are not time-barred; the amount of irregularities found, including the amount of understatement of the tax liability, the amount of overstatement of the refund of the tax difference, the refund of the input tax or the tax difference to reduce the tax due for subsequent accounting periods; the actions taken by the taxpayer after the irregularities were found to remove the effects of the irregularities.

As a result of the above adjustments, the regulations constituting the increased VAT sanction are now significantly different from those originally adopted. The legislator has limited the application of this sanction to cases of intentional action. This is a requirement that goes further than the indications of the legislator, who, in the justification of the bill, allowed its application already in the case of establishing the taxpayer's conscious participation in the questioned transaction, which in practice could also be equated with a lack of due diligence. Proving intentionality places relatively high evidentiary requirements on the tax authorities, but nevertheless reduces the risk of an increased and disproportionate sanction imposed in the case of errors caused by circumstances other than the intention to deplete tax revenues.

5.4.7. Summary

The functioning of the instrument of VAT sanctions in the Polish legal order reflects the different, even extreme attitudes of the legislator towards signals indicating the incompatibility of the legislated regulations with the norms of European law. During the period of deregulation of the economy in the first decade of the 21st century, this tool was hastily removed from the provisions of the VAT Act, without sufficiently justified factual and jurisprudential reasons, in response to the submission of a preliminary question to the European Court of Justice. Almost a decade later, on the wave of sealing the tax system in connection with the growing problem of fraud, the legislature was no longer willing to respond to the numerous objections raised by participants in the legislative process, including even government centers, pointing to the excessive automatism and repressiveness of the created regulations and the resulting incompatibility with the principles of European law. The removal of the related flaws and basing the legislation on the principle of proportionality occurred only as a result of the adaptation of the established legislation to the rulings of the Court of Justice of the European Union.

Regardless of the way in which the legislator reacted to the problems associated with the functioning of the instrument in question and the reluctance expressed recently to take into account the legitimate interests of taxpayers, the key changes in the legislation that have taken place in the almost 30-year history of VAT sanctions in Poland reflect a general tendency to move away from automatism in determining the additional tax liability and to limit excessive repression. As a result of successive changes, tax authorities are now obliged to take into account circumstances that allow them to respond adequately not only to deliberate fraud, but also to moderate sanctions in the event of proper justification and/or removal of the consequences of taxpayers' mistakes. Today, following successive modifications, the VAT sanction is a relatively sophisticated tool, the application of which requires the tax authority to consider a number of considerations, including the taxpayer's intent, his reaction to the authority's actions and the circumstances under which the irregularity occurred. The above result is largely the result of the adaptation of regulations to the norms of European law and the guidance of the Court of Justice of the European Union.

5.5. Single control file (JPK)

5.5.1. The essence of the solution and the legal status

The described solution consists in introducing an obligation to send to the tax authority in electronic form the content of records, kept by the taxpayer for the purposes of VAT settlements. The main purpose of the obligation in question is to combat certain types of fraud in this tax by improving the exchange of information between taxpayers and the tax authority and creating an advanced electronic tool for analysing this information.

This tool primarily allows cross-checking in an automated manner and assessing whether invoices on the basis of which VAT has been deducted in full or in part have been recognized by the counterparty on the side of the VAT due. This makes it possible to detect cases of issuing empty invoices, as well as typing entities involved in transactions as so-called 'poles', lending their names to cover real actors. Reporting in the format of a single control file also makes it possible to shorten inspections, reduce the cost of fulfilling tax obligations and reduce the financial and organizational costs of tax administration.

Despite the fact that the provisions of European law do not obligate the introduction of reporting in the format of the single control file, at the time of implementation of this solution in Poland, it was already functioning in numerous member states[47], which introduced in this regard the standard developed and recommended by the OECD[48]. The tools used for this purpose, based on the

47 During the implementation period, the solution in question was implemented in Austria, Belgium, Denmark, the Netherlands, Lithuania, Luxembourg, Germany, Slovenia, Sweden, Portugal and the United Kingdom, among others. Source: explanatory memorandum to the Draft Law on Amendments to the Law – Tax Ordinance and Certain Other Laws, Parliamentary Print No. 3462, p. 94.

48 Guidance on Tax Compliance for Business and Accounting Software, https://www.oecd.org/tax/forum-on-tax-administration/publications-and-products/hnwi/34910263.pdf (Accessed Oct. 31, 2023).

use of modern information technology, indicate the universality of the problems associated with the implementation of the single control file.

5.5.2. Introduction of mandatory reporting in the JPK format

In Poland, the JPK reporting obligation was introduced on July 1, 2016[49]. Initially, it applied to so-called large entrepreneurs, who were obliged to submit only records of sales and purchases of VAT in the established format. For other entrepreneurs, the absolute obligation to report in the JPK format came into force on 01.01.2018[50]. As of 01.07.2018, the scope of data, obligatorily sent in JPK format, was expanded to include VAT returns, largely created automatically on the basis of sales and purchase records data.

Files with records of purchases, sales and VAT declarations prepared on this basis are sent by taxpayers without request, in fixed monthly and/or quarterly periods. The remaining JPK structures[51] are sent at the request of tax authorities, as part of their investigations. The only way to deliver a JPK file is to send it to the dedicated server of the Ministry of Finance, without the possibility of transferring it on external data carriers.

5.5.3. Objections to the way JPK format is implemented

The subject matter scope of the record-keeping data maintained and sent by the taxpayer must correspond to the structure of the JPK schema. The content of this structure, and therefore the catalog and scope of data required of the taxpayer, are determined by the authority accepting the files sent. It has a considerable degree of discretion in this regard. The powers granted to the executive body allow it to make discretionary changes to the scope of the necessary data and the IT architecture of the files, without the need for a legislative procedure and *vacatio legis*. This is because the logical structure of the JPK is published not in the form of a regulation, but in the Public Information Bulletin on the website of the office serving the authority in question. Consequently, in order to comply with the statutory obligation to send the required recording and information

---

49 Pursuant to the provisions of the Act of September 10, 2015 on amending the Tax Ordinance Act (Journal of Laws of 2015, item 1649).

50 Article 6 of the Law of 13.05.2016 amending the Law – Tax Ordinance and some other laws.

51 Currently, there are 7 of these structures: 'Accounts', 'Bank statements', 'Warehouse', 'Invoices', 'VAT invoices – flat-rate farmers', 'Tax revenue and expense ledger' and 'Revenue records'.

data, the taxpayer must comply with the requirements, discretionarily defined and determined by the tax authority outside the constitutional system of sources of law. Due to the discretion of the authority allowed by the legislator in determining the structure of the JPK, taxpayers are also uncertain whether, and if so to what extent, the obligation to submit data in this format will be extended[52].

Given the above, the manner of implementation of the solution in question is criticized primarily for the legislator's violation of the postulate of legal certainty. The authority's ability to introduce new JPK structures, obligatory for taxpayers, make successive changes to the version of the software used and, in particular, arbitrarily introduce changes to the scope of data, obligatorily transmitted in JPK format, may also lead to numerous problems of a strictly operational nature. For example, a situation may arise in which the taxpayer's IT system will not contain all the data that the structure dictates to be sent, and/or they will be collected in a way that will not allow them to be easily generated in the scheme required by the authority. Some data may also be stored in systems other than the taxpayer's main accounting system, which will result in the need to enter it into the JPK structure at the stage of its creation[53]. Complying with these requirements may involve significant time, organizational and financial expenses. These and other risks of effective implementation are why, according to critics of the existing solution, the introduction of any changes should be preceded by a rigorous procedure for changing the law, allowing for consultations and preparation by taxpayers for the modifications.

5.5.4. Response of state authorities to objections to the way JPK format is implemented

The demand to publish the JPK structure in the form of a regulation was raised by one of the industry organizations while the legislative process was still underway[54]. The comments raised in this regard, however, did not affect the

---

52 Pietrasz P. in: L. Etel (ed.), *Ordynacja podatkowa. Tom II. Procedury podatkowe. Art. 120–344*, commentary to the Article 193a., Lex/el. (Accessed Oct. 31, 2023).

53 Pałys A. (2016). *Wybrane aspekty praktyczne wdrożenia przez podatnika Jednolitego Pliku Kontrolnego od 1.07.2016*, Przegląd Podatkowy no. 7, , p. 11–21, Lex/el. (Accessed Oct. 31, 2023).

54 Comments of 20.08.2014 to the draft law of July 9, 2014 on amendments to the Tax Ordinance Law and some other laws, submitted by the 'Lewiatan' employers' organization, p. 7.

content of the law, and the drafters did not address them in the consultations that took place. As noted above, the legal state thus adopted subsequently became the subject of criticism by representatives of the doctrine, pointing to the legitimacy of including the authority's competence in determining the structure of the PAC in the constitutional rules of lawmaking.

However, the arguments in favor of limiting the discretion of tax authorities in shaping the manner of realization of taxpayers' substantive legal obligations have not so far become the subject of evaluation by the courts. Given the silence of the drafters during the legislative process, it is therefore unclear whether the implementation of the JPK format in a way that blurs the line between the strictly technical competence of the executive body and the ability to shape the material-legal situation of taxpayers was necessary, and whether the other criteria of proportionality were met. There is no doubt that the executive body should respond in a timely manner to problems related to the ongoing adaptation of the system's IT architecture to technological changes and, in particular, respond adequately to threats to the system's security. However, the question remains open as to whether and to what extent the achievement of this goal can justify the delegation of authority to the authority to shape taxpayers' substantive liabilities.

As can be surmised, the reason for the lack of (published) case law on the subject of the executive body's competence in its relations with taxpayers is the restraint exercised so far in the use of this competence and the peculiar conciliatory attitude of the body, which, as a rule, reacted flexibly and in a relative manner for taxpayers to problems with the implementation of the standard in question. For example, the authority allowed the use of certain simplifications in the presentation of data sent in the JPK format, thus making it easier for taxpayers to adapt to the new requirements. However, it is not known whether and in what cases the authority will continue to allow these simplifications and how far they may reach. On the other hand, already after the introduction of the JPK format, the executive body did not make fundamental changes to the IT architecture and did not fundamentally alter the scope of the record-keeping data required to be sent.

However, the current manner of cooperation between the executive body and the addressees of the tax legislation does not affect the causes of objections to the imposition of obligations on taxpayers. Nor does it remove sources of uncertainty about how the authority will exercise its powers in the future. It is also pointed out that the executive body responds to taxpayers' concerns by providing explanations in the form of question-and-answer documents, published on the Finance Ministry's BIP website. However, these are de facto informal in nature. Consequently, even in the situation of following the guidance in question, taxpayers do not obtain legal protection from it, in the event of questioning the correctness of the JPK file prepared on their basis[55]. At the same time, these explanations are written in a manner that is perceived as unclear, operating in highly technical language, containing concepts that are often incomprehensible also to IT specialists[56]. Such a way of providing information is probably intended to reduce the risk of civil law liability of the authority in the event of the emergence of damages, caused by possible errors or lack of precision in the explanations provided to taxpayers. Nevertheless, the airtight and reassuring way of communicating with taxpayers heightens uncertainty about the law, resulting from the authority's discretion in setting standards for taxpayers' performance of their VAT obligations. These effects could have been avoided, provided that the constitutional path for establishing the scope of the substantive legal obligations of obligated entities is preserved.

5.5.5. Summary

The legislature's delegation of authority to the executive body to determine how taxpayers should implement their substantive legal obligations touches on the universal problem of basing legal norms on technological norms and standards. The rapid development of modern information technologies is also associated with the risk of threats, the removal of which may require the state bodies to respond in a timely manner. However, there seems to be no doubt that the powers granted in this regard to the executive bodies, as a rule, should not go beyond strictly technical issues. All the more so, therefore, in cases where the demarcation of the boundary between technical and substantive competence may be fluid, these issues should be the subject of consultations conducted in advance. In the case of the implementation of the JPK format, the legislator failed to justify the reasons for the lack of a clearly defined boundary between the strictly technical competence of the executive body and the ability to shape the substantive legal obligations of taxpayers, and neglected to clarify the doubts raised by participants in the legislative process. The result is insufficient legal certainty regarding the scope of future obligations of obligated entities.

55 Michalak W., & Stankiewicz T. (2017). *Pierwszy rok doświadczeń z Jednolitym Plikiem Kontrolnym*, Przegląd Podatkowy 2017/5, pp. 6–11, Lex/el. (Accessed Oct. 31, 2023).

56 Mariański A. (ed.). (2017). *Ordynacja podatkowa* (2nd ed.). Warszawa, commentary to the Article 193a, Legalis. (Accessed Oct. 31, 2023).

5.6. Conclusions

5.6.1. Changes in the Polish tax system in connection with its tightening

The intensity of measures taken by Polish public policy in the years under review was a particular phenomenon. First, the scale of the changes introduced was unprecedented. It included a series of actions that significantly modified the sphere of Polish taxpayers' obligations. The changes in the law that were made at the time were intended to impact on areas of particular importance. They explicitly targeted those industries in which the scope of perceived irregularities was greatest.

Here we can see the first significant feature of the changes we are writing about. They did not have the ambition to introduce broad solutions that would transform the image of Polish tax law as to its structural foundations. Of course, we do not mean that the changes were not significant. Rather, on the contrary, they were unprecedented. Considering their intensity, we can say that there was a change in the tax system, although none of the changes was strictly systemic.

Thus, it was not a matter of changing some specific tax law or procedure (Tax Ordinance). It was about ad hoc action, or rather a package of ad hoc actions. That is, the idea was to locate those areas where the most irregularities were detected and put an end to them. This is how industries were selected against which split payment was made mandatory. This is how the introduction of the fuel package was motivated. A realization that the situation of unreliable taxpayers must be worsened (so as to discourage them from similar actions) was manifested in the introduction of so-called vat sanctions. For the same reasons, the obligations for taxpayers to inform the tax authorities were increased.

It should also be noted that not all significant changes are described in this chapter. This is because we focused on those that were particularly significant from the VAT perspective. On the other hand, it is difficult to undermine, for example, the scope of the changes that were introduced under the anti-avoidance clause. Imposed on July 15, 2016, the anti-avoidance clause made a kind of 'overturn of the system'. Considering the doubts about the legislative process that we point out, it is worth noting that to this day the GAAR clause has caused far-reaching controversy as to when it can be applied – as the regulation came into effect in the middle of the year. However, it is not closely related to taxpayers' obligations under the VAT law, so we do not discuss it. In view of the content of the next chapter, however, it was not appropriate to raise issues related to the reorganization of the tax administration.

We also did not describe another very emblematic mechanism – the Polish MDR (Mandatory Disclosure Rules). We have excluded it mainly because it does not directly translate into VAT concerns. However, the legislative process and the way the regulations are implemented in this field seems extremely interesting in the Polish case. This is because the Polish legislator has definitely come out ahead of the ranks of other EU countries, introducing exceptionally far-reaching sanctions related to violations in this regard. At the same time, the Polish regulation concerned with MDR is extremely badly evaluated by practitioners and it often leads in studies indicating the most unclear legal regulation introduced in recent years .

5.6.2. The importance of the legislative procedure

We have tried to show how an important part of making successive changes to the tax system is taking care to coordinate this process appropriately by the necessity of taking into account a number of institutions that co-create the system of law in the broadest sense. As legal theorists note, today the proper way to talk about the system of law at all is to frame it within the framework of the so-called 'interpretive institutional pluralism and open textuality of law'[57]. Law today is not a hierarchical system. This is strongly demonstrated in tax law, and perhaps most notably precisely in VAT, the regulation of which must comply with the often unclear harmonization requirements.

Since we are describing an analysis of the public policy response to the VAT gap from a legislative perspective, it is important to note how diverse are the legal institutions that contribute to the discourse in this regard and, especially importantly, realistically co-create it. The VAT gap itself can be analyzed on many levels. What is important here is not only the opinion of economists, but also of practitioners who apply the law: taxpayers and their attorneys (tax advisors), tax authorities, and – above all – judges.

When creating tax policy, the role of the legislative process, including precisely its coordination, must be taken into account. Failure to take into account this institutional 'multi-voice' leads to lower quality legislation, as also demonstrated by the examples we selected.

57 Wojciechowski B. (2019). *Stosowanie prawa podatkowego przez sądy administracyjne w sytuacji interpretacyjnego pluralizmu instytucjonalnego i otwartej tekstowości prawa*, 'Państwo i Prawo', 2019, no 12, pp. 58–72.

5.6.3. Conclusions on specific mechanisms

The examples we have analyzed have allowed us to draw conclusions in evaluating the relationship between the quality of public policy and the legislative process. We will now present them in terms of specific mechanisms.

1. It seems that a model example of public policy response in the context of the relevant legislative process is the regulation of split payment. The implementation of this legal instrument was the result of the Polish legislator's ambition to tighten the tax system. Similar regulations have been introduced in other countries, but Poland remains an exceptionally diligent student here, trying to maintain the highest standard of efforts. It has succeeded in avoiding, for example, the failures that led to that in 2018. European Commission called on Romania to withdraw from the mandatory split payment mechanism. Concerns that a similar scenario awaited Poland were well-founded at the time.

First, the dialogue with the European Commission and the response to concerns raised in the course of the procedure leading to the derogation should be highly commended. Secondly, the extent of the consultations carried out, which made it possible to take into account a number of comments made by representatives of various circles, should be appreciated. As a result, this regulation avoids the criticism faced by other mechanisms fighting the VAT gap. As an aside, however, we must note that we are referring here to comments of a normative nature, relating to the quality of the regulation in question. This is because a number of objections have been expressed in the press about the economic viability of this measure.

2. On the other side is the fuel package regulation. The coordination process in this case was, as we have shown, virtually nonexistent. This regulation was quickly objected by CJEU. The second aspect of this instrument is that in the jurisprudence of Polish courts there have been quite a few problems with the proper interpretation of this regulation. The lack of clarity in the law – especially tax law – is undoubtedly a weakness of the public policy response to the fuel industry's tax problems.
3. The action of the Polish legislator in regulating VAT sanctions is completely exceptional. Preventive removal of this mechanism from the Polish legal order – in view of the fear that this one will be considered incompatible with EU standards by ECJ – is an unprecedented action. Equally surprising is the subsequent fate of this mechanism, which was reintroduced into the VAT

Act in violation of the rules of legislative technique. This resulted in giving it a much more repressive character. Subsequently, the rules for determining this sanction were corrected by the CJEU, and if the mechanism is questioned today, it is primarily with regard to the amount of the rates adopted, not with regard to the lack of proportionality of the regulation itself.

4. The regulation on Single control file (JPK) is special in nature, because in addition to reporting obligations, it does not create classic tax obligations – it does not affect settlement amounts or payment methods. Nevertheless, it grants the executive body the authority to define the scope and manner of submission of certain tax information by taxpayers, bypassing the constitutional path of lawmaking. The legislature did not resolve the doubts related to this issue during the legislative process, ignoring the questions raised as well as the demand for formal rigor in this regard. Therefore, the question of the extent of necessary freedom of executive bodies in creation and application of technological standards, which affect taxpayers' performance of their legal obligations, remains appropriate.

References

Bernat M., *VAT Sanction Again Incompatible with EU Law*. Center for Analysis and Tax Studies of the Warsaw School of Economics, https://casp.sgh.waw.pl/blog/sankcja-vat (Accessed Oct. 31, 2023).

Comments on the draft amendment law, submitted by the Polish Union of Steel Distributors, 3.10.2016, p. 2.

Comments to the draft amendment law, submitted by Związek Cyfrowa Polska, 19.10.2016, pp. 7–8.

Comments on the draft amendment law, submitted by the 'Lewiatan' employers' organizations, 3.10.2016, p. 12.

Comments on the draft amendment bill submitted by the Polish Union of Steel Distributors by letter dated 3.10.2016, p. 2.

Comments on the draft amendment law submitted by the Business Centre Club, dated 16.11.2016, p. 8.

Comments of 20.08.2014 to the draft law of July 9, 2014 on amendments to the Tax Ordinance Law and some other laws, submitted by the 'Lewiatan' employers' organization, p. 7.

Comments of 20.08.2014 to the draft law of July 9, 2014 on amendments to the Tax Ordinance Law and some other laws, submitted by the 'Lewiatan' employers' organization, p. 7.

Explanatory Memorandum of the government draft of June 26, 2006 on amendments to the Law on Goods and Services Tax and certain other laws, print 734, p. 12.

Explanatory Memorandum to the parliamentary bill of March 12, 2008 on amendments to the Law on Value Added Tax and certain other laws, print 661, p. 11.

Guidance on Tax Compliance for Business and Accounting Software, https://www.oecd.org/tax/forum-on-tax-administration/publications-and-products/hnwi/34910263.pdf (Accessed Oct. 31, 2023).

Information of July 7, 2019, on the results of the audit 'Supervision of the Minister of Finance over the collection of goods and services tax', Supreme Audit Office, p. 28

Justification of the draft law amending the VAT law, dated July 9, 2019, Print no. 3602, orka.sejm.gov.pl/Druki8ka.nsf/0/AD1A072C72B0F1CCC1258432005D0DBA/%24File/3602.pdf, p. 17 (Accessed Oct. 31, 2023).

Justification of the draft law amending the VAT law, dated September 7, 2017, Print no. 1864, https://orka.sejm.gov.pl/Druki8ka.nsf/0/1F1EC57451D0A351C12581A90046A10E/%24File/1864.pdf. (Accessed Oct. 31, 2023).

Justification of the draft law amending the VAT law, dated May 31, 2016, Print no. 554, https://orka.sejm.gov.pl/Druki8ka.nsf/0/6B73214F66D4EA16C1257FC5003BAD98/%24File/554.pdf, p. 1. (Accessed Oct. 31, 2023).

Kańtor K., & Wróblewska K. (2017). Powrót sankcji w VAT. *Przegląd Podatkowy* 2017(1), 20–27, Lex/el. (Accessed Oct. 31, 2023).

Kieszkowski W. Płatnik ma obowiązek zapłaty VAT z tytułu WNT paliwa. *Legalis.pl* (Accessed Oct. 31, 2023).

Letter from the Ministry of Finance PTI.8100.4.2016.LJU.200, dated November 15, 2016, responding to comments made on the draft law.

Mariański A. (ed.). (2023). *Ordynacja podatkowa* (2nd ed.). Warszawa, commentary to the Article 193a, Legalis. (Accessed Oct. 31, 2023).Michalak W., & Stankiewicz T. (2017). Pierwszy rok doświadczeń z Jednolitym Plikiem Kontrolnym. *Przegląd Podatkowy* 2017(5), 6–11, Lex/el. (Accessed Oct. 31, 2023). Opinion of the Minister of Foreign Affairs of 16.10.2016 on the compliance with the law of the European Union of the draft law on amendments to the Law on tax on goods and services and certain other laws, expressed by the Minister responsible for the Republic of Poland's membership in the European Union, p. 2.

Pałys A. (2016). Wybrane aspekty praktyczne wdrożenia przez podatnika Jednolitego Pliku Kontrolnego od 1.07.2016. *Przegląd Podatkowy* 2016/7, pp. 11–21, Lex/el. (Accessed Oct. 31, 2023)

Pietrasz P. [in:] L. Etel (ed.), *Ordynacja podatkowa. Tom II. Procedury podatkowe. Art. 120–344*, commentary to the Article 193a., Lex/el. (Accessed Oct. 31, 2023)

Response of the Ministry of Finance of 15.11.2016 to the comments of the Business Centre Club, p. 4.

Urbańska K. *Diagnoza systemu stanowienia prawa w Polsce z punktu widzenia organizacji pracodawców*, prezydent.pl, https://www.prezydent.pl/storage/file/core_files/2021/8/9/6c90b00587f734f247a6ce46bd9b0a78/02urbanska_katarzyna_slabosc_systemu_diagnoza.pdf. (Accessed Oct. 31, 2023).

Wojciechowski B. (2019). Stosowanie prawa podatkowego przez sądy administracyjne w sytuacji interpretacyjnego pluralizmu instytucjonalnego i otwartej tekstowości prawa. *Państwo i Prawo*, 12, 58–72.

Legislation

Act of September 10, 2015 on amending the Tax Ordinance Act (Journal of Laws of 2015, item 1649).

Annex No. 15 to the VAT Act (Journal of Laws of 201, item 1751).

Council Directive 2006/112/EC of 28 November 2006 on the common system of value added tax (*OJ L 347, 11.12.2006, p. 1–118*) ('VAT Directive').

European Union, *Consolidated version of the Treaty on the Functioning of the European Union*, 26 October 2012, OJ L. 326/47-326/390; 26.10.2012 (hereinafter cited as 'TFUE').

Pursuant to the Law of November 7, 2008 amending the Law on Value Added Tax (Journal of Laws of 2008, No. 209, item 1320).

Regulation of the Prime Minister of June 20, 2002 on 'Principles of Legislative Techniques' (Journal of Laws of 2016, item 283).

The Law on Value Added Tax and certain other laws (Journal of Laws of 2016, item 2024).

VAT Law, as amended by the Law of May 26, 2023, amending the Law on Goods and Services Tax and certain other laws (Journal of Laws of 2023, item 1059).

Case law

Judgment of the CJEU judgment of April 15, 2021 (C-935/19, Grupa Warzywna sp. z o.o., ECLI:EU:C:2021:287).

Judgment of the ECJ of January 15, 2009 (C-502/07, *K-1*, ECLI:EU:C:2009:11, pts 19, 20 and 28).

Judgments of the Polish Constitutional Court of June 16, 1986 (U 3/86).

Judgments of the Polish Constitutional Court of April 20, 1993 (U 12/92).
Judgments of the Polish Constitutional Court of October 19, 1993 (K 14/92).
Judgments of the Polish Constitutional Court of November 30, 1993 (K 18/92).
Judgments of the Polish Constitutional Court of April 4, 1995 (K 10/94).
Judgments of the Polish Constitutional Court of November 19, 1996 (K 7/95).
Judgment of the Polish Constitutional Court of April 29, 1998 (K 17/97).
Judgments of the Supreme Administrative Court of July 31, 2007 (I FSK 1062/06).
Judgment of the Supreme Administrative Court of October 16, 2006 (I FPS 2/06).
Judgment of the Supreme Administrative Court of October 22, 2021 (I FSK 489/21).
Judgments of the Supreme Administrative Court of December 8, 2022 (I FSK 1561/22).
Judgment of the Regional Administrative Court in Warsaw of May 29, 2007 (III SA/Wa 159/07).
Judgments of the Regional Administrative Court in Warsaw of September 30, 2020 (III SA/Wa 66/20).

Konrad Buczkowski (Polish Academy of Sciences),
Paweł Ostaszewski (University of Warsaw)

Chapter 6 Criminal policy response - Motives for criminalisation and the statistical picture

Abstract: This chapter presents the statistical background for the entire period of the new criminal law on VAT fraud, i.e. 2017–2022, and discusses in detail (on the basis of documents related to the legislative process of the Act amending the Criminal Code) the motives for introducing new types of crimes against documents into the Polish criminal law system.

Key words: VAT fraud, Poland, criminal policy, legislation process, Criminal Code, statistical data

6.1. General comments

The issue of combating VAT fraud has existed in the Polish legal system since this tax was introduced in 1993[1]. However, the first criminal provisions concerning the prosecution of acts of this type appeared in 1997, when the Fiscal Penal Code introduced provisions referring directly to behaviours violating the obligations set out in the VAT Act[2]. A further extension of the scope of criminal sanctions took place in the Fiscal Penal Code of 10th September 1999[3]. However, in the

1 With the enactment of the VAT Act of 8th January 1993 (Journal of Laws No. 11, item 50), replaced by the current VAT Act of 11th March 2004 (i.e. Journal of Laws 2023, item 1570)

2 The Act on Amending the Act on VAT and Excise Duty and Amending the Fiscal Penalty Act of 21st November 1996 (Journal of Laws No. 137, item 640) amended the Fiscal Penalty Act of 26th October 1971 (i.e. Journal of Laws of 1984, No. 22, item 103, as amended) by changing the content of Article 102 and adding a new Article 104a, in which liability is introduced for a person who, contrary to the provisions of the Act on VAT and Excise Tax or the Act on Tax Liabilities, does not issue an invoice or bill for a service rendered, refuses to issue an invoice or bill or does not keep copies of issued invoices or bills, or issues an invoice or bill for the supply of goods or services containing information inconsistent with reality, or uses such an invoice or bill, and furthermore fails to keep records of turnover and amounts of output VAT with the use of a cash register, or makes a sale without the use of a cash register, or fails to issue a document from the cash register confirming the sale to the buyer.

3 Journal of Laws 2023, item 654.

opinion of the legislator, they still did not meet the expectations as regards the actual combating of VAT offences. The problem highlighted was the need to establish and prove the depletion of tax receivables, which made the prosecution of these acts ineffective and the penalties imposed did not ensure effective combating of this type of crime. Other measures of an administrative nature to combat VAT fraud that existed independently of criminal sanctions also proved to be insufficient. Therefore, the idea arose to change this state of affairs through the introduction of criminal provisions – detached from the necessity of proving a connection between the act and tax depletion – which would penalise the very fact of issuing an unreliable document in the form of an invoice (material falsification) or invoices fraudulently confirming untrue circumstances which may be significant for the determination of the amount of public liability (intellectual falsification). Its implementation took place through the adoption on 10th February 2017 of the Act amending the Act on the Penal Code and certain other acts[4] by adding articles 270a, 271a and 277a – 277d to Chapter XXXIV – Offences against the credibility of documents.

In this part, we present the statistical background for the entire period in which these new provisions were in force, i.e. between 2017 and 2022, and discuss more generally (on the basis of documents related to the legislative process of the Act amending the Penal Code) the motives behind the introduction of new types of offences against documents into the Polish criminal law system.

6.2. Criminal law provisions to combat VAT offences: The legislative process

The idea of amending the legislation – mainly the Penal Code – to combat crimes related to VAT fraud arose in the wake of press reports and expert estimates indicating that the so-called VAT gap, i.e. the difference between actual and expected VAT revenues, had increased from 0.6 % of GDP in 2007 to 2.9 % of GDP in 2013, only to decrease slightly to 2.4 % of GDP in 2014. It was estimated that reducing the VAT gap to its 2007 level would generate an additional PLN 42.7 billion for the Treasury in 2015[5]. The Ministry of Finance estimated that between 2007 and 2015 the Treasury lost around PLN 200 – 250 billion through

4 Journal of Laws 2017, item 244.

5 *Wyłudzenia VAT – luka podatkowa w 2014 roku i prognoza na 2015 [VAT fraud – tax gap in 2014 and forecast for 2015]*, 25th September 2015, PWC (report), https://www.pwc.pl/pl/pdf/luka-vat-pwc-wrzesien-2015.pdf (Accessed Oct. 31, 2023).

VAT fraud[6]. In 2015. Poland was in 6th place (after Romania, Slovakia, Greece. Lithuania and Italy) in terms of the VAT gap calculated as a percentage of tax revenue[7].

It should therefore come as no surprise that the tightening of regulations has become one of the priorities of the new government of Law and Justice (which won the elections in 2015). In addition to taking a number of measures of an administrative and fiscal nature, such as the extension in 2015 of the scope of application of the reverse charge of VAT to include electronic equipment and mobile phones, or the continued expansion of the industries covered by the principle of so-called joint and several liability for the payment of VAT due if it has not been paid by the counterparty, or the introduction from the beginning of 2016 of the obligation to use the Single Control File submitted in a specific form every month to the tax authorities, it was also decided to make changes to the regulations of criminal and procedural law, introducing new types of offences aimed at combating VAT fraud.

The draft bill on amendments to the Acts on the Penal Code and certain other acts, prepared by the Ministry of Justice, was published on the website of the Government Legislation Centre[8] on 29th July 2016. This short draft, only five pages long, in addition to amending the provisions of the Act of 6th June 1997, the Penal Code[9], which was included in its title, provided for the introduction of amendments to: the Act of 6th June 1997, the Code of Criminal Procedure[10], the Act of 28th September 1991 on Fiscal Control[11] (later replaced by the Act of 16th November 2016 on the National Fiscal Administration[12]), the Act of 6th April 1990. on the Police[13], the Act of 12th October 1990 on the Border Guard[14],

6 *Kulisy Spraw: karuzele VAT-owskie* [*Backstage of Affairs: VAT carousels*], Polskie Radio, 17/08/2017, https://polskieradio24.pl/130/5561/Artykul/1821346,kulisy-spraw-karuzele-vatowskie (Accessed Oct. 31, 2023).

7 Sarnowski J., Selera P. (2018). *Zmniejszenie luki VAT w Polsce w latach 2016 – 2017. Przyczyny, środki, dalsze perspektywy [Reducing the VAT gap in Poland in 2016 – 2017. Causes, measures, further perspectives].* Polish Economic Institute, Warsaw, , p. 13.

8 https://legislacja.rcl.gov.pl/projekt/12288207.

9 Journal of Laws 2022, item 1138.

10 Journal of Laws 2022, item 1375.

11 Journal of Laws 2016, item 720, repealed by virtue of Article 159 of the Act of 16th November 2016. – Provisions introducing the National Fiscal Administration Act (Journal of Laws of 2016, item 1948) as of 1st March 2017.

12 Journal of Laws 2023, item 615.

13 Journal of Laws 2023, item 171.

14 Journal of Laws 2023, item 1080.

the Act of 24th August 2001 on the Military Gendarmerie and Military Order Authorities[15] and the Act of 9th June 2006 on the Central Anti-Corruption Bureau[16]. It should be noted here that the amendments to the aforementioned laws consisted of extending the powers of all the authorities covered by the subject matter of these laws to include the possibility of ordering the procedural monitoring and recording of the content of telephone conversations (amendment to the content of Article 237 of the Code of Criminal Procedure) and conducting operational and investigative activities with regard to the offences added to the Criminal Code by the draft law amending the Criminal Code and certain other laws.

In the explanatory memorandum to the draft law[17], it is stated that the main reasons for working on the amendments to the Criminal Code include the fact that the state budget loses billions of zloty every year as a result of the actions of criminals engaged in value-added tax (VAT) fraud. It was pointed out that in the period from 2014 to 2016, 253 people were sentenced in cases involving fraudulently obtaining undue VAT refunds of at least a large value, of which only 31 were sentenced to imprisonment without conditional suspension. On the other hand, in the same period (2014–2016), according to the data of the National Public Prosecutor's Office, 360 pre-trial proceedings were conducted, the subject of which was fraudulently obtaining an undue refund of VAT of at least high value in the meaning of Article 53 § 15 of the Fiscal Penal Code[18], and in which the fraudulent VAT amounted to almost PLN 10 billion (approximately EUR 2.2 billion according to the exchange rate of August 2023). In addition, based on the data of the Supreme Chamber of Control, the volume of fictitious activities detected by the fiscal control authorities is systematically increasing. While in 2013 the fiscal control authorities detected fictitious VAT invoices amounting to almost PLN 20 billion, already in 2015 it was almost PLN 82 billion[19].

---

15 Journal of Laws 2023, item 1266.

16 Journal of Laws 2022, item 1900.

17 Explanatory Memorandum to the Draft Act on Amendments to the Act on the Penal Code and Certain Other Laws, 8th Legislature, Parliamentary Print No. 888, https://orka.sejm.gov.pl/Druki8ka.nsf/0/EA8BC112272EA7CEC125804200323EDD/%24File/888.pdf (Accessed Oct. 31, 2023).

18 Article 53 § 15 of the Penal Code specifies that great value is the value which, at the time the criminal act is committed, exceeds one thousand times the minimum wage. The Act of 10th September 1999, the Fiscal Penal Code (i.e. Journal of Laws of 2023, item 654).

19 Explanatory memorandum…, p. 2.

The most common ways of defrauding the tax authorities with regard to output VAT and input VAT and tax refunds are as follows: (1) issuing invoices by an entity that actually exists, for an activity that actually took place but the taxable person was another entity, (2) issuing invoices for an activity that did not take place at all, (3) issuing of invoices by a completely fictitious entity that has only been created for the purpose of issuing these documents; (4) the supply of goods, which *de facto* do not leave the country, is declared as an intra-Community supply of goods or export (fictitious export), (5) services are provided on the territory of the country, but are fictitiously declared as provided outside the territory of the country (fictitious place of supply)[20].

Therefore, it was pointed out that 'apart from the necessity to counteract such practices with amendments to tax regulations and regulations on administrative and penal-fiscal proceedings, the legislator also considers it necessary to combat VAT fraud with criminal law instruments. The point is that this type of behaviour, aimed at the illegal acquisition of financial resources at the expense of the state budget, should become unprofitable and an adequately severe criminal sanction should have a deterrent effect on potential perpetrators. (…) Threatening these acts only with sanctions stemming from the Fiscal Penal Code can hardly be considered sufficient, especially in the situation where they result in a significant depletion of budget revenues'[21]. It was also emphasised that the entrepreneurs themselves (e.g. companies related to trade in liquid fuels, tobacco products or spirits) put forward proposals for the introduction of broader criminal law protection in the area of VAT fraud, 'pointing out that such activity not only significantly distorts competition and the rules of the free market, but it is also a kind of invitation to move the entire activity to the 'black market'. (…) The advisability of such activities has also been pointed out by an organisation operating within the UN structure – Global Compact Network Poland'[22].

With regard to the detailed justification of the proposed amendments to the Penal Code, the project proponents stated that their aim is to 'focus on counteracting and combating crime involving the creation of untrue, unreliable documents that relate to factual circumstances that may be of significance for the determination of a public law receivable. Such a situation directly leads to VAT fraud on a scale that is very extensive for state finances'[23]. Such a presentation

20 Explanatory memorandum…, p. 1.
21 Explanatory memorandum…, pp. 1–2 .
22 Explanatory memorandum…, p. 3.
23 Explanatory memorandum…, p. 4.

of the object of criminalisation was considered more appropriate for the system of common criminal law, as the criminalisation of the depletion of public-law receivables takes place on the basis of the provisions of fiscal criminal law. It was pointed out that the construction of criminal law provisions would lead to the elimination of the most important instrument for VAT evasion, i.e. the unreliable invoice.

In the Explanatory Memorandum to the bill, it was emphasised that 'behaviour related to VAT fraud was also previously threatened by criminal sanctions. However, both the threat provided for in the system of fiscal criminal law and the formulation of the elements of these acts – closely related to the need to establish the depletion of receivables – meant that the prosecution of these acts and the penalties imposed did not ensure an effective fight against this crime. Measures of an administrative and legal nature cannot be considered effective in this regard, as their severity is in no way commensurate with the extent of the general social damage caused by these behaviours. (…) The scale of this criminal activity directly affects society as a whole and every individual member of society because the state budget is far less able to cope with the redistributive needs'[24]. For this reason, it was considered reasonable to introduce the threat of severe criminal punishment (of up to 15 years and 25 years of imprisonment) for acts related to offences concerning large-scale receivables, which place them among the offences punishable by the most severe penalties, such as murder (Article 148 § 1 and 2 of the Penal Code) or offences against peace or humanity or the counterfeiting of money (Article 310 § 1 of the Penal Code).

At the same time, it has been emphasised that the proposed provisions introduce a gradation of types of prohibited acts (basic and qualified), the acceptance of which depends on the total amount of receivables indicated on an invoice. However, it was pointed out at the outset that it is possible to apply to the perpetrator of the offence of falsifying an invoice a provision which establishes a privileged type – a less serious offence (Article 270a § 3 and Article 271a § 3 of the proposal to amend the Code of Criminal Procedure), which may be applied regardless of the amount stated on the invoice, if such an invoice does not have significant negative consequences (the unlawful benefit obtained by the perpetrator is insignificant or the invoice is not used to obtain an unlawful benefit despite its actual issue).

It was also pointed out that 'the proposed shape of the features of the types of offences against documents is intended to ensure that criminal sanctions are

24 Explanatory memorandum…, pp. 5 – 6.

only applied to persons, often acting in a larger group, who commit material falsification [counterfeiting or falsification of an invoice – author's note] and intellectual falsification [using a counterfeited or falsified invoice – author's note] in relation to VAT invoices with regard to factual circumstances which may have significance for the determination of the amount of the public law receivable, acting intentionally. Persons who accidentally make a mistake when issuing an invoice, even if it arises as a result of negligence or even recklessness, will not be subject to this liability. This is because these offences are intentional in nature and in order for criminal liability to apply, it will be necessary to demonstrate not only the material or intellectual characteristics of the act, but also the subjective characteristics, i.e. the intention of the perpetrator to commit the act. (…) It is therefore out of the question to penalise traders who make mistakes, who act without the intention of issuing a false invoice or who use such an invoice in the knowledge that it does not reflect actual economic events.'[25].

Another intention of the legislator was to break the solidarity of criminal groups involved in organised VAT fraud and to obtain testimony or statements from individual members of such groups, which would allow the illegal activities of such groups to be terminated. To this end, 'it is desirable to institutionalise the possibility of a certain mitigation of criminal repression for those who decide to express so-called active contrition in a certain form or return the unlawfully obtained financial benefit. (…) The legislator [also] provided for the possibility of the perpetrator returning only a significant part of this benefit – to the extent dependent on the possibility of making independent determinations (Article 8 § 1 of the Code of Criminal Procedure) in a given criminal proceedings'[26]. The solutions are in the draft articles 277c and 277d of the penal code.

The legislative process at the governmental work stage, in accordance with the established procedure, included agreements with individual ministries, members of the Council of Ministers and the Governmental Legislation Centre.

The comments made by the Ministry of Finance mostly boiled down to a discrepancy between the wording used in the draft amendments to the Penal Code and that used under other legislation, including tax legislation[27].

25 Explanatory memorandum…, pp. 8 – 9.

26 Explanatory memorandum…, p. 10.

27 Letter from the Ministry of Finance No. PR2.021.744.2016.MTS.SOD, 10th August 2016, https://legislacja.rcl.gov.pl/docs//2/12288207/12370133/12370136/dokument243123.pdf (Accessed Oct. 31, 2023).

In its comments, the Ministry of Development drew attention to the need to clarify the relationship between the proposed provisions of the Act on the Penal Code enabling the imposition of a fine in addition to the imposed prison sentence and the provisions of Article 61 § 1 and 2 of the Penal Code, which provide only a fine as a sanction for failing to issue an invoice or bill for the performance of a service, issuing such documents in a defective or unreliable manner, refusal to issue them or using a defective or unreliable document[28].

The Ministry of Foreign Affairs, on the other hand, drew attention to the need to consider whether the proposed high penalties for VAT fraud offences, in addition to having a deterrent element, are also proportionate. In justifying its position, the Ministry of Foreign Affairs referred to the content of Article 2(1) of the Convention on the Protection of the European Communities' Financial Interests, which indicates that the penalties imposed by a Member State for serious fraud are to be not only effective and dissuasive, but also proportionate to the act, which does not exclude the use of imprisonment against the perpetrator. Furthermore, the Ministry of Foreign Affairs pointed to the need to demonstrate precisely whether the extension of the powers of certain authorities to apply certain operational measures (in particular, telephone tapping and monitoring of correspondence) does not infringe Directive 2002/58/EC of the European Parliament and of the Council of 12th July 2002 concerning the processing of personal data and the protection of privacy in the electronic communications sector[29].

There was also a public consultation on the draft law. During this process, the Lewiatan Confederation and the Supreme Court submitted their comments.

The Polish Confederation of Private Employers drew attention to the fact that the proposed provisions (Articles 270a, 271a and 277a of the Penal Code) do not meet the criteria for defining the circumstances and conditions for imposing a penalty and for linking the amount of the penalty to the amount of tax evasion and the contribution to its occurrence, which creates a risk that these provisions will be applied in cases where there is no tax evasion or where the amount of the tax evasion is disproportionate to the amount of the penalty[30].

---

28 Letter from the Ministry of Development No. 176441/16, 16th August 2016, https://legislacja.rcl.gov.pl/docs//2/12288207/12370133/12370136/dokument243122.pdf (Accessed Oct. 31, 2023).

29 Letter from the Ministry of Foreign Affairs No. DPUE.920.1196.2016/2/JS of 11th August 2016, https://legislacja.rcl.gov.pl/docs//2/12288207/12370133/12370136/dokument243119.pdf (Accessed Oct. 31, 2023).

30 Letter from the Lewiatan Confederation, 12th August 2016, https://legislacja.rcl.gov.pl/docs//2/12288207/12370139/12370142/dokument243127.pdf (Accessed Oct. 31, 2023).

The comments submitted by the Supreme Court indicated that the proponent did not demonstrate a rational need to shape new types of offences as crimes, as well as to introduce criminal sanctions in the form of the threat of imprisonment for at least 5 years or 25 years in the case of the offences specified in Article 270a § 1 of the Penal Code or Article 271a § 1 of the Penal Code. Furthermore, the Supreme Court pointed out that there is no need to create separate grounds for extraordinary mitigation of punishment provided for in Articles 277c and 277d of the Penal Code, since such grounds are already set out in Article 60 § 3 of the Penal Code[31].

Work on the bill continued until 13th September 2016, when it was adopted by the Council of Ministers[32].

The bill was submitted to the Sejm on 22nd September 2016. It was referred under Article 118(1) of the Constitution of the Republic of Poland of 2nd April 1997[33] granting the legislative initiative to the Council of Ministers, by the then Prime Minister Beata Szydło. On 4th October 2016, the draft was referred to the first reading at the session of the Sejm. Following the rejection of the motion to reject the draft in the first reading, it was referred for work to the Standing Subcommittee on Amendments to the Criminal Code, which adopted a resolution to reject the submitted draft on 15th December 2016. However, the Subcommittee's resolution was not taken into account by the Extraordinary Committee on Amendments to the Codification and the draft was recommended for further work[34].

After the bill was sent to Parliament, the National Council of the Judiciary submitted its opinion. Without denying the need to combat the phenomenon of VAT fraud by means of criminal law instruments, it pointed out that the criminal sanctions provided for were inappropriate to the nature of the legal interest protected by the law, that they were excessively restrictive and that their introduction into the

31 Comments of the Supreme Court – Regulatory Impact Assessment, https://legislacja.rcl.gov.pl/docs//2/12288207/12370166/12370167/dokument243523.pdf (Accessed Oct. 31, 2023).

32 Memorandum of agreement No. 32/2016 of the meeting of the Council of Ministers on 13th September 2016, https://legislacja.rcl.gov.pl/docs//2/12288207/12370166/12370171/dokument248205.pdf (Accessed Oct. 31, 2023).

33 Journal of Laws No. 78, item 483.

34 Report of the Extraordinary Committee for Amendments to the Codifications on the Government Bill on Amendments to the Act on the Penal Code and Certain Other Acts (Print No. 888), 8th Kadence, Print No. 1189, https://orka.sejm.gov.pl/Druki8ka.nsf/0/771B8224CEC320F8C12580A6004FCD95/%24File/1189.pdf (Accessed Oct. 31, 2023).

legal system would render the system of criminal sanctions internally inconsistent. It was pointed out that 'the proposed provisions violate the coherence of the system of criminal sanctions, as they provide for a more severe criminal reaction in the case of offences against a legal good such as property than in the case of goods such as life or personal or sexual freedom. Thus, the proposed regulation also violates the principle of proportionality of the criminal response. According to this principle, the legislator should not resort to an excessively severe sanction when legislating, and in determining the type and amount of punishment the legislator should be guided by the type of protected good and the degree of social harmfulness of the criminalised act'[35].

On 26th January 2017, the second and third reading of the bill took place. It was passed by a majority of 238 votes, with 191 against and 11 abstentions. Given that the effective date of the amendment was set for 1st March 2017, the enacted text of the law was immediately transmitted to the Senate.

The Senate had already communicated its position on 2nd February 2017 by introducing one amendment to the text of the Act with regard to amending the content of Article 237 § 3 of the Code of Criminal Procedure. It aimed to exclude the right to use the monitoring and recording of telephone conversations when the pending proceedings or a justified fear of a new offence concerns offences under Article 234, Article 235 or Article 236 of the Code of Criminal Procedure, insofar as they relate to the commission of a misdemeanour or disciplinary offence. In the opinion of the Senate, leaving the possibility of monitoring, in particular wiretapping, in misdemeanour and disciplinary proceedings will violate the right to privacy of the person subject to monitoring in a manner disproportionate to the good violated by that person, which raises doubts in the light of the provisions of the Constitution of the Republic of Poland[36]. The Senate's amendment, as recommended by the Sejm's Extraordinary Committee for Amendments to Codifications[37], was adopted at the session on 10th February

35 Opinion of the National Council of the Judiciary of 16th September 2016 on the Draft Law on Amendments to the Law on the Penal Code and Certain Other Laws, https://orka.sejm.gov.pl/Druki8ka.nsf/0/E15BE69E0D01DAA4C12580520058A0B0/%24File/888-001.pdf (Accessed Oct. 31, 2023).

36 Resolution of the Senate of 1st February 2017 on the Act on Amendments to the Act on the Penal Code and Certain Other Laws, 8th Legislature, print no. 1260, https://orka.sejm.gov.pl/Druki8ka.nsf/0/E492987D7B97DD33C12580BB004DA14B/%24File/1260.pdf (Accessed Oct. 31, 2023).

37 Report of the Extraordinary Committee for Amendments to the Codifications on the Resolution of the Senate on the Act on Amendments to the Act on the Penal Code and

2017 and with it the Act as a whole. On 11th February, the Act was signed by the President of the Republic of Poland and published in the Journal of Laws on 13th February 2017 under item 244.

6.3. Statistical picture of new criminal policy instruments

The subject of this study is the practical application of the provisions introduced by the Act of 10th February 2017 amending the Act – Penal Code and certain other acts (Journal of Laws of 2017, item 244) criminalising the falsification of invoices. Therefore, it is also worth outlining the statistical picture of these offences from 2017–2022, i.e. from the full period of their validity, including: the number of proceedings initiated by the police, the number of offences identified, offences and suspects detected, and tried and convicted persons[38]. We have chosen to present these data in the context of data on all offences under Chapter XXXIV of the Criminal Code on offences against the reliability of documents.

The available statistics include details of the seven offences:

1. Material forgery of invoices in the basic type – article 270a § 1 of the Code of Criminal Procedure, punishable with imprisonment from 6 months to 8 years.

Certain Other Acts, 8th Legislature, print no. 1262, https://orka.sejm.gov.pl/Druki8ka.nsf/0/20ED2E976C1F7CE9C12580C1004FA9C4/%24File/1262.pdf (Accessed Oct. 31, 2023).

38 The concepts presented require a brief explanation. Initiated proceedings are proceedings initiated by an organisational unit of the police in connection with an event suspected of being a crime, or initiated by the public prosecutor's office and handed over to the police for further direct conduct. An identified offence is an offence that is a crime or misdemeanour prosecuted by public indictment, including a fiscal offence, that is the subject of pre-trial proceedings that have been completed and as a result of which the offence has been confirmed. A detected offence is an identified offence in which at least one suspect has been identified in completed pre-trial proceedings. A suspect is a person against whom a decision on the presentation of charges has been made (Article 313 § 1 of the Code of Criminal Procedure) or who has been charged without such a decision in connection with the commencement of questioning as a suspect. An adjudicated person is a person against whom a court decision has been made (conviction, acquittal, discontinuance of proceedings). A convicted person is a person against whom a final criminal sentence has been passed. See: https://statystyka.policja.pl/download/20/232288/Uwagiidefinicje.docx (Accessed Oct. 31, 2023).

2. Material forgery of invoices in the qualified type – Article 270a § 2 of the Code of Criminal Procedure, punishable with imprisonment for a term no shorter than 3 years.
3. Material forgery of invoices in the privileged type – Article 270a § 3 of the Code of Criminal Procedure, punishable with a fine, restriction of freedom or imprisonment for up to 2 years.
4. Intellectual forgery of invoices in the basic type – Article 271a § 1 of the Code of Criminal Procedure, punishable with imprisonment from 6 months to 8 years.
5. Intellectual forgery of invoices in the qualified type – Article 271a § 2 of the Code of Criminal Procedure, punishable with imprisonment for a term not shorter than 3 years.
6. Intellectual forgery of invoices in the privileged type – Article 271a § 3 of the Code of Criminal Procedure, punishable with imprisonment for up to 3 years.
7. Forgery of invoices with the amount due exceeding PLN 10 million – Article 277a of the Penal Code, punishable with imprisonment for a term no shorter than 5 years or 25 years of imprisonment (unfortunately, statistical data does not distinguish in this case between paragraph 1 and paragraph 2 which defines a privileged type, which is a case of lesser gravity)[39].

Since 2017, the number of initiated proceedings and established offences of invoice forgery has steadily increased (cf. Table 6.1) – in 2017, the police recorded only 15 such acts, while in 2022 it was already 981. However, in the context of all offences against the credibility of documents, the number of cases involving invoice forgery is very low – it accounts for approximately only 1 % of them. Looking in more detail at the data presented in Table 6.1, it can be seen that, of the individual articles and paragraphs of the newly introduced provisions, Article 270a § 1 and Article 271a § 1 of the Penal Code predominate. These offences have a very high detection rate (this is, of course, related to the very process of reporting them, which will be discussed in detail later when describing the

39 As a side note, it is worth noting that as of 1st October 2023, the amount of punishment provided for the offences of Article 270a § 2 of the Penal Code and Article 271a § 2 of the Penal Code has changed and they are now punishable by imprisonment from 3 to 20 years and Article 277a of the Penal Code, which is punishable by imprisonment from 5 to 25 years. See the Act of 7th July 2022 amending the Act on the Penal Code and certain other acts (Journal of Laws of 2022, item 2600 as amended by Journal of Laws of 2023, item 403).

results of the file research) and the fact that most often one suspect committed a minimum of several of these offences (the number of suspects is many times lower than the number of detected offences).

Table 6.1. Number of prosecutions initiated, offences identified, offences detected and suspects in relation to the falsification of invoices

	Proceedings initiated					
	2017	**2018**	**2019**	**2020**	**2021**	**2022**
Offences against the credibility of documents	29049	27350	25498	20086	19915	18390
Falsification of invoices	39	117	182	244	256	346
Art. 270a § 1 CC.	30	80	105	130	128	147
Art. 270a § 2 CC.	0	1	0	1	2	7
Art. 270a § 3 CC.	2	5	14	20	22	36
Art. 271a § 1 CC.	5	25	51	81	82	115
Art. 271a § 2 CC.	1	2	4	7	12	15
Art. 271a § 3 CC.	1	3	7	4	10	20
Art. 277a CC.		1	1	1	0	6
	Offences identified					
	2017	**2018**	**2019**	**2020**	**2021**	**2022**
Offences against the credibility of documents	68070	60608	57790	54873	57675	84285
Falsification of invoices	15	167	236	515	514	981
Art. 270a § 1 CC.	11	62	155	406	219	322
Art. 270a § 2 CC.	1	2	14	26	3	16
Art. 270a § 3 CC.	2	95	28	19	63	110
Art. 271a § 1 CC.	1	7	25	44	71	426
Art. 271a § 2 CC.			1	12	16	14
Art. 271a § 3 CC.		1	3	4	135	89
Art. 277a CC.			10	4	7	4
	Offences detected					
	2017	**2018**	**2019**	**2020**	**2021**	**2022**
Offences against the credibility of documents	54208	47945	45800	45862	49202	76566
Falsification of invoices	8	144	206	487	464	913
Art. 270a § 1 CC.	4	41	134	385	180	271
Art. 270a § 2 CC.	1	2	14	25	3	15
Art. 270a § 3 CC.	2	93	23	17	59	104

(continued)

Table 6.1. Continued

		Offences detected				
	2017	**2018**	**2019**	**2020**	**2021**	**2022**
Art. 271a § 1 CC.	1	7	23	40	67	418
Art. 271a § 2 CC.			1	12	16	12
Art. 271a § 3 CC.		1	1	4	134	89
Art. 277a CC.			10	4	5	4
		Suspects				
	2017	**2018**	**2019**	**2020**	**2021**	**2022**
Offences against the credibility of documents	8698	7857	7290	6503	6202	5929
Falsification of invoices	5	26	54	636	132	143
Art. 270a § 1 CC.	3	16	40	28	61	53
Art. 270a § 2 CC.	1	1	1	0	2	8
Art. 270a § 3 CC.	0	4	2	122	12	10
Art. 271a § 1 CC.	1	5	10	23	40	52
Art. 271a § 2 CC.			0	10	8	15
Art. 271a § 3 CC.		0	0	40	9	4
Art. 277a CC.		0	1	0	0	1

Source: Police Headquarters data.

Similarly to the number of offences and suspects, the number of convictions from the articles of the Penal Code analysed is also increasing from year to year. In 2017, there were four convictions and in 2022 there were already 161 (cf. Table 6.2).

Table 6.2. Number of people convicted of offences consisting of the falsification of invoices between 2017 and 2022

	2017	2018	2019	2020	2021	2022
Offences against the credibility of documents	7573	7 660	6897	6032	6348	4561
Falsification of invoices	4	26	22	47	128	161
Art. 270a § 1 CC.	0	9	11	28	81	85
Art. 270a § 2 CC.	0	5	0	1	1	5
Art. 270a § 3 CC.	4	10	5	4	0	0
Art. 271a § 1 CC.	0	1	6	10	39	53
Art. 271a § 2 CC.	0	0	0	4	2	10
Art. 271a § 3 CC.	0	0	0	0	0	0
Art. 277a CC.	0	1	0	0	3	3

Source: Data from the Ministry of Justice. Data for 2017–2020 refers to final convictions and data for 2021–2022 refers to non-final convictions (at first instance).

For the last two years (2021 and 2022), we have provided more detailed data on court decisions and sentences imposed for the offences analysed based on statistical reports on convictions at first instance (cf. Table 6.3 and 6.4). The most common form of termination of a case involving falsification of an invoice brought before the court is the conviction of the offender – such sentences were passed in 96 % of cases in 2021 and 93 % of cases in 2022. Discontinuations and conditional discontinuations of proceedings are much rarer in these cases than in other cases of offences against document reliability. While among cases for falsification of invoices discontinuations constituted only 6 % of decisions in 2022, cases for all crimes against document credibility ended in this way in as many as 20 % of cases. Also less frequent in the cases analysed (as compared to other falsifications) are acquittals and sentences passed as a result of accepting a motion for voluntary submission to punishment, sentencing without trial or without taking evidence (cf. Table 6.3).

Table 6.3. The structure of adjudications for offences involving the falsification of invoices in 2021 and 2022.

	Total adjudications	Convictions		Discontinuation*		Acquittal**		Convictions as a result of the granting of an application under Articles: 335, 338a and 387 of the Code of Criminal Procedure.	
		n	%	n	%	n	%	n	% of convictions
2021									
Offences against the reliability of documents	7413	6348	85.6	908	12.2	157	2.1	3400	53.6
Falsification of invoices	134	128	95.5	6	4.5	0	0.0	18	14.1
Art. 270a § 1 CC.	89	83	93.3	6	6.7	0	0.0	17	20.5
Art. 270a § 2 CC.	1	1	100	0	0.0	0	0.0	0	0.0
Art. 270a § 3 CC.	0	0	–	0	–	0	–	0	–
Art. 271a § 1 CC.	39	39	100	0	0.0	0	0.0	1	2.6
Art. 271a § 2 CC.	2	2	100	0	0.0	0	0.0	0	0.0
Art. 271a § 3 CC.	0	0	–	0	–	0		0	–
Art. 277a CC.	3	3	100	0	0.0	0	0.0	0	0.0
2022									
Offences against the credibility of documents	5961	4561	76.5	1208	20.3	192	3.2	1645	36.1
Falsification of invoices	174	161	92.5	11	6.3	2	1.1	58	36.0
Art. 270a § 1 CC.	102	90	88.2	11	10.8	1	1.0	21	23.3
Art. 270a § 2 CC.	5	5	100	0	0.0	0	0.0	5	100
Art. 270a § 3 CC.	0	0	–	0	–	0	–	0	–
Art. 271a § 1 CC.	54	53	98.1	0	0.0	1	1.9	29	54.7
Art. 271a § 2 CC.	10	10	100	0	0.0	0	0.0	3	30.0
Art. 271a § 3 CC.	0	0	–	0	–	0	–	0	–
Art. 277a CC.	3	3	100	0	0.0	0	0.0	0	0.0

Source: Data from the Ministry of Justice statistical reports MS-S6r and MS-S6o.

* Includes discontinuance and conditional discontinuance.

** Includes acquittal and waiver of sentence.

Those convicted for the offences of falsifying invoices were definitely more often punished with imprisonment (24–26 % of convictions, while for all offences from Chapter XXXIV of the Penal Code this occurred only in about 5 % of cases – cf. Table 6.4) and with community service. This means that falsification of invoices is generally punished more severely than other counterfeiting offences. With such small numbers of imprisonment convictions, it would be unauthorised to draw far-reaching conclusions about the exact dimensions of this punishment, but it is worth pointing out that they were not particularly high. In 2022, they did not exceed 1.5 years in prison and only for the so-called 'invoice felony' defined in Article 277a of the Penal Code did it amount to 3 and 5 years in prison.

6.4. Summary

The problem of the so-called VAT gap has been the subject of public debate for many years. Statistics show that its size is constantly changing. According to data published by the Ministry of Finance, the VAT gap has decreased in recent years from around 24 % in 2015 to less than 5 % in 2022[40]. This does not change the fact that any gap between expected and actual state budget revenues should prompt state authorities to take measures to reduce it further. Such measures may be of various types, including an increase in the number of inspections carried out by the tax authorities, but also the introduction of a legislative initiative.

One such amendment was the introduction of provisions into the Penal Code criminalising the falsification of an invoice – as a necessary element of conduct aimed at fraudulently evading VAT. Work on the amendment was relatively short, as it took less than seven months from the drafting of the first version to its adoption. It was the legislator's intention that the new provisions would significantly facilitate criminal proceedings and the punishment of perpetrators of false invoicing. It was assumed that the new types of offences would take over the task of punishing the perpetrators of the most serious VAT fraud, which was previously carried out on the basis of offences typified by the Fiscal Penal Code. An analysis of the statistical data on the number of proceedings initiated on the basis of Articles 270a, 271a and 277 of the Criminal Code, as well as on the offences established and detected, shows that these offences belong to

40 Luka w VAT urosła. Oto jak skomentowało to ministerstwo [The VAT gap has grown. Here is how the ministry commented on it], Business Insider, 25th April 2023, https://businessinsider.com.pl/gospodarka/podatki/luka-w-vat-urosla-oto-jak-skomentowalo-to-ministerstwo/lk5697j (Accessed Oct. 31, 2023).

Table 6.4. The structure of non-final convictions for invoice forgery offences in 2021 and 2022

	Total convictions	Imprisonment		Suspended imprisonment		Community service		Fine	
		n	%	n	%	n	%	n	%
2021									
Offences against the credibility of documents	6348	348	5.5	3117	49.1	374	5.9	2496	39.3
Falsification of invoices	128	33	25.8	25	19.5	32	25.0	38	29.7
Art. 270a § 1 CC.	83	24	28.9	18	21.7	17	20.5	24	28.9
Art. 270a § 2 CC.	1	1	100	0	0.0	0	0.0	0	0.0
Art. 270a § 3 CC.	0	0	–	0	–	0	–	0	–
Art. 271a § 1 CC.	39	4	10.3	6	15.4	15	38.5	14	35.9
Art. 271a § 2 CC.	2	1	50.0	1	50.0	0	0.0	0	0.0
Art. 271a § 3 CC.	0	0	–	0	–	0	–	0	–
Art. 277a CC.	3	3	100	0	0.0	0	0.0	0	0.0
2022									
Offences against the credibility of documents	4561	247	5.4	926	20.3	314	6.9	3069	67.3
Falsification of invoices	161	38	23.6	66	41.0	18	11.2	39	24.2
Art. 270a § 1 CC.	90	26	28.9	25	27.8	13	14.4	26	28.9
Art. 270a § 2 CC.	5	0	0.0	5	100	0	0.0	0	0.0
Art. 270a § 3 CC.	0	0	–	0	–	0	–	0	–
Art. 271a § 1 CC.	53	5	9.4	30	56.6	5	9.4	13	24.5
Art. 271a § 2 CC.	10	4	40.0	6	60.0	0	0.0	0	0.0
Art. 271a § 3 CC.	0	0	–	0	–	0	–	0	–
Art. 277a CC.	3	3	100	0	0.0	0	0.0	0	0.0

Source: data from the Ministry of Justice statistical reports MS-S6r and MS-S6o. The table does not include the mixed penalty due to the small number – 7 convictions for this penalty for all offences against document reliability in 2021, 1 in 2022 and none for falsification of invoices.

one of the less frequently applied provisions of Chapter XXXIV of the Penal Code, relating to offences against the authenticity of documents. In 2022, they accounted for only about 2 % of all proceedings initiated under the provisions of this chapter and just over 1 % of the offences identified and detected. The statistics are slightly better for the number of suspects. In this case, they accounted for more than 2 % of all suspects for any of the offences against the reliability of documents. In 2022, 161 persons were convicted for falsifying invoices, which is more than 3.5 % of all persons convicted for offences under Chapter XXXIV of the Penal Code.

It is of course difficult to assess the effectiveness of the new legislation on the basis of statistics alone. However, it is worth noting that since 2017, when the analysed provisions were introduced into the Penal Code, the number of proceedings conducted has increased in each subsequent year. These are proceedings that require the collection of a number of documents and, in many cases, are preceded by control proceedings conducted by the tax authorities. This may explain the relatively low number of such cases. In addition, not all (or perhaps even most) cases of falsification of invoices reach the criminal court with qualification under the provisions of the Criminal Code, but are qualified as fiscal offences under the provisions of the Fiscal Penal Code. This does not change the fact that the analysed provisions of the Penal Code provide additional assistance to law enforcement authorities in the fight against crimes related to VAT fraud in Poland.

References

Sarnowski J., & Selera P. (2018). *Zmniejszenie luki VAT w Polsce w latach 2016 – 2017. Przyczyny, środki, dalsze perspektywy [Reducing the VAT gap in Poland in 2016 – 2017. Causes, measures, further perspectives].* Warsaw: Polish Economic Institute.

Comments of the Supreme Court – Regulatory Impact Assessment, https://legislacja.rcl.gov.pl/docs//2/12288207/12370166/12370167/dokument243523.pdf (Accessed Oct. 31, 2023).

Explanatory Memorandum to the Draft Law on Amendments to the Law – Penal Code and Certain Other Laws, 8th Legislature, Parliamentary Print No. 888, https://orka.sejm.gov.pl/Druki8ka.nsf/0/EA8BC112272EA7CEC125804200323EDD/%24File/888.pdf (Accessed Oct. 31, 2023).

https://statystyka.policja.pl/download/20/232288/Uwagiidefinicje.docx (Accessed Oct. 31, 2023).

Kulisy Spraw: karuzele VAT-owskie [*Backstage of Affairs: VAT carousels*]. Polskie Radio, 17 August 2017, https://polskieradio24.pl/130/5561/Artykul/1821346,kulisy-spraw-karuzele-vatowskie (Accessed Oct. 31, 2023).

Letter from the Ministry of Finance No. PR2.021.744.2016.MTS.SOD, 10th August 2016, https://legislacja.rcl.gov.pl/docs//2/12288207/12370133/12370136/dokument243123.pdf (Accessed Oct. 31, 2023).*Letter from the Ministry of Foreign Affairs No. DPUE.920.1196.2016/2/JS of 11*th *August 2016*, https://legislacja.rcl.gov.pl/docs//2/12288207/12370133/12370136/dokument243119.pdf (Accessed Oct. 31, 2023).

Letter from the Lewiatan Confederation, 12th August 2016, https://legislacja.rcl.gov.pl/docs//2/12288207/12370139/12370142/dokument243127.pdf (Accessed Oct. 31, 2023).

Luka w VAT urosła. Oto jak skomentowało to ministerstwo [*The VAT gap has grown. Here is how the ministry commented on it*]. Business Insider, 25th April 2023, https://businessinsider.com.pl/gospodarka/podatki/luka-w-vat-urosla-oto-jak-skomentowalo-to-ministerstwo/lk5697j (Accessed Oct. 31, 2023).

Memorandum of Understanding No. 32/2016 of the meeting of the Council of Ministers on 13th September 2016, https://legislacja.rcl.gov.pl/docs//2/12288207/12370166/12370171/dokument248205.pdf (Accessed Oct. 31, 2023).

Ministry of Development letter No. 176441/16, 16th August 2016, https://legislacja.rcl.gov.pl/docs//2/12288207/12370133/12370136/dokument243122.pdf (Accessed Oct. 31, 2023).

Opinion of the National Council of the Judiciary of 16th September 2016 on the Draft Law on Amendments to the Law – Penal Code and Certain Other Laws, https://orka.sejm.gov.pl/Druki8ka.nsf/0/E15BE69E0D01DAA4C12580520058A0B0/%24File/888-001.pdf (Accessed Oct. 31, 2023).

Regulatory Impact Assessment of 08/09/2016 of the Draft Law on Amendments to the Law – Penal Code and Some Other Laws, https://legislacja.rcl.gov.pl/docs//2/12288207/12370133/12370134/dokument259751.docx (Accessed Oct. 31, 2023).

Resolution of the Senate of 1st February 2017 on the Law on Amendments to the Law – Penal Code and Certain Other Laws, 8th Legislature, print no. 1260, https://orka.sejm.gov.pl/Druki8ka.nsf/0/E492987D7B97DD33C12580BB004DA14B/%24File/1260.pdf (Accessed Oct. 31, 2023).

Report of the Extraordinary Committee for Amendments to the Codifications on the Government Bill on Amendments to the Act – Penal Code and Certain Other Acts (Print No. 888), 8th Kadence, Print No. 1189, https://orka.sejm.gov.pl/Druki8ka.nsf/0/771B8224CEC320F8C12580A6004FCD95/%24File/1189.pdf (Accessed Oct. 31, 2023).

Report of the Extraordinary Committee for Amendments to the Codifications on the Resolution of the Senate on the Act on Amendments to the Act – Penal Code and Certain Other Acts, 8th Legislature, print no. 1262, https://orka.sejm.gov.pl/Druki8ka.nsf/0/20ED2E976C1F7CE9C12580C1004FA9C4/%24File/1262.pdf

(Accessed Oct. 31, 2023). *Wyłudzenia VAT – luka podatkowa w 2014 roku i prognoza na 2015* [*VAT fraud – tax gap in 2014 and forecast for 2015*], 25th September 2015, PWC (report), https://www.pwc.pl/pl/pdf/luka-vat-pwc-wrzesien-2015.pdf (Accessed Oct. 31, 2023).

Legislation

Criminal fiscal law of 26th October 1971 (i.e. Journal of Laws of 1984 No. 22, item 103 as amended).

The Act of 6th April 1990 on the Police (i.e. Journal of Laws of 2023, item 171).

The Act of 12th October 1990 on the Border Guard service (i.e. Journal of Laws of 2023, item 1080).

The Act of 28th September 1991 on fiscal control (i.e. Journal of Laws 2016, item 720).

The Act of 8th January 1993 on VAT (Journal of Laws No. 11, item 50).

The Act amending the Act on VAT and Excise Tax and amending the Fiscal Penalty The Act of 21st November 1996 (Journal of Laws No 137, item 640).

The Constitution of the Republic of Poland of 2nd April 1997 (Journal of Laws No. 78, item 483).

The Act of 6th June 1997, the Penal Code (i.e. Journal of Laws 2022, item 1138).

The Act of 6th June 1997, the Code of Criminal Procedure (i.e. Journal of Laws 2022, item 1375).

The Act of 10th September 1999, the Fiscal Penal Code (i.e. Journal of Laws 2023, item 654).

The Act of 24th August 2001 on Military Police and Military Order Authorities (i.e. Journal of Laws of 2023, item 1266).

The Act of 11th March 2004 on VAT (i.e. Journal of Laws of 2023, item 1570).

The Act of 9th June 2006 on the Central Anti-Corruption Bureau (i.e. Journal of Laws of 2022, item 1900).

The Act of 16th November 2016 on the National Fiscal Administration (i.e. Journal of Laws 2023, item 615).

The Act of 16th November 2016, the Provisions introducing the Act on the National Fiscal Administration (Journal of Laws of 2016, item 1948).

The Act of 10th February 2017 amending the Act on the Penal Code and certain other acts (Journal of Laws of 2017, item 244).

The Act of 7th July 2022 amending the Act on the Penal Code and certain other acts (Journal of Laws 2022, item 2600 as amended by Journal of Laws 2023, item 403).

Konrad Buczkowski (Polish Academy of Sciences),
Joanna Klimczak (Institute of Justice),
Paweł Ostaszewski (University of Warsaw)

Chapter 7 Criminal policy response - Case files research

Abstract: This chapter presents the functioning of the new provisions of Polish Criminal Code in practice, based on the research conducted on criminal cases, including in particular, whether they have fulfilled the expectations raised when they were introduced to effectively combat crimes related to extorting the VAT. The study covered 194 criminal cases.

Key words: VAT fraud, court file study, VAT extortion, Criminal Code, offence

7.1. General comments

In the legislator's opinion, the provisions of the Fiscal Penal Code[1], which have been applied up to now, have not played their proper role in combating the so-called 'VAT gap', due to their connection with the need to prove the depletion of the State Treasury's revenues. Therefore, work has been carried out on the introduction of provisions into the Penal Code that would facilitate the conduct of proceedings in cases of VAT extortion and penalise behaviour that constitutes a prelude to the unlawful deduction of input VAT or its undue refund. The falsification of an invoice (both formally and intellectually) was considered to be such behaviour.

These provisions were implemented by the adoption on 10 February 2017 of the Act amending the Act on the Penal Code and certain other acts by adding Articles 270a, 271a and 277a – 277d to Chapter XXXIV – Offences against the credibility of documents.

In this study, we analyse the functioning of these provisions in practice based on the research conducted on criminal cases, including in particular, whether they have fulfilled the expectations raised when they were introduced to effectively combat crimes related to extorting the VAT.

---

1 The Act of 10th September 1999, the Fiscal Penal Code (i.e. Journal of Laws 2023, item 654).

7.2. Methodology of the case file study and characteristics of the examined sample

As stated at the outset, the main objective of the file survey carried out was to analyse the functioning in practice of the provisions of Articles 270a, 271a and 277a-d introduced into the Penal Code, to diagnose the most serious problems arising in the conduct of cases of invoice falsification, to determine the duration of these proceedings, the effectiveness of the penalties and measures of a financial nature imposed and the effectiveness of the enforcement of these penalties and measures.

In order to achieve these objectives, we decided to carry out a case file study of all court cases for the offences analysed that were finalised between 2017 and 2022. We requested files for the study from all courts that showed a minimum of one conviction from the aforementioned articles. At the time of the study (May-July 2023), only data on final convictions from 2017–2020 and non-final convictions (at first instance) from 2021–2022 were available. We used both data sources to compile the list of courts from which we requested files.

The study covered 194 cases tried before 90 courts, mostly district courts (93 % of cases) and a small number before county courts (7 %).

The body that informed the law enforcement authorities of the fact that an offence of falsifying invoices had been committed was most often the tax office – 37 % of the cases (cf. Table 7.1) – and the victim in the broadest sense of the term (it was most often the company on whose account the falsified invoices were issued). About a dozen of the cases examined were initiated as a result of activities carried out by: the Border Guard, the Police and the Customs and Fiscal Office, and in individual cases as a result of actions of other institutions, including: the Central Anti-Corruption Bureau, the Provincial Inspectorate for Plant and Seed Protection, the General Inspector of Financial Information, the Director of the Fiscal Administration Chamber and the Customs Office. Five cases (3 % of those investigated) were initiated after self-incrimination by one of the perpetrators – most often playing the role of a 'stooge' in the illegal procedure. There was no information on who filed the complaint in 13 cases that were opened because the material of a particular perpetrator was excluded for separate examination and the original complaint was not included in the file.

Table 7.1. Who reported suspected offences?

	N	%
Tax office	66	36.5
Customs and Tax Administration	16	8.8
Border Guard activities	13	7.2
Police activities	14	7.7
Other institution	7	3.9
Victim	60	33.2
Self-denunciation	5	2.8
Total	**181**	**100.0**
No data available	13	

Source: Own compilation based on case file study.

The cases examined ended most frequently with an 'ordinary' conviction (46 % of all cases – cf. Table 7.2), in 28 % of cases, a sentence was passed as a result of an 'agreement' between the convicted person and the prosecutor (most frequently under Article 335 of the Code of Criminal Procedure – 42 cases, less frequently under Article 387 of the Code of Criminal Procedure – 12 cases and one case under Article 338a of the Code of Criminal Procedure)[2] In 17 % of the cases, there was a final injunction judgment, in twelve cases a decision on conditional discontinuance of proceedings, in four cases an acquittal, and in the last two cases a decision on discontinuance of the case.

Table 7.2. Type of final termination of the case

	N	%
Injunction	32	16.5
Consensual judgment	55	28.4
Ordinary conviction	89	45.9
Judgment of acquittal	4	2.1
Discontinuance of proceedings	2	1.0
Conditional discontinuance of proceedings	12	6.2
Total	**194**	**100.0**

Source: Own compilation based on case file study.

2 These are so-called consensual modes, which allow for a faster conclusion of proceedings as a result of an agreement between the prosecution and the accused on guilt and punishment.

The average duration of pre-trial proceedings in the cases analysed was 412 days (13.5 months), with a lower median of 277 days, i.e. 9 months, from the notification of the commission of the offence to the submission of the indictment or the request for punishment to the court. The shortest lasted only 4 days (when the material was excluded from separate consideration) and the longest lasted five and a half years. The most common duration was between six months and one year (28 %) and between one year and two years (25 %).

While pre-trial proceedings were lengthy, which was mainly due to the volume of evidence collected in the course of these proceedings, proceedings before the court were already mostly quick and not very extensive. Proceedings at first instance lasted on average 162 days (just over 5 months, median 112 days – over 3.5 months). The longest case examined lasted 1242 days, i.e. almost three and a half years. The duration of first instance proceedings was most frequently in the range of up to three months – 44 % – and between three and six months – 29 %.

Only 18 cases (9 %) were appealed against the first instance judgment. In eight of these, the appeal was dismissed and the judgment was upheld. In one case, the verdict was overturned and the case was sent back for retrial, and in nine cases the substance of the sentence was changed. These changes mainly involved minor changes in the legal classification of acts and penalties, most often in favour of the convicted person.

On the other hand, the average duration of the proceedings before the court of second instance was 209 days (almost seven months, median 165 days or five and a half months, minimum 98 days – three months, maximum 595 days – one and a half years) and in most cases more than three months to one year.

In 47 cases (24 % of all cases examined), at least one expert opinion was ordered. These were commissioned exclusively by the Public Prosecutor's Office in the course of pre-trial proceedings. These opinions concerned the analysis of documents in 20 cases (43 %) – mainly the authorship of signatures on invoices in dispute, the state of mind and sanity of the accused in 18 cases (38 %), the analysis of the contents of a computer or mobile phone in seven cases (15 %) and both the analysis of documents and the state of mental health of the accused in two cases.

7.3. Description of case file study results: Characteristics of perpetrators and the measures taken by the State against them

A total of 244 people were tried in the 194 cases examined. The details described below relate to 234 defendants[3]. In almost all cases (87 %), there was only one

3 For practical reasons, the study included data on a maximum of four defendants.

defendant on trial. In 16 cases there were two defendants, in eight cases there were between 3 or 5 defendants and in one case the court sentenced 11 defendants. It should be noted that the cases we examined often involved defendants whose case was excluded for separate trial because of the possibility of faster sentencing in this consensual mode. Therefore, the number of co-defendants convicted in our study does not correspond to the number of persons involved in the particular criminal activity in each case.

In almost all the cases, more than one legal basis was used to charge (and subsequently convict) the perpetrators. Respondents were most often convicted under Article 270a of the Criminal Code (144 perpetrators) and Article 271a of the Criminal Procedure Code. (90 perpetrators). Convictions were often based on provisions of the Fiscal Code – Article 62(2) of the Fiscal Code (79 perpetrators), Article 56 of the Fiscal Code (59 perpetrators), Article 61 of the Fiscal Code (30 perpetrators). Only one offender was convicted under Article 277a-d of the Penal Code. Quite often fraud appeared in the qualification of the prosecution (Article 286 of the Penal Code – 33 convicted people), certification of falsities, i.e. Article 271 of the Penal Code (32 convicted people) and use of a document certifying falsities (Article 273 of the Penal Code – 24 perpetrators). With regard to five convicted offenders, the court found that they participated in an organised criminal group (Article 258 § 1 of the Penal Code). Two perpetrators were convicted under Article 77.1 of the Accounting Act of 29/09/1994.

It is worth mentioning that the legislator, in the justification of the draft act introducing new types of offences related to falsification of invoices to the Penal Code, assumed that they would take over the role in combating VAT fraud from the penal provisions contained in the Fiscal Penal Code, with the simultaneous possibility of preserving the qualification of behaviours of lesser social harmfulness of an act on the basis of the latter, in particular Article 62 § 1 and 2 of the Fiscal Penal Code. At the same time, it was emphasised that 'There is, of course, the possibility of a coincidence of legal qualifications of the general criminal law and the fiscal penal law with regard to the same criminal offence. It should then be resolved on the basis of the disposition of Article 8 § 1 of the Fiscal Penal Code, according to which, if the same act, which is a fiscal offence or a fiscal misdemeanour, at the same time exhausts the elements of an offence or a misdemeanour specified in the penal provisions of another act, each of these provisions is applied. (…) As a result of the application of the directive expressed in Article 8 of the Fiscal Penal Code, as many offences or misdemeanours are attributed to the perpetrator as many elements of the type of a prohibited act defined in the scope of application of the sanctioning norms decoded from the converging provisions defining the elements of a fiscal offence or a general offence or a general misdemeanour are realised by the same act of the same perpetrator constituting the basis for the criminal law assessment.'[4]. Therefore, cumulative qualifications of the provisions of the Penal Code and the Fiscal Penal Code were noted in the cases analysed. Mainly, it was the qualification from Article 271a of the Penal Code and Article 62 § 2 of the Criminal Fiscal Code[5].

The defendants were Polish (94 % of those examined), with the exception of a dozen people – 13 of Ukrainian origin and one of Belgian origin. The majority of the defendants in the cases we examined were men (77 %), which is in line with the national gender statistics for those convicted of falsifying invoices.

On the day the notice of possible criminal offence was received by the law enforcement authorities, the youngest respondent was 20 years old and the oldest was 72 (cf. Table 7.3). On average, the defendants in the examined cases were about 43 years old (median=42)[6]. The low percentage of defendants under the age of 30 shows that the defendants in the cases studied differed from typical criminal offenders, whose criminal activity is estimated by criminologists to peak between the ages of 16 and 30[7].

Table 7.3. Age of the offender

	N	%
Up to 30 years	30	14.0
31–40 years	62	29.0
41–50 years	68	31.8
51–60 years	54	25.2
Total	**214**	**100.0**
No data available	*20*	*8.5*

Source: Own compilation based on case file study.

4 Explanatory memorandum…, p. 4.

5 More on this topic: Gruszka M. (2022). Zbieg przepisów przy przestępstwach związanych z podatkiem VAT oraz problematyka należytej staranności w VAT w aspekcie prawnokarnym [Confluence of regulations in VAT offences and the problematic of due diligence in VAT in the aspect of criminal law], [in:] Sz. Pawelec (ed.), *Karuzele VAT. Wybrane regulacje prawa karnego materialnego i procesowego* [VAT carousels. Wybrane regulacje prawa karnego materialnego i procesowego]. Wolters Kluwer, Warsaw , pp. 187–252.

6 Data on the age of defendants is based on 214 questionnaires (20 missing data).

7 Cf. e.g. D.P. Farrington, *Age and Crime*, Crime and Justice, 1986, vol. 7.

The defendants were mostly residents of large and medium-sized Polish cities. Every fifth defendant lived in a rural area (cf. Table 7.4). In contrast to the perpetrators of common crimes, in the majority of these cases examined the defendants graduated at least from secondary school or university (a total of 79 % – Table 7.5).

Table 7.4. Place of residence of the offender

	N	%
Village	51	21.9
Town up to 10 000 inhabitants	13	5.6
Town of between 10,000 and 50,000 inhabitants	40	17.2
Town of between 50,000 and 100,000 inhabitants	27	11.6
City of between 100,000 and 500,000 inhabitants	60	25.8
City with more than 500,000 inhabitants	42	18.0
Total	**233**	**100.0**
No data available	*1*	*0.4*

Source: Own compilation based on case file study.

Table 7.5. Education of the offender

	N	%
Primary	12	5.1
Vocational	37	15.8
Secondary	104	44.4
Higher	81	34.6
Total	**234**	**100.0**

Source: Own compilation based on case file study.

The perpetrators studied were mostly self-employed, within the framework of which they committed the act tried in the criminal case under analysis (just under 49 % of the perpetrators). Almost 17 % indicated that they were working on a permanent basis (employment contract) and about 10 % were working on a casual basis. One in ten defendants declared to law enforcement that they were not working. Among them, there were unemployed people who, due to the detection of crimes, had to terminate their business activities, as well as unemployed people who used the opportunity to earn money in criminal activities, as so-called 'stooges'. The explanation of one of them serves as an example:

My son M. suggested to me in the summer of 2018 that a friend of his – I don't know the details – I saw him once during the signing of the contract – needed someone to be president of the company and that it was possible to make money. My son knew that I was not working professionally, I had financial problems. My son told me that my job was to buy back the company – and sign VAT invoices. I agreed. (…) Before going to the notary, I dressed nicely and shaved, because now I have a beard which frightens me when I look in the mirror. I did not pay at the notary, everything was paid for. The man who drove me walked into the notary with me. It was obvious that he knew the notary, they spoke to each other by name. (….) The documents were already waiting for me to sign, I signed them where they showed me where to sign. I myself would not have known where to sign. (…) He [J.] also told me that M. (the son) would drop off documents for me to sign, I was to sign them. He said that I would receive PLN 200 a week regardless of the number and value of the documents I signed. (…) My son would bring me 10, sometimes 20 invoices a week, I did not count them, I judged the number by its appearance. I read the first bills, then I didn't read them any more because I didn't care. I don't know who the recipients of these invoices were, I don't know what they were about, I remember some pallets, but I don't know if I sold goods or provided services (…) My son brought me the invoices and showed me where to sign. I would have had a problem signing such a document myself, I never wrote out invoices myself, I wouldn't have been able to do it. I had the stamp of my company (…). It was based at my address, that is where I lived. (…) I earned about 4 thousand zloty on this whole business, which I spent on living. I feel exploited, I wanted to earn money and I made trouble for myself. (…) This year I've been drinking alcohol since the holidays, in February this year my legs failed and I started treatment for thrombosis, I gave up alcohol. (…) Before that, I used to drink every day. When I was going to the notary or had to go to the bank I would not drink from the morning until 4pm to go to the bank to collect the money. Then I didn't drink until I went to the bank, I drank afterwards. My son asked me not to smell of alcohol when he went to the bank with me. He would tell me in the morning that there would be a transfer that day, then I was not to drink until the money was withdrawn (Case No 163).

It is also worth adding that the perpetrators performed various functions in the course of their activities. They were not only sole traders, but also persons in managerial positions, including members of the management boards of companies, who could issue unreliable or falsified invoices themselves or instruct another person to issue such invoices. In addition, a noticeable group of perpetrators were accountants operating independently or within companies, who issued or posted unreliable invoices.

acting with short intervals of time and with premeditated intent, as a person commissioning an accounting service, acting as an employee of an accounting office, as a partner of a civil partnership and a person actually managing it, and therefore being a person authorised to issue documents on behalf of this company – instructed a person providing accounting services for the company to issue invoices concerning services rendered for (…) – cleaning and care of outdoor areas, certifying falsities as to the circumstances of the actual performance of services in the amount of PLN 808,920, which were not performed and then used these documents by submitting them for accounting and tax settlements. (Case No. 65)

The defendants usually declared that they earned quite high incomes – one in four, above PLN 5,000 per month. The average earnings of the defendants was PLN 5,835[8]. Half of them had incomes above PLN 3,100. The lowest amount a suspect declared as their monthly income was PLN 302 and the highest was PLN 50,000. More than 14 % of the defendants indicated that they did not earn any income. It should also be borne in mind that income amounts are collected by law enforcement authorities only on the basis of suspects' declarations (Table 7.6).

Table 7.6. The average monthly net income of offenders

	N	%
No income	30	14.4
PLN 200–1000	14	6.7
PLN 1001–2000	23	11.0
PLN 2001–3000	51	24.4
PLN 3001–5000	40	19.1
Over PLN 5,000	51	24.4
Total	**209**	**100.0**
No data available	*25*	*10.7*

Source: Own compilation based on case file study.

The majority of defendants pleaded guilty during the criminal proceedings (74 %). Such a result is not surprising given that often the cases studied were concluded consensually and that many cases were initiated as a result of exclusion from other proceedings against those defendants about whom there was no doubt of guilt and a conviction could be handed down against them.

The vast majority of respondents had no previous convictions (78 %). One in five defendants had a previous conviction and most had been to court before. The record holder had 38 previous convictions.

The largest number of respondents had previously been convicted of offences against property (33 people), the most common of which was fraud (Article 286 of the Criminal Code – 19 people). Another group of offences for which the respondents had been previously convicted were offences against the

8 Data for 179 defendants. There are no data or no income for the remainder.

credibility of documents (18 people) and offences against the safety of transport (15 people). Nineteen people had previously been convicted of offences under the Penal Code, the most common of which were offences under Article 56 of the Penal Code (7 persons), Article 61(1) of the Penal Code, Article 62(2) of the Penal Code and Article 54 of the Penal Code. Three perpetrators had previously been convicted for participation in an organised criminal group (Article 258 of the Fiscal Penal Code) and five for acts under the Act on Counteracting Drug Addiction.

Turning to the justice system's response to the offences investigated, it is necessary to start with the fact that 33 suspects (out of 234 people investigated) were subjected to preventive measures by law enforcement authorities. The most severe measure – pre-trial detention – was applied to five people. The longest arrest lasted nearly two years (620 days) and the shortest just over a month (42 days). The other preventive measures were often applied to a single suspect. Thus, property surety was applied to 24 suspects and a ban on leaving the country was applied to 13, while other preventive measures were applied to 26 suspects (police supervision being the most common measure).

Security of assets was applied with regard to 56 people (24 % of respondents). It was not uncommon for the object of the security to be the suspects' cars or real estate, and the average value of the property subject to security was approximately PLN 30,000.

As already mentioned, in the cases examined, the defendants answered mainly under the following provisions of the Penal Code of interest to us: articles 270a and 271a of the Penal Code carrying the threat of imprisonment (cf. point 2). However, in the cases examined, the courts most often applied other types of penalties on the basis of Article 37a of the Penal Code[9]. The courts sometimes imposed more than one sentence on the same defendant (e.g. a fine and a suspended prison sentence).

In the majority of cases analysed, the courts applied for a fine (79 %) and in every third case for a suspended imprisonment sentence of (34 %). It was rare for perpetrators to be sentenced to imprisonment (6.2 %) or community service (5.7 %).

---

9 Article 37a § 1 of the Penal Code. If the offence is punishable only by deprivation of liberty for a term not exceeding 8 years and the punishment imposed for it would not be more severe than one year, the court may, instead of that punishment, impose a sentence of restriction of liberty of not less than 3 months or a fine of not less than 100 daily rates if it simultaneously imposes a penal measure, a compensatory measure or forfeiture.

In addition, seven offenders were ordered by the court to compensate by paying, in part or in full, the lost amount to the injured party (which was sometimes the Tax Office). In one case, the court banned the convicted person from running a business for six years.

In only 12 cases did the court order the forfeiture of the financial gain from the offence. This measure affected 14 offenders. The highest amount of forfeiture from a convicted person was PLN 300,000 and the lowest was PLN 1,500.

The most severe sentence – unsuspended imprisonment – was handed down to 13 offenders. The shortest sentence was 8 months and the longest was 3 years and 8 months.

The courts sentenced 12 offenders to a community service, in each case a penalty consisting of the obligation to perform unpaid, monitored work for social purposes[10]. The highest level of this penalty was nearly two years (22 months) of work at 24 hours per month, and the lowest level was six months of work at 20 hours per month.

In the case of 85 convicts, the court applied a sentence of suspended imprisonment. Most often it was one year of imprisonment conditionally suspended for 2 or 3 years of probation.

As has already been indicated, the most frequent, i.e. in the case of 188 convicted people, the courts imposed a fine. Its average amount in the cases examined was PLN 12,633.88. However, in the case of half of the convicted people, the amount of the fine did not exceed PLN 6000. The lowest amount of this penalty was PLN 400 (20 daily rates of PLN 20 each) and the highest – PLN 132,500 (530 rates of PLN 250 each) – Table 7.7.

---

10 In Poland, the penalty of community service may be executed in two ways – as an obligation to perform unpaid, controlled work for social purposes or as a deduction from 10 % to 25 % of the remuneration for work on a monthly basis for a social purpose indicated by the court (Article 34 of the Penal Code). As evidenced by the results of research, the application of this punishment in the form of community service is the most common on a national scale. Cf. Wzorek D., Zielińska E., & Klimczak J. (2022). *Kara ograniczenia wolności i jej rola w resocjalizacji sprawców przestępstw [Penalty of community service and its role in the rehabilitation of offenders]*, Publishing House of the Institute of Justice, Warsaw.

Table 7.7. The amount of the fine imposed

	N	%
up to PLN 1000	12	6.4
> PLN 1000 to PLN 4000	59	31.4
> PLN 4,000 to PLN 7,000	29	15.4
> PLN 7,000 to PLN 10,000	19	10.1
> PLN 10,000 to PLN 20,000	36	19.1
> PLN 20,000	33	17.6
Total	**188**	**100.0**

Source: Own compilation based on case file study.

More than one in three of the cases we examined were accompanied by an enforcement file (36 % of cases). This information allowed us to check, to some extent, how the sentence imposed by the court was carried out by offenders. Unfortunately, as most of the cases we examined had been convicted relatively recently, it was sometimes the case that the sentences imposed were still being served. We were able to confirm that in 105 cases the sentence imposed by the court had been carried out, of which in 22 cases it had been partially carried out at the time of the study. The partial execution of the sentence was due to the fact that, for example, the convicted person had paid the fine imposed but the probation period of the suspended prison sentence against him or her was still in progress. In 15 cases, the sentence imposed in the conviction was changed by the court to another sentence – a fine was changed to imprisonment (11 cases) or restriction of liberty (4 cases). In two cases, the perpetrators requested (and the courts granted) that the penalty of restriction of liberty in the form of community service be changed to a penalty in the form of deduction from their monthly salary.

To summarise the above analysis, the average offender convicted in the cases analysed was a bachelor with no previous convictions, with secondary or higher education, who was running his own business, in the course of which he committed a VAT invoice falsification offence. In the majority of cases, the perpetrators pleaded guilty and were mostly sentenced to fines of around PLN 6,000 (median).

7.4. Description of case file study results: Types of cases and criminal acts

The analysis focused on the question of whether the new criminal law actually enables a more efficient combating of VAT fraud. Within the 194 investigations examined, approximately 10% of the investigations were identified as containing elements of organised activity aimed at the understatement of taxes, primarily VAT. In this group, the *modus operandi* included, among others, 'empty invoice factories', which were used by many entities to overstate the cost of doing business:

> The *investigation uncovered a mechanism for committing tax fraud related to the issuing of unreliable invoices and 'I'll give costs' type advertisements. Persons interested in acquiring such documents contacted, among others, telephone numbers (…) and (…). They then made payments of commission fees for their issuance into bank accounts belonging to the money brokers. (…)*
>
> *The mechanism of this criminal offence consisted of the publication by members of the group, acting under the leadership of S., who was hiding abroad, on local internet advertising portals, internet domains created for this purpose and in emails sent to groups of recipients selected from databases created for this purpose, of offers of sale of falsified VAT invoices to interested parties with the aim of using these documents in the poorly understood so-called tax optimisation. Parties interested in purchasing this type of falsified documents, using instructions from these offers, were redirected to the main domains, in particular (…).ru and (…).com, where, using a contact gateway, they declared their intention to purchase unreliable cost-creating VAT invoices. In response to the request, they were provided with an email address (…) and a contact telephone number, where they carried out further correspondence and conversations to agree on details, such as the expected content of the invoice, the method of its transfer and the cost of obtaining it (…).*
>
> *During these telephone conversations, the interested parties were instructed to provide, via email correspondence, any details they wished to be included on the VAT invoice. An invoice was then issued to them and sent to them in response also by email. The message stated that they had to pay an amount of 5% of the gross value indicated on the VAT invoice representing the remuneration to the forgers of these documents for issuing them.*
>
> *In addition, the numbers of the bank accounts to which the described payment was to be made were indicated. These accounts were mainly held in Polish banks and their holders were, in particular: G. and the late J.*
>
> *A significant proportion of the cash that constituted the proceeds of crime was transferred abroad from these accounts to Cypriot and Turkish accounts and then withdrawn at ATMs there or used to purchase virtual currencies.*
>
> *The criminal group, whose activities were uncovered, indicated in the VAT invoices, as issuers, the subject and address data of at least 65 Polish economic entities of various activity profiles, whose representatives were not aware that the documents were being issued. As a result, these entities did not provide the services and sales of goods indicated in the invoices and did not record them in their books, including in the structures of the Single Control File, and did not include them in their VAT returns and annual PIT/CIT returns. The recipients of these VAT invoices, on the other hand, despite the fact that they did not reflect actual economic events, recorded these documents in their books and included their values in their tax declarations on the side of input VAT and deductible costs, which enabled them to evade due VAT and income tax and, in some cases, enabled them to obtain undue refunds of the allegedly overpaid tax or its declared excess. (Case No. 75)*

There were also a few cases reported that were in the nature of 'VAT carousels', the operation of which involved the transfer of a manufactured good or service between a number of entities, some of which bore the character of a 'disappearing taxpayer':

during a period no shorter than from the beginning of (…) to at least (…), in various places in the country, including (…), (…) and (…), acting at short intervals, in the execution of a premeditated intention, in order to derive a financial benefit, within the framework of an organised criminal group and an adopted division of tasks, jointly and in agreement with the convicted person W., whom he induced to commit the following acts and provided him with assistance in their execution, and other identified persons.

Being a person actually involved in economic and financial matters and acting on behalf of [X] company, then [Y] company, not conducting any real economic activity, having previously acquired shares in this entity, being authorised to accept and issue documents within the framework of the aforementioned economic entity performing the role of the so-called 'disappearing taxpayer' in the tax fraud consisting of the pretence of supplies and their fictitious documentation with VAT invoices between an established group of entities involved in the procedure in order to evade payment and reduce the amount due to the State Treasury, being authorised to accept and issue documents within the framework of the aforementioned economic entity performing the role of the so-called 'disappearing taxpayer' in a tax fraud consisting of fictitious supplies and their fictitious documentation with VAT invoices between an established group of entities involved in the procedure in order to evade payment and reduction of public receivables due to the State Treasury in the form of tax on goods and services by virtue of conducting business activity by the final recipients of these documents and beneficiaries of the procedure, in the period from (….) to (…) in order to use them for the purpose of authenticity, he used VAT invoices fully forged by an unidentified perpetrator, by impersonating the below-mentioned entities, in the scope of factual circumstances which may be of significance for the determination of the amount of a public liability in the scope of the goods and services tax, and VAT invoices certifying falsities in this scope with the total gross value of PLN 3,345,702.13., net value of PLN 2,720,083. and VAT in the amount of PLN 625,619.13, which were to confirm that [X] had not purchased goods from [5] entities.

Then, in the period from (…) to (…), consecutively in relation to the aforementioned documents of the alleged purchase of goods, he certified falsities in documents as to the factual circumstances which could be of significance for the determination of the amount of a public receivable or its refund in tax on goods and services, i.e. the occurrence of a transaction subject to tax on goods and services, which did not take place, by issuing under [company X] VAT sales invoices, containing the total amount due, the total value of which is significant and amounts to PLN 4,898,108.18 gross, and PLN 3,986,592.00 net and VAT at the amount of PLN 909,101.18, after which he used these invoices as authentic by handing them over to [two] recipients and entered them in the register of purchases and sales of VAT referred to in article 109.3 of the Act of 11/03/2004. on tax on goods and services, and disclosed for the period from November 2018 to February 2019 in monthly tax information having the form of electronic accounting documents called the Single Control

File, showing therein false data on purchases and sales documented with counterfeit VAT invoices allegedly originating from [five entities] and with untruthful VAT invoices issued by [company X] to: [17 entities], with a total gross value of PLN 8,243,810.31, and net value of PLN 6,706,675.00 and the VAT amounting to PLN 1,534,720.31 in such a way that he sent them in the described electronic form by electronic means of communication to the Head of the National Fiscal Administration, (…), i.e. an act under Article 270a § 1 of the Penal Code in conjunction with Article 271a § 2 of the Penal Code in conjunction with Article 270 § 1 of the Penal Code in conjunction with Article 271 § 1 of the Penal Code in conjunction with Article 18 § 2 and § 3 of the Penal Code in conjunction with Article 271a § 2 of the Penal Code in conjunction with Article 271 § 1 of the Penal Code in conjunction with Article 11 § 2 of the Penal Code in conjunction with Article 12 § 1 of the Penal Code in conjunction with Article 65 § 1 of the Penal Code. (Case No. 162)

In order to carry out the procedure related to the circulation of invoices in order to obtain the refund of unpaid VAT, it is necessary to organise a chain of entities that ensure the flow of such documents between them. These entities must have all the attributes of a trader and, at the same time, the status of an active taxpayer of goods and services tax, and at the same time fulfill the tax obligations related to the transmission of electronic records of purchases and sales of VAT and the submission of tax returns as defined by law. As stated in the Explanatory Memorandum to the indictment in the example cited above: 'The specific nature of VAT and the choice of the form of taxation and business activity determine the actions of entities that, to a greater or lesser extent, engage in the creation of documents to authenticate companies created solely for criminal purposes. The creation of fictitious documents, including, in particular, VAT invoices, creates the groundwork necessary for the crime of 'artificially reducing' tax liabilities, which aims at the illegal reduction or elimination of the tax burden or at obtaining this public claim at the expense of the Treasury'. (Case No. 162).

In the cases analysed, there were between 3 and 108 actors involved, with more than 50 % of the cases involving between 3 and 5 actors, a further 30 % involving between 7 and 23 actors, and the remaining 20 % involving between 99 and 108 actors.

What sectors did the participants come from? The overwhelming majority came from construction, transport and distribution of liquid fuels (oil, petrol, gas) and solid fuels (coal), scrap metal, waste collection and disposal, and repair services. They accounted for more than 70 % of all cases analysed in this group. Other activities included car washes, machinery hire, consultancy and accountancy, window dressing, event organisation, wholesale of food products (including markets), repair services and even funeral services. In 2 % of cases, these were purely fictitious companies whose only role was to issue so-called 'empty invoices'. Illegal activities aimed at obtaining a refund of undue VAT, but also of income tax, thus sectors where it is easy to conceal the real object of taxation and to deliberately overstate (or understate) the value of goods or services. These types of activities are generally considered to be the most vulnerable to VAT fraud:

> *In the course of the investigation it was established that [company X] was to purchase approximately 201,885 kg of various types of scrap, including 47,100 kg of lead waste and 154,785 kg of battery scrap, with a total value of PLN 779,120.50. It was also to sell 199,028 kg of various types of scrap, including 44,402 kg of lead waste and 154,626 kg of battery scrap, with a total value of PLN 779,120.50. At the same time, it was to sell 199,028 kg of various types of scrap, including 44,402 kg of lead waste and 154,626 kg of battery scrap with a total value of PLN 785,633.26. The analysis carried out by the USA in (…) shows that the company would have to concentrate approximately 10,625 kg of scrap per day. From the submitted documentation, 816 proofs of purchase were found from thirteen non-business persons (…) in the month of May 2018. None of the witnesses interviewed were able to identify the individuals from whom they purchased or received scrap in significant quantities, averaging 15,530 kg of scrap per person with an average value of PLN 59,932. None of the witnesses – customers – ran a business from which they could even buy the scrap metal in question. The witness statements contain numerous inconsistencies and lack any logical coherence. Despite the number of witnesses, it is impossible to determine from their content the addresses of households, garages, shops in the area (…) mining and metallurgical heaps in the area (…) from which scrap metal was to be obtained.*
>
> *The interviewees were unable to say what they had done with the large sums of money they had received for selling scrap metal. At the same time, they were unable to indicate why, despite such good results, they had stopped collecting scrap metal in June 2018.*
>
> *At the same time, [company X] did not have the physical, technical and human capacity to store, sort, deliver, issue and transport approximately 201,885 kg of scrap metal in the month of May 2018. The company had one garage, one collection point in (…), transport vehicles with a permissible weight of 3.5 tonnes, which allowed the transport of no more than 2 tonnes of scrap metal at a time. The company employed an employee, the accused, who was authorised to collect scrap metal. At the same time, [the defendant] carried out many other activities in the form of construction and maintenance services, as well as handling scrap batteries. During the period in question, the company did not have any fixed assets, including property, from which to purchase scrap metal. In addition, carrying out such an extensive activity entails the accumulation of a large amount of waste, whereas this circumstance was not found during the visual inspection carried out during the tax inspection in both L., K. and T. At the same time, it is physically impossible for [the accused] and occasionally [another person] to unload 201,885 kg of scrap metal by hand in the month of May 2018. It is relevant that [the accused] should personally deliver approximately 10,770 kg of scrap metal to the scrap metal collection point in the month of May 2018, while at the same time personally dealing with the collection point. (Case No. 192)*

The possible nature of the attempts to obtain a refund of undue tax was further indicated by the type of goods and services for which the falsified invoices were submitted. The invoices issued covered the purchase or sale of goods such as: cement, mineral wool wall panels, fibre reinforced adhesive, silicon plaster, facade mesh, sand extraction, diesel fuel, rods, building boards, fabrics, battery scrap, lead waste, sanitary ceramic products, chemical products (pellets), europallets, filters (air, oil), computers, flowers, carbon dust, washing powders, wooden lumber, sports equipment, bookbinding services, repair and maintenance of coffee machines or estimation services.

In cases of this kind, analyses of the Single Control File (SCF), the purpose of which is to provide the tax authorities with information on all sales invoices and cost invoices issued by the economic entity in a given period, were extremely helpful in demonstrating and proving the criminal activity of the entities. The comparison of SCFs of different companies makes it possible to determine whether a given transaction – documented by a VAT invoice – actually took place and whether its value on the part of the seller and the buyer was the same. In one of the cases analysed, the SCF analysis uncovered 396 taxpayers who, between January 2018 and September 2019, entered VAT invoices allegedly issued and not recorded by the issuer in the SCF records into the electronic accounting system, allowing further steps to be taken and charges to be brought against three individuals.

What is, however, an important conclusion of the analysis is the finding that in the remaining 90 % of the cases analysed from 2017 to 2022, no elements of organised action to defraud undue value added tax were observed. Although the criminal actions were aimed at overestimating the costs of doing business and thus underestimating the public law receivable in the form of income tax and reducing the VAT receivable, they were actions of single entities or on behalf of single entities using a falsified invoice not documenting a real economic event. As W. Kotowski notes: 'The VAT invoice has three essential functions. The first one is indicated directly in the content of Article 106b(1)(1) of the VAT Act and in the title of Section XI of the VAT Act, it is the documentation of the supply of goods or services. A VAT invoice correctly issued and recorded in the tax books is an accounting document and allows for the identification of the taxable activity and making it subject to the appropriate regime of application of the VAT regulations (...). Another function of a VAT invoice is the control function. The issue of a VAT invoice allows the tax administration to carry out control activities and verify the correctness of the sales declared by the taxable person (...). The third and, from the perspective of the VAT taxable person, the most important function of the VAT invoice is to ensure the neutrality of taxation by allowing the input tax at the preceding stage of turnover to be deducted from the output tax. The VAT invoice is, as it were, a vehicle for input tax and, as a rule, the exercise of the right to deduct input tax cannot take place without an invoice (…). The mere fact that a certain amount is indicated as the value of the tax due in the text of the invoice does not entitle the recipient to exercise the right to deduct input tax in relation to that amount. In its judgment of 13/12/1989, the Court of Justice made it clear that the deduction of input tax by a purchaser requires the taxable person to be in possession of a VAT invoice that includes the value of the input tax specific to the supply of goods or services in question. According to the Court of Justice, this is the circumstance on which the right to deduct input tax depends. Consequently, the amount of tax allegedly due, which is erroneously calculated in a given transaction – either because of an incorrect (inflated) VAT rate or because of the taxation of an activity that falls outside the scope of VAT – cannot be deducted as input tax. The Court also pointed out that a different interpretation of the Directive's provisions, allowing any amount shown on an invoice as output tax to be deductible, would in fact facilitate an abuse of the law'[11].

Detection of an offence of material or intellectual falsification of an invoice occurred in almost 50 % as a result of control undertaken by the tax authority within the National Fiscal Administration. In 2 % of cases, the detection of an offence was a result of the police's own actions, in another 2 % of cases the analysed proceedings were excluded from other proceedings, in 6 % of cases an unreliable invoice was revealed by a control of the Border Guard (mainly on Poland's eastern border with Ukraine). More than 30 % of the notifications on the possibility of committing a crime were cases in which the notification was submitted by entities aggrieved by a crime, whose data was used to issue a falsified VAT invoice. The remaining cases of detection of offences covered by the study concerned notifications by other entities, including the General Inspector of Financial Information or a municipal authority.

It should be noted that in the cases analysed, trade in false invoices mainly took place between Polish enterprises (about 70 % of the cases). Only in 1 % of cases did Polish companies issue unreliable invoices to foreign companies and

---

11 Kotowski W. (2021). Pusta faktura. Faktura niedokumentująca rzeczywistego zdarzenia gospodarczego [Empty invoice. An invoice undocumenting a real economic event], [in:] O. Ożóg, J. Rudowski (eds.), *Karuzele i inne oszustwa podatkowe. Metody przeciwdziałania unikaniu opodatkowania* [*Carousels and other tax evasion. Methods of counteracting tax avoidance*], Wolters Kluwer, Warsaw, pp. 151 – 152.

vice versa. In the remaining cases, the falsified invoice was detected in some other way or there was no exchange of invoices between economic operators (e.g. use of company data to issue an 'empty' invoice – i.e. an invoice that does not confirm a real business transaction). There were no special relationships between the perpetrators analysed in this study, apart from purely business relationships (over 90 % of cases). Only in slightly more than 5 % of cases was it possible to establish that the perpetrators had family or friendship links or that they worked in the same company.

The modus operandi of the perpetrators can be grouped under several patterns of action, some of which may overlap:

1. the issuing of invoices by a real entity in respect of an activity which has actually been carried out, but where the taxable person is a different entity:

in August 2018. (…) acting for the purpose of gaining a pecuniary benefit and creating the appearance of the existence of circumstances justifying a VAT refund, while running a business (…) and being responsible for the affairs of that company, submitted to the Accounting Office X (….) as genuine four falsified VAT invoices (…) issued by company X as the alleged seller (…), where they were subsequently entered in the books and a VAT-7 return was prepared (…), as a result of which output tax was understated by the amount of input VAT in the amount of PLN 16,308. (Case No. 175)

2. invoicing for activities that did not occur at all:

in the period …., in the execution of the same intention and using the same opportunity, within the framework of the business activity conducted, he accepted unreliable VAT invoices that did not document real economic events, and then used unreliable VAT invoices instructing to enter them into the VAT purchase register of the business activity conducted, thus unreliably keeping VAT records pursuant to article 109 paragraph 3 of the VAT Act, as well as submitting VAT-7 tax return, he provided false information regarding the right to reduce input tax by input tax resulting from unreliable purchase invoices, in relation to which pursuant to article 88 section 3a point 1a and 4a of the VAT Act the taxpayer is not entitled to reduce the amount of output tax by input tax, thus causing depletion of VAT by the amount of PLN 11,270. (Case No. 78)

3. the issuing of invoices by an entity that was not subject to VAT, or the issuing of so-called 'empty invoices' by an entity created for the sole purpose of issuing invoices:

"despite not having the status of a VAT taxpayer, issued the below-mentioned invoices […] by which he certified untruths as to factual circumstances which could be of significance for the determination of the amount of the public law receivable." (Case No 150)

the perpetrator used unreliable invoices, containing a total amount of receivables of a significant value, which were untrue as to the facts (…) – a total of PLN 308,023.00, and the invoices in question were used to deduct input tax not paid at an earlier stage of trade in the amount of PLN 57,597.81. The perpetrator purchased these invoices from three companies which the office traced as being wholesalers of invoices. When questioned by the customs and tax office, the perpetrator claimed that these were actual services, but he did not know and could not give any details about these companies. At the prosecutor's office, he refused to give an explanation. (Case no. 138)

4. falsification of invoices in order to use them as authentic:

   falsifying invoices for the purpose of authenticity by writing them and forging the seller's signature on them to document a sale of potatoes which in fact did not take place and which was important for determining the amount of the public debt in the form of income tax, and then using these invoices by entering them in the income and expense ledger of a non-agricultural business activity and in the course of control, as well as in the annual PIT-36 return, in which a falsity was stated, inflating the costs of income generation, as a result of which due income tax was understated and the State Treasury revenues in the amount of PLN 1,292 were exposed to a depletion (Case No. 48)

5. the issuing of invoices by an existing company for amounts that do not correspond to the actual economic turnover or for sales that have not taken place, with a view to settling accounts with the Tax Office:

   intention that other persons used for tax settlements unreliable invoices, bills and provided untruth in VAT returns, providing 15 entities with 332 unreliable invoices issued to 4 entities with the total value of PLN 2,025,682.53, including PLN 384,245.72 in VAT and used 7 unreliable bills with the total value of PLN 30,196.00 and provided other entities with 26 unreliable invoices for the total amount of PLN 113,896 concerning the sale of services or goods, which were not realised and which were untrue, i.e. he helped to disclose falsities in tax declarations and to expose the State Treasury to a loss of tax on goods and services (Case no. 61)

6. services are indicated as having been provided on the national territory but are fictitiously declared as having been provided outside the national territory (fictitious place of supply):

   In the period from … to … in (…), as the owner of the transport company [Z] (…) and the actual operator of the registered [in the name of another person – author's note] company [X] and the registered [in the name of another person – author's note] [Y], at short intervals, in the execution of a premeditated plan, in order to derive a financial benefit, acting with the intention of leading the State Treasury to a disadvantageous disposition of property, attempted to obtain an undue refund of VAT of a significant value in the amount of PLN 423,837 on account of international sales of goods and passenger transport services as well as agricultural services by the company [X], by misleading the officials of the Tax Office in (….) with a view to forging 68 CMR documents and 68 VAT invoices of intermediate contractors for the purpose of authenticating them and – being a person authorised to do so – certified the invoices with untruths in the amount of PLN 423,837, certified the falsity in VAT invoices from the companies [Z] – 32 invoices, [Y] – 36 invoices and [X] – 132 invoices as to the performance of freight, passenger transport and agricultural [products] services for foreign entities, which altogether contained the amount of receivables of the total considerable value of PLN 3,028,929, which constituted circumstances of legal significance, in particular of importance for the determination of the amount of VAT refund. (Case No. 89)

7. the use of a so-called 'stooge' who was unaware of the purpose of the action he or she had taken:

"I received the invoice (…) in the town of (…) from a shop with the sign 'Bar' (…) The goods I was carrying in the cars – me in mine, him in his – together with my colleague (…) [convicted in another case – author's note] were washing powder. The goods were to be transported to us across the border from Poland into Ukraine by a Ukrainian citizen whose first and last name I do not know. I had no idea that there was anything wrong with this document.(…) I was supposed to get PLN 100 for the transport. I have no job in Ukraine and I have a dependent wife and two children." (Case no. 44)

"I received the invoice from a colleague (…), I cannot remember his name. [He] was the one who hired me to transport him the goods from Poland to Ukraine across the border. (…) I met [him] in the queue to Poland and he offered me money for transporting the goods from Poland. I was to receive USD 40 for the fare. For this goods I received from [him] a retained invoice. Giving it to me he said that everything was in order." (Case No. 42)

The research has shown that the actions undertaken by perpetrators of acts specified in the analysed provisions of the Penal Code as a result of a material or intellectual falsification of an invoice – in terms of its compliance with the actual state of affairs, confirming an economic event which took place and the value of receivables on account of such an activity as a result of an unreliable invoice – also cause significant depletion on the revenue side of the State Treasury. Within the framework of the file analysis in 151 cases (on the basis of a verdict), it was possible to determine the total value of false invoices at the net amount of PLN 182,793,250 and the amount of all receivables due on account of VAT, which was not paid or which was undue refunded at the amount of PLN 31,830,956.98. Obviously, these values are small in relation to the actual scale of depletion. As Szymon Pawelec notes, the estimated scale of VAT evasion and the size of the VAT gap in Poland in 2013–2016 was recorded at between 27 and 20% of the total theoretical VAT receipts, which translated from more than PLN 42 billion to nearly PLN 34 billion per year respectively[12].

12 Pawelec Sz. (2022). Karuzele *VAT* – wybrane zagadnienia prawa karnego materialnego i procesowego. Wprowadzenie do problematyki [VAT carousels – selected issues of

Looking at specific values of amounts established in the judgments analysed (151 cases) and included in false invoices (net amounts documenting the value of goods or services), it should be noted that in over 63 % of cases these amounts were between PLN 300 and 500,000, in another 35 % of cases they were between PLN 501,000 and PLN 10,000,000. In the remaining 2 % of cases (3 cases) they exceeded the value of PLN 10,000,000 – a maximum of PLN 40,716,678.14. (Table 7.8).

Table 7.8. The value of unreliable invoices established in final judgment

	N	%
up to PLN 100 000	52	34.4
from PLN 101,000 to PLN 500,000	43	28.5
from PLN 501,000 to PLN 1 million	27	17.9
>PLN 1 million to PLN 10 million	26	17.2
> PLN 10 million	3	2.0
Total	**151**	**100.0**
No data available	33	

Source: Own compilation based on case file study.

When considering the total amount of all VAT debts evaded as a result of the crime (data for 119 cases), we notice that less than 60 % of the understated tax was within the range from PLN 81 to 100,000, another 30 % was evaded or undue tax in the amount from PLN 101,000 to PLN 500,000. In just over 9 % of cases it exceeded PLN 500,000. The maximum amount of VAT evasion recorded in the study was PLN 9,364,835.96. (Table 7.9).

substantive and procedural criminal law. Introduction to the issues], [in:] Sz. Pawelec (ed.), *Karuzele VAT. Wybrane regulacje prawa karnego materialnego i procesowego* [*VAT carousels. Selected regulations of substantive and procedural criminal law*]. Wolters Kluwer, Warsaw, p. 15.

Table 7.9. The value of VAT evasion established in final judgment

	N	%
up to PLN 10,000	24	20.2
from PLN 10001 to PLN 100000	47	39.5
From PLN 101,000 to PLN 200,000	24	20.2
from PLN 201,000 to PLN 500,000	13	10.9
> PLN 500,000	11	9.2
Total	**119**	**100.0**
No data available	75	

Source: Own compilation based on case file study.

When analysing individual cases, it should be noted that the action of the legislator, whose aim – by introducing new types of offences related to falsification of invoices into the Penal Code – was to facilitate preparatory proceedings related to combating crime aimed at depletion of budget revenues through issuing and using a counterfeited or falsified invoice, has not been fully implemented in practice. This is due to the fact that, in the cases analysed, the charges relating to offences under the Penal Code often occurred in parallel to charges relating to tax offences under the Fiscal Penal Code. The same conduct of the perpetrator, in the case of establishing the use of an invoice for tax settlement purposes, was qualified on the basis of the provisions of the Fiscal Penal Code, while in the case of establishing the attestation of a falsity in an issued invoice – on the basis of the Penal Code. Due to the fact that the statutory elements of fiscal offences (in the majority of analysed cases these were Articles 56 and 62 of the Fiscal Penal Code) overlap with the elements of common offences from the Penal Code (Articles 270a of the Penal Code, 271a of the Penal Code, but also 271 and 273 of the Penal Code) – in accordance with the rule set out in § 8 (1) of the Fiscal Penal Code – each of these provisions will be applied (perfect concurrence of provisions). Thus, the legislator's intention, which was to transfer the burden of prosecuting tax fraud offences from the provisions of the fiscal penal law to the penal code, led to a 'duplication' of charges against the same criminal behaviour of perpetrators in a situation where they simultaneously issued an unreliable invoice and used it for tax settlements.

It is worth remembering, however, that proceedings in cases related to VAT fraud, especially when the procedure itself involves a number of persons and economic entities, are extremely demanding to conduct due to the nature of the activity of the perpetrators, who try to conceal their criminal nature through supposedly genuine economic transactions. As in other proceedings of an economic nature, the detection of this type of crime and its proof, ending with the indictment of the participants in the procedure, are often preceded by many months of painstaking investigative activities.

7.5. Summary: The response of Polish criminal policy to the problem of VAT fraud

VAT fraud crime is such a group of acts, which not only constitutes a significant cost for public finances, but also violates the certainty of economic turnover and distorts competition rules. Therefore, the process of sealing the tax law and combating the pathologies related to it is a necessary task, but extremely difficult to implement due to its multidimensional nature. This is because any legislative changes must not only meet constitutional requirements in such a way as to guarantee each citizen's fundamental rights and the certainty that the actions he or she takes are in compliance with the law, so that the law does not become 'a kind of trap for the citizen and so that he or she can arrange his or her affairs in the confidence that he or she is not exposed to legal consequences that he or she could not foresee when taking decisions and actions and in the conviction that his or her actions taken in compliance with the law in force will also be recognised by the legal order in the future'[13], but also the requirements of correct legislative technique. Legislative solutions must be followed by organisational changes to ensure the correct collection, control and enforcement of tax laws.

It is therefore not surprising that, over time, successive attempts have been made to curb unfavourable phenomena in order to reduce not only the grey tax zone and behaviour that significantly affected budget revenues. To this end, the tax law introduced, among others, split payment, Single Control File, reverse charge in domestic trade or joint and several liability of the purchaser in connection with the purchase of so-called sensitive goods. A new sanction of an administrative nature for abuse of the law in the form of an additional tax liability has emerged.

However, all these measures, in the opinion of the legislator, were not sufficient to properly combat tax crime. Therefore, on the grounds of criminal law and proceedings, provisions appeared introducing the so-called extended

---

13 Judgment of the Constitutional Court of 7th February 2001, ref. K 27/00, https://isap.sejm.gov.pl/isap.nsf/download.xsp/WMP20010060099/T/M20010099TK.pdf (Accessed Oct. 31, 2023).

confiscation or admitting the so-called fruit of the poisoned tree as evidence in a criminal trial. Another step was the amendments to the Penal Code introducing liability for falsification of an invoice, subject to much more severe sanctions than those previously provided for in the provisions of the Fiscal Penal Code.

This is because the legislator considered that the provisions used so far to combat VAT fraud were not sufficient to achieve the objective of limiting the scale of this phenomenon. By including these new provisions in the Penal Code, the legislator also considered that this would be a much more effective way of combating this type of crime than adding further types of offences to the specialised Fiscal Penal Code. According to the legislator's assessment, a necessary element for the initiation of the VAT fraud procedure is the falsification of a VAT invoice, which will then be used in order to obtain an undue reimbursement of this tax, and thus, 'by focusing on the criminalisation of offences against documents (credibility of invoices), it is possible to achieve the effect of annihilating the most important instrument for VAT fraud'[14]. At the same time, thanks to the introduction of new types of offences into the Penal Code, they are expected to fulfill (mainly through the level of sanctions) a much broader preventive function than if they were a supplement to tax offences in the Fiscal Penal Code.

So, have the provisions introduced into the Penal Code to regulate the material and intellectual falsification of a VAT invoice fulfilled the intended reduction of VAT crime?

The answer to this question is not clear-cut. If this aspect were to be considered solely in terms of the number of proceedings completed during the period in which these provisions were in force (from 2017 to 2022) and the number of persons convicted under them, it could be concluded that their actual effectiveness was not great. During the period analysed, 677 people were convicted (finally or not) on the basis of all the added provisions, while in 2020 alone, 473 people were legally convicted only on the basis of Article 62 of the Fiscal Penal Code (failure to comply with obligations to issue invoices and bills for services rendered). Also, the value of potential and actual tax evasion that can be established on the basis of sentences in the analysed cases (over PLN 31 million) in relation to the estimated size of the actual VAT gap is not great. However, this does not give grounds to unequivocally state that the new criminal provisions introduced in 2017 did not have a preventive effect on reducing attempts to defraud VAT, both by individual taxpayers and organised groups aimed at defrauding VAT.

---

14 Explanatory memorandum...., p. 5.

The VAT gap observed in Poland has been gradually decreasing since 2015. In 2015, it was over 24 %, a year later just over 20 %, to drop to around 14 % in 2017 and to only 3.1 % in 2021 (with a slight rebound, to 4.9 % in the following year)[15]. Therefore, the effectiveness of the operation of the criminal provisions on VAT invoice fraud should be seen in the broader context of legislative changes aimed at reducing VAT fraud and narrowing the VAT gap. And this objective, as can be seen in the official data published by the Ministry of Finance, has been largely achieved.

References

Farrington D. P. (1986). Age and Crime. *Crime and Justice*, 7.

Gruszka M. (2022). Zbieg przepisów przy przestępstwach związanych z podatkiem VAT oraz problematyka należytej staranności w VAT w aspekcie prawnokarnym [The concurrence of regulations in VAT offences and the issue of due diligence in VAT in the legal and criminal aspect], [in:] Sz. Pawelec (ed.), *Karuzele VAT. Wybrane regulacje prawa karnego materialnego i procesowego* ['VAT Carousels. Wybrane regulacje prawa karnego materialnego i procesowego']. Warsaw: Wolters Kluwer.

Kotowski W. (2021). Pusta faktura. Faktura niedokumentująca rzeczywistego zdarzenia gospodarczego [Empty invoice. An invoice undocumenting a real economic event], [in:] I. Ożóg, J. Rudowski (eds.), *Karuzele i inne oszustwa podatkowe. Metody przeciwdziałania unikaniu opodatkowania* ['Carousels and other tax evasion. Methods of counteracting tax avoidance']. Warsaw Wolters Kluwer, pp .151–152.

Pawelec Sz. (2022). Karuzele VAT – wybrane zagadnienia prawa karnego materialnego i procesowego. Wprowadzenie do problematyki [VAT carousels – selected issues of substantive and procedural criminal law. Introduction to the issues, [in:] Sz. Pawelec (ed.), *Karuzele VAT. Wybrane regulacje prawa karnego materialnego i procesowego* ['VAT carousels. Wybrane regulacje prawa karnego materialnego i procesowego']. Warsaw: Wolters Kluwer.

Wzorek D., Zielińska E., & Klimczak J. (2022). *Kara ograniczenia wolności i jej rola w resocjalizacji sprawców przestępstw* [Penalty of community service and its role in the rehabilitation of offenders]. Warsaw: Publishing House of the Institute of Justice.

---

15 *Luka w VAT urosła. Oto jak skomentowało to ministerstwo [The VAT gap has grown. Here's how the ministry commented on it]*, Business Insider, 25th April 2023, https://businessinsider.com.pl/gospodarka/podatki/luka-w-vat-urosla-oto-jak-skomentowalo-to-ministerstwo/lk5697j (Accessed Oct. 31, 2023).

Explanatory Memorandum to the Draft Law on Amendments to the Law – Penal Code and Certain Other Laws, 8th Legislature, Parliamentary Print No. 888, https://orka.sejm.gov.pl/Druki8ka.nsf/0/EA8BC112272EA7CEC12580420 0323EDD/%24File/888.pdf (Accessed Oct. 31, 2023).

Judgment of the Constitutional Court of 7th *February 2001*, ref. K 27/00, https:// isap.sejm.gov.pl/isap.nsf/download.xsp/WMP20010060099/T/M2001009 9TK.pdf (Accessed Oct. 31, 2023).

Luka w VAT urosła. Oto jak skomentowało to ministerstwo [*The VAT gap has grown. Here is how the ministry commented on it*], Business Insider, 25th April 2023, https://businessinsider.com.pl/gospodarka/podatki/luka-w-vat-urosla-oto-jak-skomentowalo-to-ministerstwo/lk5697j (Accessed Oct. 31, 2023).

Legislation

The Act of 6th June 1997, the Penal Code (i.e. Journal of Laws 2022, item 1138).

The Act of 10th September 1999, the Fiscal Penal Code (i.e. Journal of Laws 2023, item 654).

Polish Studies in Economics

Edited by Ryszard Kokoszczyński

Vol. 1 Wojciech Grabowski: Employee Stock Options, Payout Policy, and Stock Returns. Shareholders and Option Holders in Large U.S. Technology Corporations. 2012.

Vol. 2 Jan Jakub Michałek/Michał Brzozowski/Andrzej Cieślik (eds.): The Relationship between Human Development, Exports and Foreign Direct Investments in Emerging Europe. 2013.

Vol. 3 Tomasz Żylicz: The Economics of International Environmental Cooperation. 2015.

Vol. 4 Juliusz Jabłecki / Ryszard Kokoszczyński / Paweł Sakowski / Robert Ślepaczuk / Piotr Wójcik: Volatility as an Asset Class. Obvious Benefits and Hidden Risks. 2015.

Vol. 5 Janusz Kudła / Konrad Walczyk / Robert Kruszewski / Katarzyna Kopczewska / Agata Kocia: Modeling Fiscal Policy in the European Union. 2015.

Vol. 6 Andrzej Cieślik / Jan Jakub Michałek (eds.): Liberalization of Transportation Services in the EU: the Polish Perspective. 2015.

Vol. 7 Katarzyna Metelska-Szaniawska: Economic Effects of Post-Socialist Constitutions 25 Years from the Outset of Transition. The Constitutional Political Economy Approach. 2016.

Vol. 8 Elżbieta Czarny / Andżelika Kuźnar / Jerzy Menkes (eds.): The Impact of the Transatlantic Trade and Investment Partnership on International Cooperation. 2017.

Vol. 9 Adam Czarnecki: Going Local? Linking and Integrating Second-Home Owners with the Community's Economy. A Comparative Study between Finnish and Polish Second-Home Owners. 2017.

Vol. 10 Adam Biela (ed.): European Questionnaire for Job Analysis (EQJA). 2018.

Vol. 11 Gabriela Grotkowska: Public-Sector Wage Premium in Poland. 2018.

Vol. 12 Piotr Dybka: What Determines International Competitiveness of the Economy? Evidence from Bayesian Model Averaging. 2022.

Vol. 13 Damian Bębnowski: The Importance of Constitutional Rules and Property Rights. The German Economy in 1990–2015. 2022.

Vol. 14 Wojciech Łątkowski: Projections of Demand for Care among the Elderly in Poland Including Health Status and Living Arrangements. 2024.

Vol. 15 Dominik J. Gajewski (ed.): *VAT Gap* in Poland: Policy Problem and Policy Response. 2024.

www.peterlang.com

www.ingramcontent.com/pod-product-compliance
Ingram Content Group UK Ltd.
Pitfield, Milton Keynes, MK11 3LW, UK
UKHW041826031026
15587UKWH00002B/600

9 783631 908747